Globalisation and Enlargement of the European Union

On 1 January 1995, Austria and Sweden joined the European Union (EU). This book analyses why the two countries joined the EU at a moment when the latter's development towards a neo-liberal economic policy, embodied in the Internal Market and the convergence criteria of the Economic and Monetary Union, endangered their traditional Keynesian economic policy-making, and when the steps towards a Common Foreign and Security Policy threatened their neutrality.

It is argued that the processes leading to Austria's and Sweden's accession have to be analysed against the background of globalisation, a structural change experienced since the early 1970s and characterised by the transnationalisation of production and finance and a shift from Keynesianism to neo-liberalism. Neo-functionalist and intergovernmentalist theories are unable to explain instances of structural change, because they take existing power structures as given. Consequently, a neo-Gramscian perspective is developed as an alternative approach to European integration. Most importantly, its focus on social forces, engendered by the production process, allows the approach to conceptualise globalisation.

Applying this perspective to the Austrian and Swedish case, it is established that alliances of internationally-oriented and transnational social forces of capital and labour respectively, supported by those institutions linked to the global economy such as the Finance Ministries, were behind the drive towards the EU. Resistance by national capital and labour, but also the Green Parties in both countries and additionally the Left Party in Sweden, could not prevent membership. Although not of primary importance, changes in the international structure – Gorbachev's liberal foreign policy and a general decline in the power of the Soviet Union in the case of Austria, and the end of the Cold War in the case of Sweden – allowed the pro-EU forces in both countries to redefine neutrality in a way that made it compatible with membership. A chapter on the possible EU enlargement to Central and Eastern Europe completes the arrangement of the book.

Andreas Bieler is a Lecturer and Director of Studies in Social and Political Sciences at Selwyn and Newnham College, University of Cambridge, UK. He is a co-editor of *Non-State Actors and Authority in the Global System*, also published by Routledge.

Routledge/Warwick Studies in Globalisation

Edited by Richard A. Higgott and published in association with the Centre for the Study of Globalisation and Regionalisation, University of Warwick.

What is globalisation and does it matter? How can we measure it? What are its policy implications? The Centre for the Study of Globalisation and Regionalisation at the University of Warwick is an international site for the study of key questions such as these in the theory and practice of globalisation and regionalisation. Its agenda is avowedly interdisciplinary. The work of the Centre will be showcased in this new series.

This series comprises two strands:

Routledge/Warwick Studies in Globalisation is a forum for innovative new research intended for a high-level specialist readership, and the titles will be available in hardback only. Titles include:

1. Non-State Actors and Authority in the Global System
Edited by Richard A. Higgott, Geoffrey R. D. Underhill and Andreas Bieler

2. Globalisation and Enlargement of the European Union
Austrian and Swedish social forces in the struggle over membership
Andreas Bieler

Warwick Studies in Globalisation addresses the needs of students and teachers, and the titles will be published in hardback and paperback. Titles include:

Globalisation and the Asia-Pacific
Contested territories
Edited by Kris Olds, Peter Dicken, Philip F. Kelly, Lily Kong and Henry Wai-chung Yeung

Regulating the Global Information Society
Edited by Christopher Marsden

Globalisation and Enlargement of the European Union

Austrian and Swedish social forces in the struggle over membership

Andreas Bieler

London and New York

First published 2000
by Routledge
11 New Fetter Lane, London EC4P 4EE

Simultaneously published in the USA and Canada
by Routledge
29 West 35th Street, New York, NY 10001

Routledge is an imprint of the Taylor and Francis Group

© 2000 Andreas Bieler

Typeset in Baskerville by Curran Publishing Services Ltd,
Norwich
Printed and bound in Great Britain by T. J. International Ltd,
Padstow, Cornwall

British Library Cataloguing in Publication Data
A catalogue record for this book is available
from the British Library

Library of Congress Cataloging in Publication Data
Bieler, Andreas
    Globalisation and enlargement of the European Union:
    Austrian and Swedish social forces in the struggle over
    membership / Andreas Bieler
    208 pp. 156 x 234 mm (Routledge/Warwick Studies in
    Globalisation
    Includes bibliographical references and index
    1. European Union – Austria. 2. European Union – Sweden.
    3. Austria – Economic conditions – 1945– . 4. Sweden –
    Economic conditions – 1945– . I. Title. II. Series
    HC240.25.A9 B54 2000
    337.1'42–dc21   99-058062

ISBN 0-415-21312-6

Contents

Tables

Foreword

The Centre for the Study of Globalisation and Regionalisation, founded in October 1997, is funded by the Economic and Social Research Council of the UK with an initial grant of over £2.5 million. The Centre is rapidly becoming an international site for the study of key issues in the theory and practice of globalisation and regionalisation, and has an avowedly inter-disciplinary agenda. Research staff in CSGR are drawn from international relations, political science, economics, law and sociology. The Centre is committed to scholarly excellence but also strives to be problem-solving in methodological orientation.

Three broad categories of enquiry inform and underwrite the research programme of the Centre. What is globalisation? Can we measure its impacts, and if so, how? What are its policy implications? Understandings of globalisation are seen to be multi-dimensional – political, economic, cultural, ideological – so CSGR sees globalisation in at least two broad ways: first as the emergence of a set of sequences and processes that are increas-ingly unhindered by territorial or jurisdictional barriers and that enhance the spread of trans-border practices in economic, political, cultural and social domains; second as a discourse of political and economic knowledge offering one view of how to make the post-modern world manageable. For many, globalisation as 'knowledge' constitutes a new reality. Centre research will ask what kinds of constraints globalisation poses for inde-pendent policy initiatives on the part of national policy makers and under what conditions these constraints are enhanced or mitigated.

Within these broad contexts empirical work at CSGR focuses on, first, particular regional projects in Europe, North America and the Asia-Pacific; second, the enhancement of international institutions, rules and policy competence on questions of trade competition and international finance and investment; third, normative questions about governance, sovereignty, democratisation and policy-making under constraints of globalisation. Indeed, Centre research is sensitive to the wider normative nature of many of these questions, especially in research into the counter-tendencies towards, or sites of resistance to, globalisation at regional and local levels that give rise to different understandings of the importance of space and territoriality. Warwick/Routledge Studies in Globalisation will provide an avenue for the publication of scholarly research monographs, policy-oriented studies and collections of original themed essays in the area of the research agenda of CSGR.

Andreas Bieler's study of the enlargement of the EU to include Austria and Sweden is the fourth volume in the series, but it is the first research monograph. We are particularly pleased to publish the book given that most of the research and writing was undertaken while Andreas was employed as a research assistant at Warwick. The book is an important contribution for three reasons. First, it offers an alternative explanation to that found in more established neo-functional and inter-governmentalist theories of integration. Second, Bieler's discussion of the European integration experience is firmly located within a wider analysis of the impact of globalisation on this process. Third, not only does this study add an important new empirical dimension to the story of widening European integration, its marriage of theory and practice demonstrates the utility of a neo-Gramscian perspective not only as a critique of established theories of International Relations, but also as a useful tool for detailed empirical analysis. Bieler's study represents one of the first serious efforts to bring a neo-Gramscian perspective to a detailed empirical study; it thus represents important ground-breaking work in the study of globalisation and regionalisation.

Richard Higgott
Director, CSGR

Acknowledgements

This book, with the exception of chapter six, is a rewritten version of a doctoral dissertation presented in March 1998 at the University of Warwick, UK. Earlier versions of parts of chapters three and four first appeared as 'Austria's application to the EC: a neo-Gramscian case study of European integration', in *New Political Economy* 3, 1 (1998): 27–43; and 'Globalisation, Swedish trade unions and European integration: from Europhobia to conditional support', in *Cooperation and Conflict* 34, 1 (1999): 21–46.

I am indebted to my two supervisors Peter Burnham and Richard Higgott, the two examiners Henk Overbeek and Anthony Payne, two anonymous referees and Adam Morton for comments on earlier drafts. Special thanks go to Otto Holman, Julie Smith and Simon Smith for their remarks on chapter six. I am also grateful to Ian Bartle, Cecilia Goria, Jens Mortensen, Mića Panić, Magnus Ryner, Geoffrey Underhill and Bastiaan van Apeldoorn for their help on one or the other aspect of the book. The assistance of Craig Fowlie and Milon Nagi from Routledge, and Chris Carr and Paul Simmonds of Curran Publishing Services in the production of the book is gratefully acknowledged.

I would further like to thank all the interviewees in Austria and Sweden for their time and effort in assisting me with my research. Without their openness, this project could not have been carried out. In particular, I want to mention Dr Peter Henseler from the Austrian Finance Ministry, who supported the research beyond the interview. Finally, I am thankful to the staff of the Library of the Finance Ministry, Vienna and the Riksdagbiblioteket, Stockholm. Their assistance during my research trips is much appreciated.

Andreas Bieler
Cambridge, February 2000

Abbreviations

AK	Chamber of Labour (Austria)
ANB	Austrian National Bank
AS	Austrian Schilling
AWS	Solidarity Electoral Action (Poland)
BWK	Chamber of Commerce (Austria)
CAP	Common Agricultural Policy
CEE	Central and Eastern Europe
CEE-5	Poland, the Czech Republic, Hungary, Slovenia and Estonia
CEE-10	Poland, the Czech Republic, Hungary, Slovenia, Estonia, Latvia, Lithuania, Slovakia, Bulgaria and Romania
CFSP	Common Foreign and Security Policy
CMKOS	Czech and Moravian Confederation of Trade Unions
CP	Centre Party (Sweden)
CSCE	Conference on Security and Co-operation in Europe
CSSD	Czech Social Democratic Party
DM	German Mark
EA	Europe Agreement
EBRD	European Bank for Reconstruction and Development
ECB	European Central Bank
ECE	Economic Commission for Europe (of the UN)
ECJ	European Court of Justice
ECU	European currency unit
EEA	European Economic Area
EFTA	European Free Trade Area
EMS	European Monetary System
EMU	Economic and Monetary Union
EP	European Parliament
EPC	European Political Co-operation
ESP	Economic and Social Partnership (Austria)
ETUC	European Trade Union Confederation
EU	European Union
FDI	foreign direct investment
FIDESZ	Alliance of Young Democrats (Hungary)

FP	Liberal Party (Sweden)
FPÖ	Austrian Freedom Party
FTA	Free Trade Agreement
GA	Green Alternative Party (Austria)
GP	Green Party (Sweden)
GPA	White Collar Workers' Union (Austria)
IGC	intergovernmental conference (of the EU)
IMF	International Monetary Fund
IR	International Relations
KSCM	Communist Party (the Czech Republic)
LK	Chamber of Agriculture (Austria)
LO	Swedish Trade Union Confederation
LRF	Federation of Swedish Farmers
MDF	Hungarian Democratic Forum
MIEP	Party of Hungarian Truth and Life
MP	Workers' Party (Hungary)
MS	Moderate Party (Sweden)
MSZP	Hungarian Socialist Party
NATO	North Atlantic Treaty Organisation
ÖAAB	Austrian League of Blue and White Collar Workers (ÖVP)
ÖBB	Austrian Farmers' League (ÖVP)
ODS	Civic Democratic Party (the Czech Republic)
OECD	Organisation for Economic Co-operation and Development
ÖGB	Austrian Federation of Trade Unions
ÖVP	Austrian People's Party
ÖWB	Austrian Business League (ÖVP)
PSL	Polish Peasant Party
QMV	qualified majority voting
ROP	Movement to Rebuild Poland
SACO	Swedish Confederation of Professional Associations
SAF	Confederation of Swedish Employers
SAP	Social Democratic Party (Sweden)
SEA	Single European Act
SI	Federation of Swedish Industries
SKr	Swedish Krona
SLD	Democratic Left Alliance (Poland)
SPÖ	Austrian Social Democratic Party
SPR-RSC	Republican Party (the Czech Republic)
TCO	Swedish Confederation of Professional Employees
TNC	transnational corporation
UN	United Nations
UNICE	Union of Industrial and Employers' Confederations
VÖI	Federation of Austrian Industrialists
VP	Left Party (Sweden)
WEU	West European Union

1 Introduction

Theories of integration and Austria's and Sweden's accession to the European Union – a critique and alternative

Introduction

On 1 January 1995, Austria and Sweden acceded to the European Union (EU).[1] Historically, membership had been rejected in both countries for two main reasons. First, a majority of forces in Austria and Sweden agreed that their neutral status excluded the possibility of membership in a supranational economic organisation such as the EU as it would imply a loss of national sovereignty and possible participation in measures such as one-sided embargoes of weapon exports and, thus, undermine neutrality (Huldt 1994: 111; Neuhold 1992: 89). Second, the domination of the EU by christian democratic parties and big capital appeared to imply a threat to the social democratic achievements in both countries. The greater part of Austria's heavy industry had been nationalised after the Second World War, mainly in order to protect it against reparation demands by the occupying allies. For much of the Austrian Social Democratic Party (SPÖ), however, nationalisation was also a precondition for the achievement of full employment and the maintenance of state authority over the economy. 'Rightly, the Socialists argued that the contribution of the state-owned sector in economic stabilization, full employment, and regional development would be menaced if Austria were forced to accept supranational direction from Christian Democratic governments' (Kurzer 1993: 207).

Similarly in Sweden, in particular the left wing of the Social Democratic Party (SAP) and the Communist Party, since 1990 known as the Left Party (VP), both argued that 'Swedish involvement in the political integration of the [EU] would harm rather than sustain her capacity to pursue a welfare programme based on the principles of equal rights and advanced state-intervention' (Jerneck 1993: 26).

Why, then, did Austria and Sweden join the EU at a moment when it had moved towards positions which contributed even further to the dangers outlined? The Single European Act (SEA) of 1987 not only spelt out the goals of the Internal Market, that is, the four freedoms of goods, services, capital and labour, it also strengthened the supranational institutions. The European Court of Justice (ECJ), for example, became the arbiter of the Internal Market, while the European Parliament (EP) gained a second reading and the potential to influence legislation through amendments with the introduction of the co-operation procedure. The Treaty of Maastricht, signed in 1991, laid out among other changes the plan for Economic and Monetary Union (EMU), including a single currency. This together with monetary policy in general was to be administered by a supranational and independent European Central Bank (ECB). On 1 January 1999, eleven of the fifteen EU members, including Austria, carried out this step, when they irrevocably fixed their exchange rates. In order to become a member, countries had to fulfil neo-liberal convergence criteria, focusing on low inflation, price stability and 'sound' budgetary targets. Sweden, despite its decision not to participate in the final stage of EMU, had to pursue the same neo-liberal policies from 1 January 1995 onwards. The Treaty of Maastricht had specified that all members had to draw up a convergence programme outlining the measures the countries intended to undertake in order to meet the criteria, regardless of their eventual participation, and this also applied to Sweden. In short, the revival of European integration since the mid-1980s consisted of a combination of liberalisation, deregulation and further supranational policy co-ordination and, therefore, threatened to undermine national policy autonomy in general, and policies of full employment and a generous welfare state in particular, even further. Moreover, the Treaty of Maastricht established first steps towards a Common Foreign and Security Policy (CFSP), designed eventually to include a common defence policy, leading perhaps even to a common defence. The West European Union (WEU) was declared an integral part of the development of the EU, responsible for the elaboration and implementation of all EU decisions with defence implications.[2] Even after the Treaty of Amsterdam in 1997, the CFSP remained an intergovernmental institution, while the link to the WEU was unclear and the question of a defence policy unresolved. Nevertheless, the clear potential for future pooling of sovereignty in this area represents a threat to Austria's and Sweden's neutral status (Nugent 1999: 48–98).

In this book, the processes in the two countries leading first to application and eventually to accession to the EU are analysed in order to solve the puzzle outlined above. It is argued that the 1995 enlargement of the EU has to be analysed against the background of structural change since the early 1970s, often referred to as globalisation. The exact nature of globalisation and its implications for Austria and Sweden are discussed in detail in chapter two. Here, it suffices to define globalisation briefly as the transnationalisation of production and finance at the material level, expressed in the rise in size and numbers of transnational corporations (TNCs) and a world-wide deregulation of national financial markets, together with a change from Keynesian ideas to neo-liberalism at the ideological level (Cox 1993: 259–60, 266–7). An analysis of established neo-functionalist and intergovernmentalist theories of integration in the next section of this chapter demonstrates that they are unable to explain such instances of structural change. The third section, therefore, outlines a neo-Gramscian alternative, which guides the empirical investigation of the rest of the book. Overall, this book, first, contributes to understanding why these two countries chose to join the EU in 1995. Second, it adds to both International Relations (IR) and European integration theory by applying a neo-Gramscian perspective to a case of European integration for the first time.

Some limitations of integration theories

Neo-functionalist and intergovernmentalist approaches have dominated the explanation of European integration. The former assume that integration starts when it is realised that certain economic problems yield higher welfare gains, if they are dealt with at the supranational level. The notion of spill-over is crucial for the neo-functionalist explanation of integration. It can be divided into three different processes (Tranholm-Mikkelsen 1991: 4–6). First, functional spill-over occurs in the economic sphere; because of the interdependence between industrial sectors, the integration of one sector makes the integration of another necessary to reap the full welfare benefits of the first integration. Second, this is accompanied by political spill-over. Interest groups of an integrated sector are expected to shift their focus to the new decision-making centre in order to influence the decisions that are important to them, and to press for further integration of related sectors. Finally, cultivated spill-over refers to the independent capacity of the supranational institutions to push for further integration. Overall, the 'main thesis was that sectoral integration was inherently expansive' (Tranholm-Mikkelsen 1991: 6), and, once started, would lead to an automatic process of further integration (Haas 1958: 297; Lindberg 1963: 294).

Various studies of Austria's and Sweden's accession to the EU incorporate one or the other aspect of neo-functionalism. Jerneck, for example, touches upon the notion of political spill-over as a force towards further integration by highlighting the increasing involvement of Swedish transnational actors in Brussels (Jerneck 1993: 42). Other studies outline the important role of central institutions such as the Commission. Gstöhl, for example, highlights the Commission's (and especially Jacques Delors') role in starting the European Economic Area (EEA) process in January 1989 (Gstöhl 1996: 55). Pedersen utilises all three versions of spill-over in his explanation of the move from the EEA to membership. The attempt to establish an Internal Market comprising all members of the EU and European Free Trade Area (EFTA) created functional spill-over, which led to an expansion of the negotiation agenda. This pressure was intensified by political spill-over of EFTA interest groups, which shifted their loyalty to the EU. Eventually, to prevent the loss of involvement in decision-making in too many areas, EFTA governments opted for membership, which gave them co-decision making power. An explanation along the line of cultivated spill-over focuses on directed change and political leadership. 'One may thus interpret the apparent failure of the EEA as a success in disguise, as part of an incrementalist strategy aimed at integrating EFTA in the [EU]' (Pedersen 1994: 16). Overall, these studies employ neo-functionalist concepts only as partial explanations.

In general, neo-functionalist approaches are characterised by two main problems. First, being based on an ahistorical understanding of human beings as rational, utility-maximising individuals, the notion of spill-over implies an inevitable, teleological process of further integration along an objective economic rationality. The analysis in this book demonstrates, however, that there were strong forces in Austria and Sweden which opposed membership. A closer economic relationship short of full membership was debated as an alternative and eventual accession was not the result of economic necessity, but the outcome of an open-ended struggle. Second, neo-functionalism explains European integration through an emphasis on the internal dynamics of European politics. The wider structure within which European integration is situated is completely neglected. It is, therefore, impossible to take into account structural changes such as globalisation and the end of the Cold War.

During the two decades of relative stagnation between 1965 and 1985, neo-functionalism lost a great deal of its attraction as an explanation of European integration. Only since the revival of European integration in the mid-1980s has neo-functionalism regained the attention of scholars (e.g. Burley and Mattli 1993; Mutimer 1989; Tranholm-Mikkelsen 1991). The notion of spill-over is still seen as a useful tool of analysis, although only as part of an eclectic and less ambitious theoretical framework (George 1996: 275–83). A neo-functionalist explanation of entire instances of European integration is neither attempted nor deemed to be possible.

In contrast to neo-functionalism, which emphasises the importance of non-governmental interest groups in the process of European integration, intergovernmentalism, closely related to the theory of neo-realism in IR, takes into account the international structure. It is considered to be an anarchic system, in which states, as the only significant actors, pursue rational policies of power maximisation and security enhancement to ensure their survival. The most important explanatory variable is the distribution of capabilities between states. Changes in this distribution lead to actions by states to counter possible losses (Waltz 1979).

With reference to European integration, Hoffmann concludes that a convergence of national preferences is the precondition for European integration. Europe 'has to wait until the separate states decide that their peoples are close enough to justify the setting up of a European state' (Hoffmann 1966: 910). Thus, states are seen as 'gate-keepers' between their people and Europe. They carefully guard their sovereignty, which is ensured by the principle of unanimity voting in the Council of Ministers.

There are a number of explanations of Austria's and Sweden's accession to the EU along intergovernmentalist lines. Koch, for example, argues that Austria responded to the pressure of economic necessity. Its close economic links with the EU and its poor economic performance in comparison to other Western European countries from the early 1980s onwards left no other option than membership (Koch 1994). Similarly, Miles points to economic imperatives which drove Sweden towards membership. The end of the Cold War and the concomitant changes in the international structure facilitated this move in that they 'removed the shackles of keeping a rigid neutrality policy' (Miles 1994a: 83). In short, both countries joined the EU in response to changes in the distribution of economic and military capabilities between states. However, these explanations are also unsatisfactory. Although intergovernmentalism takes into account the international structure, its exclusive focus on states in the international arena limits changes to those purely at the level of state structures. It cannot account for structural changes such as globalisation, which go beyond the state structure. By the same token, the explanation is still deterministic, since states as the main actors can only adapt to structural change. Austrian and Swedish EU membership again appears to have been inevitable.

The criticism of intergovernmentalism for taking states as unitary actors led to the proposal of complementing it with a domestic perspective (Bulmer 1983). The analysis of domestic politics explains the construction of national interests, the strategies adopted by states, and it shows when national ratification of international agreements is possible (Milner 1992). Putnam combines the domestic perspective with intergovernmentalism by suggesting that 'the politics of many international negotiations can usefully be conceived as a two-level game' (Putnam 1988: 434). Level I refers to agreements between states at the international level, whereas Level II looks at the ratification process at the domestic level. Putnam's hypothesis is that a government only concludes an international agreement, for which it expects to be able to construct a majority coalition between societal groups at the domestic level.

The convergence of national interests around a neo-liberal, deregulatory programme with the focus on low inflation was a precondition for the revival of European integration in the mid-1980s. Cameron points to the move towards conservative and christian democratic governments in Britain, Belgium, the Netherlands, Denmark and Germany in the late 1970s and early 1980s to explain the shift from Keynesianism to neo-liberalism (Cameron 1992: 57). When applied to the cases of Austria and Sweden, however, this explanation based on domestic politics shows deficiencies. As outlined in chapter two, the turn to neo-liberalism occurred under a social democratic government in Sweden, while in Austria it was not only the inclusion of the christian democratic People's Party (ÖVP) in a coalition government in 1987, but also the internal change of the SPÖ, the stronger party in government, which led to the adoption of neo-liberal policies. The European left changed during the 1980s and this cannot be explained by pointing to structural and domestic events alone. Rather, the independent impact of neo-liberalism as a set of economic ideas has to be investigated to explain the general turn to neo-liberalism by parties of the right and the left.

This approach is further limited, because it considers that lobbying by interest groups only takes place within a country's domestic realm. Thereby, the significance of transnational actors such as transnational corporations (TNCs) is neglected. Their level of action is European if not world-wide, maintaining production sites in several countries at the same time. This allows them, first, to develop initiatives with the Commission and to lobby several governments at the same time. Second, they can put pressure on national governments by either threatening to transfer production units to other countries or by actually carrying out this threat, if certain conditions are not met. State-centric approaches can only account for TNCs by regarding them as several, unconnected actors in their individual domestic sphere, not as transnational actors transgressing the line of separation between international and domestic politics. As outlined in chapters three and four, the role of TNCs was particularly important in Sweden's accession to the EU.

In order to tackle these shortcomings, Moravcsik developed the most sophisticated state-centric approach to date, which he labelled 'liberal intergovernmentalism'. He, first, connects a liberal theory of national preference formation, that is, 'domestic politics', with an intergovernmentalist analysis of inter-state negotiations in a two-level game, and then adds a regime theory component. States as rational decision-makers, first, use EU institutions and are prepared to transfer parts of their sovereignty to increase the efficiency of inter-state co-operation. Second, they accept the restriction of their external sovereignty, because EU 'institutions strengthen the autonomy of national political leaders *vis-à-vis* particularistic social groups within their domestic polity' (Moravcsik 1993: 507; see also Moravcsik 1998: 18-85).

None the less, even 'liberal intergovernmentalism' suffers severe deficiencies. It provides no insight into how the independent role of ideas is to be investigated or how transnational actors can be accounted for. TNCs' behaviour, such as the investment boom of the 1980s in the EU, is interpreted as rational adaptation to credible intergovernmental commitments, while policy ideas are merely viewed as the result of intergovernmental demands, not as an independent force (Moravcsik 1995: 618). In short, this predominant emphasis on states as main actors in international relations prevents all types of intergovernmentalism from dealing with ideas and transnational actors as independent forces behind integration.

A further problem with intergovernmentalist approaches in general is the prioritising of questions of international security and military capabilities over economic issues. An analysis of the security implications of

Austria's and Sweden's accession to the EU in chapter five, however, shows that the decision regarding application was taken on economic grounds in 1989 and 1990 respectively, and only subsequently was neutrality redefined in a way which made it compatible with membership. The end of the Cold War facilitated this redefinition, but it did not push Austria and Sweden towards EU membership.

Finally, the exclusive state-centric focus makes all varieties of intergovernmentalism concentrate on inter-state negotiations as the crucial event of further integration. Wincott, however, points out that instances of integration are not so much the result of intergovernmental negotiations, but emerge from the 'everyday grind of the Community' (Wincott 1995). In other words, the process leading to negotiations and setting the agenda should be more important than the negotiations themselves, as should the sites of social struggle related to the ratification of negotiation agreements. Consequently, chapter three analyses the processes behind the Austrian and Swedish application in detail, while chapter four concentrates on the struggle over the referendum in both countries. The accession negotiations themselves are only dealt with in the first section of chapter four, and it is argued that, although not without importance, they were only a link between the original decision to apply and the final decision in the referendum to accept the terms of membership.

In order to overcome the shortcomings of neo-functionalist and intergovernmentalist integration theories, several scholars suggest combining intergovernmentalism with neo-functionalism in respect of EU enlargement (e.g. Pedersen 1994; Miles *et al.* 1995). However, this would be misleading. As Puchala had already observed in 1972, 'attempts to juxtapose or combine the conventional frameworks for analytical purposes by and large yield no more than artificial, untidy results' (Puchala 1972: 276–7). Neo–functionalist approaches cannot be combined with state-centric approaches, as their basic assumptions are diametrically opposed. While the former speak about the supersession of states, the latter consider sovereignty to be unchangeable.

Another attempt to overcome the impasse of established integration theories has been a shift away from International Relations (IR) and towards Comparative Politics. It is argued that the EU can be regarded as a political system similar to national political systems and that, therefore, EU policy-making or politics can be better accounted for by Comparative Politics approaches (Hix 1994; 1999). To mention some examples, the 'policy networks' approach, which offers a model of interest group intermediation, has been transferred to EU politics for the understanding of sectoral policies (e.g. Peterson 1995). 'Multi-level governance', moreover, understands the EU as a political system 'in which authority and policy-making influence are shared across multiple levels of government – subnational, national, and supranational' (Marks *et al.* 1996: 342). Finally, new (or historical) institutionalism concentrates on how actors' behaviour is structured and shaped by EU institutions, which are themselves often the result of choices in the past (e.g. Bulmer 1998). These approaches clearly help to account for the variety of actors within the complexity of EU policy-making. Nevertheless, the turn towards Comparative Politics implies a dangerous distinction between European integration and EU policy-making. The two areas are closely connected and should not be separated analytically. As has been argued, day-to-day policy-making may set the agenda for further European integation via major treaty revisions. Moreover, the fact that established integration theories are insufficient in the analysis of European integration does not signify that IR theory as such is useless. Hence, a neo-Gramscian alternative, derived from developments in IR, is suggested in the next section.

A neo-Gramscian alternative

Cox argues that in order to explain structural change we need a 'critical' theory, which 'does not take institutions and social and power relations for granted but calls them into question by concerning itself with their origins and how and whether they might be in the process of changing' (Cox 1981: 129). In other words, 'critical' theory is a theory of history in that it is concerned with understanding the process of change. It, therefore, adopts a historical-structures perspective, which regards 'human nature and the other structures that define social and political reality – ranging from the structure of language through those of laws, morals, and institutions, and including the state and world-order structures like the balance of power – as being themselves products of history and thus subject to change' (Cox 1989: 38).

In short, in contrast to the state-centric and neo-functionalist approaches, it treats human nature, the state and the international system not as unchanging substances, but as a continuing creation of new forms (Cox 1981: 132). Additionally, 'critical' theory realises that 'theory is always for someone and for some purpose' (Cox 1981: 128). Hence, it not only identifies the purpose behind established integration theories – further integration in the case of neo-functionalism, the preservation of modern state power and national sovereignty in the case of intergovernmentalism – but is also capable of comprehending the social purpose behind a particular phase of European integration (van Apeldoorn 1997). In chapters three and four, it is outlined how a continuation and deepening of neo-liberal restructuring of state–society relations was the purpose behind Austrian and Swedish EU membership.

In two seminal articles in the 1980s, Cox developed a neo-Gramscian perspective as 'critical' theory, based on the work of the Italian Communist Antonio Gramsci (Cox 1981 and 1983). In the wake of Cox's work, a whole range of different studies along neo-Gramscian lines were published, which mainly had the task of understanding hegemony at the international level as well as the structural change of world order (e.g. Agnew and Corbridge

1995; Augelli and Murphy 1993; Cox 1987; Gill 1990 and 1993a; Murphy 1994; Overbeek 1993; Rupert 1995). While these neo-Gramscian studies show many similarities in the way they built on Gramsci's concepts, they are also clearly different from each other. Nevertheless, there has been a tendency, mainly by critics, to identify a cohesive neo-Gramscian 'school' (e.g. Burnham 1991; Moran 1998: 56–8; Smith 1996: 202). According to Morton, however, a 'school' label of this type should be resisted, since this entails the danger of simplifying internal contradictions and transforming neo-Gramscian research into an orthodoxy, which could imply the loss of its original 'critical' intentions (Morton 1998: 1–6). In this book, Morton's suggestion of labelling these studies neo-Gramscian perspectives is adopted. The emphasis on the plural form is crucial. 'It immediately accepts the diversity of contributions within the perspectives whilst also permitting the flexibility to realise commonalities and overlaps' (Morton 1998: 8). Consequently, by drawing on Gramsci and a range of neo-Gramscian thinkers, this book attempts to develop a neo-Gramscian perspective which constitutes an analytical framework, capable of understanding the processes behind Austria's and Sweden's accession to the EU against the background of global structural change. The label 'neo-Gramscian' perspective is preferred to 'Gramscian' perspective, since the use of the latter 'mistakenly conveys a parallel or coexistence, without any significant change, of the historical moment that Gramsci occupied' (Morton 1998: 6).

It was recently argued that Gramsci's thought needs to be historicised and understood against the background of his own time. The transfer of his concepts to contemporary analyses would be both a misinterpretation of Gramsci and unhelpful for the understanding of current empirical events (Germain and Kenny 1998). Morton, however, outlines that Gramsci himself thought that the concrete study of past history in order to construct a new history was an essential part of a theory of praxis. In other words, Gramsci himself was engaged in the appropriation of ideas from the past for the understanding and transformation of the present.

> Thus whilst one has to bear an attentiveness to the peculiarities of history, to pay consistent attention to the specificities of alternative historical and cultural conditions, Gramsci's insights and concepts can still be adapted, as he indeed adapted and enriched his own concepts to changing circumstances, to new conditions.
>
> (Morton 1999: 5).

Social forces and the analysis of structural change

The neo-Gramscian perspective adopted here focuses on social forces, engendered by the production process, as the most important collective actors. The concept of class is crucial for the definition of social forces. For the purpose of this study, classes are regarded 'as social forces whose

cohesion derives from the role played in a mode of production'
(Holman and van der Pijl 1996: 55). Consequently, class is defined as a
relation and the various fractions of labour and capital can be identified
by relating them to their place in the production system.

The capitalist mode of production based on private enterprise and wage
labour is characterised by the opposition between capital, the entrepre-
neurial, property-owning stratum on the one hand, and free labour, which
is the stratum of those forced to sell their labour-power, on the other.
Labour and capital are, consequently, two collective actors opposing each
other, engendered by the production process as social forces. There are,
however, further differences within the capitalist mode of production.
Importantly for this study, while production was organised on a national
basis in the post-war era, significant parts have been transnationalised since
the early 1970s as part of the globalisation processes. As a consequence,
capitalist accumulation is no longer necessarily inscribed in national paths
of economic development (Radice 1997: 5). A basic distinction can,
therefore, be drawn between transnational social forces of capital and
labour, engendered by those production sectors which are organised on a
transnational scale, and national social forces of capital and labour
stemming from national production sectors. These forces are located in the
wider structure of the social relations of production, which do not *determine*
but *shape* their interests and identity. Their actual position on questions
such as EU membership still has to be empirically investigated.

Overall, the identification of the various fractions of labour and capital by
relating them to their place in the production system makes structural
changes such as globalisation accessible, since the emergence of new social
forces engendered by the transnationalisation of production and finance can
be incorporated. Globalisation, thus, is not only understood as an exogenous
structural impact to which actors can only respond. It is also regarded as
enabling with transnational forces playing an active role, responding to and
bringing about global structural change at the same time.

It is frequently argued that it is not possible to speak of class, if there is
a lack of class consciousness and class activity at the political level. Hence,
it is impossible to speak of transnational class fractions, unless these fractions have formed political alliances with fractions in other countries. Ste.
Croix, however, points out that class, according to Marx, is a group of
persons identified by their position in the mode of production. 'The individuals constituting a given class may or may not be wholly or partly
conscious of their own identity and common interests as a class, and they
may or may not feel antagonism towards members of other classes as such'
(Ste. Croix 1981: 44). In other words, class exists as such at the economic
level without necessarily having developed a political consciousness. It is in
this respect that it is possible in the rest of the book to speak of Austrian
and Swedish transnational class fractions of capital and labour, regardless
of whether they have formed political connections with fractions in other

countries. It is the position in the production system and not political activity, which designates the membership of a particular class.

Through his emphasis on social forces, Cox reintroduces the sphere of production into the analysis, arguing that it 'creates the material basis for all forms of social existence, and the ways in which human efforts are combined in productive processes affect all other aspects of social life, including the polity' (Cox 1987: 1). In other words, the relations which organise material production are considered to be crucial for the wider institutional reproduction of social orders on both a national and an international level. Importantly, production is not understood simply in the narrow sense of the production of physical goods or in the form of different economic sectors. 'It covers also the production and reproduction of knowledge and of the social relations, morals, and institutions that are prerequisites to the production of physical goods' (Cox 1989: 39). Cox does not disregard 'non-class' issues such as peace, ecology, and feminism. However, while they are not to be set aside, they must be 'given a firm and conscious basis in the social realities shaped though the production process' (Cox 1987: 353).

The definition of class as a relation implies that the emphasis for the understanding of structural change has to be on class struggle, since 'the very existence of classes . . . involves tension and conflict between the classes' (Ste. Croix 1981: 49). This neo-Gramscian perspective, consequently, 'rejects the notion of objective laws of history and focuses upon class struggle [be they intra-class or inter-class] as the heuristic model for the understanding of structural change' (Cox with Sinclair 1996: 57–8). The essence of class struggle is exploitation and the resistance to it, and this confrontation of opposed social forces in concrete historical situations implies the potential for alternative forms of development. It is thus clear that there are no inevitable developments in history. Instances of European integration are as much the outcome of an open-ended struggle as are other political developments.

Van der Pijl shows how a concern with the degradation of human and environmental conditions can be incorporated into empirical analyses through the lens of class struggle. He distinguishes three terrains of capitalist discipline. First, original accumulation and resistance to it predominantly took place during the early history of capitalism, when the new mode of production was imposed on social relations via the subordination of the use value of a product to the exchange value aspect (van der Pijl 1998: 36–8). Second, the capitalist production process represents the exploitation of labour at the workplace. Human autonomy is subordinated to the process of expanding value in order to increase surplus value and, thus, profit. Class struggles take place in the labour market and directly at the workplace (van der Pijl 1998: 40).

More recently, capitalist discipline has gone beyond the workplace and also affected the process of social reproduction in its entirety, leading to the exploitation of the social and natural substratum. For example, education, health and the public sector as such have been submitted to capitalist profit criteria. Moreover, 'the tightening discipline of capital on the reproductive sphere also implies the destruction/exhaustion of the biosphere' (van der Pijl 1998: 46). The ozone layer is destroyed and the air, soil and water polluted and exhausted in the relentless search for profit. As a response, new social movements and Green parties supporting issues such as feminism, gay rights and environmental protection emerged from the late 1960s onwards to defend the personality and environment against further exploitation. Partly as a backlash against these new social movements, popular resentment against the disruption of social life by increased capitalist exploitation has emerged and is frequently channelled into political action around xenophobic and racist programmes by extreme-right political parties (van der Pijl 1998: 47–8).

In short, struggles led by new social movements, Green and extreme-right parties against increased exploitation of the social and natural sphere of reproduction are as much part of class struggle as are struggles between trade unions and employers' association over wage increases. In chapters three and four, it can be seen how the struggles about EU membership in Austria and Sweden included all three dimensions of capitalist discipline. Austria in particular provides an example of right-wing and green opposition to intensified capitalist exploitation of the reproduction sphere as manifested in accession to the EU.

Furthermore, the neo-Gramscian perspective used in this study 'enlarges the [state-centric] perspective through its concern with the relationship between the state and civil society' (Cox 1981: 134). Cox speaks about various forms of states and shows that the '*raison d'état*' cannot be separated from society, as it depends on the configuration of social forces at the state level. Forms of state are defined in terms of the apparatus of administration and of the historical bloc or class configuration that defines the *raison d'état* for that form (Cox 1989: 41). This implies that states cannot be treated as unitary actors, but as structures within and through which social forces operate. Gramsci's concept of the integral state is analytically useful for the conceptualisation of the relation between state and society (Rupert 1995: 27–8). On the one hand, the integral state consists of 'political society', which comprises the coercive apparatus of the state more narrowly understood including ministries and other state institutions. On the other, it includes 'civil society', made up of political parties, unions, employers' associations, churches, and so on, which 'represents the realm of cultural institutions and practices in which the hegemony of a class may be constructed or challenged' (Rupert 1995: 27).

The concept of the integral state implies, first, that the focus on social forces does not exclude an analysis of state institutions, that is, political society. As discussed in chapter two, due to the internationalisation of the state in the process of globalisation, those state institutions, which are linked to the global economy (such as finance ministries, central banks), are given priority within a country's governmental set-up over those institutions which deal with predominantly national problems (for example, labour ministries). Similarly, the emphasis on social forces as the main actors does not imply that political parties and interest associations, or civil society, are considered to be unimportant. Nevertheless, in contrast to pluralist and corporatist policy-making approaches (e.g. Lehmbruch and Schmitter 1982), they are not considered to be rational, unitary actors. Rather, they are regarded as institutional frameworks within and through which different class fractions of capital and labour attempt to establish their particular interests and ideas as the generally accepted, or 'common sense', view.

Additionally, regarding the state as a structure through which social forces operate makes it possible to overcome the artificial separation of domestic and international spheres of state-centric theories. 'Social forces are not to be thought of as existing exclusively within states. Particular social forces may overflow state boundaries, and world structures can be described in terms of social forces just as they can be described as configurations of state power' (Cox 1981: 141). Thus, a neo-Gramscian perspective helps us to understand a world order as stemming from the same basic social structures, which are the foundation of the forms of state within this order.

Finally, neo-Gramscian perspectives take into account the independent role of ideas. On the one hand, they are considered to be a part of the overall structure in the form of 'intersubjective meanings'. Hence, ideas establish the wider frameworks of thought, 'which condition the way individuals and groups are able to understand their social situation, and the possibilities of social change' (Gill and Law 1988: 74). On the other hand, ideas may be used by actors as 'weapons' in order to legitimise particular policies and are important in that they form part of a hegemonic project by organic intellectuals (which is discussed later) (Bieler 1998: 72–80). Strategies are likely to be successful in those cases, where the legitimising ideas correspond to the 'intersubjective meanings' of the structure, because they will appear logical. Conversely, it might be difficult to carry out actions legitimised with ideas which are in contradiction to the 'intersubjective meanings'. Nevertheless, 'intersubjective meanings' are not only constitutive of social practices. They are also instantiated by them, and human consciousness thus embodies a transformative quality. Hence, actors themselves, who use certain ideas to legitimise particular policies, may change 'intersubjective meanings' of the social totality. This treatment of ideas indicates a dialectical conceptualisation of structure and agency more generally. 'Structures are formed by collective human activity over time. Structures, in turn mould the thoughts and actions of individuals. Historical change is to be thought of as the reciprocal relationship of structures and actors' (Cox 1995: 33). Structures may limit the possible strategies of action, but they do not determine outcomes, which are the result of struggle, and structures themselves may be changed through agency.[3]

Historical bloc, hegemony and the role of organic intellectuals

The centrepiece of this neo-Gramscian perspective is Gramsci's concept of a historical bloc. At a basic level of understanding, a historical bloc is an alliance of classes or fractions of classes, which attempts to establish a particular form of state and/or world order preferable to them. Nevertheless, a historical bloc is more than a simple alliance of social forces. It is 'the term applied to the particular configuration of social classes and ideology that gives content to a historical state' (Cox 1987: 409). It forms a complex, politically contestable and dynamic ensemble of social relations which includes economic, political and cultural aspects (Rupert 1995: 29–30). It is a solid structure of political society and civil society and consists of structure and superstructure, 'in which precisely material forces are the content and ideologies are the form' (Gramsci 1971: 377). The relationship between structure and superstructure is reciprocal, 'which is nothing other than the real dialectical process' (Gramsci 1971: 366). 'Superstructures of ideology and political organisation shape the development of both aspects of production [that is, the social relations and the physical means of production] and are shaped by them' (Cox 1983: 168).

Another important neo-Gramscian concept is hegemony. Unlike the neo-realist notion of this phenomenon, in which a hegemonic state controls and dominates other states and the international order thanks to its superior amount of economic and military capabilities (Gilpin 1981: 29; Keohane 1984: 32–3), it describes a type of rule, which predominantly relies on consent rather than on coercion. Additionally, a hegemonic order is based on a historical bloc that does not necessarily coincide with the boundaries of a state, but may be established at a transnational level. Hegemony 'is based on a coherent conjunction or fit between a configu- ration of material power, the prevalent collective image of world order (including certain norms) and a set of institutions which administer the order with a certain semblance of universality' (Cox 1981: 139). On the one hand according to Cox, a 'historic[al] bloc cannot exist without a hegemonic social class' (Cox 1983: 168). Thus, it can be seen that the establishment of a historical bloc implies that this bloc enjoys hegemonic rule. Gill, on the other hand, distinguishes between the two concepts. He states that a historical bloc 'may at times have the potential to become hegemonic' (Gill 1993b: 40), but does not necessarily do so. For the purpose of this study, Gill's definition is used. It offers the analytical advantage of enabling the identification of a strong combination of material and ideological forces, the historical bloc, without immediately leading to the conclusion that this is combined with hegemonic rule and, thereby, the absence of significant opposition.[4]

Organic intellectuals play a crucial role in achieving hegemony. According to Gramsci,

> every social group, coming into existence on the original terrain of an essential function in the world of economic production, creates together with itself, organically, one or more strata of intellectuals which give it homogeneity and an awareness of its own function not only in the economic but also in the social and political fields.
> (Gramsci 1971: 5).

Social groups do not simply produce ideas, but they concretise and articulate strategies in complex and often contradictory ways, which is possible because of their class location, their proximity to the most powerful forces in production and the state. It is their task to organise the social forces they stem from and to develop a hegemonic project which is able to transcend the particular interests of this group so that other social forces are able to give their consent. Such a hegemonic project must be based on, and stem from, the economic sphere. It must, however, also go beyond economics into the political and social sphere, incorporating issues such as social reform or moral regeneration, to result in a stable hegemonic political system. It 'brings the interests of the leading class into harmony with those of subordinate classes and incorporates these other interests into an ideology expressed in universal terms' (Cox 1983: 168).[5]

Burnham criticises the role attributed to ideas and organic intellectuals by neo-Gramscian perspectives. He alleges that they pursue a pluralist road of investigation through giving equal importance to ideas and materialist forces. Similarly, part of the overall structure such as the polity, the economy and civil society are given real autonomy without any analysis of the relation between these parts. Burnham argues that this position

> lacks the power to explain either the systematic connection between values, social relations and institutions or the extent to which the historical appearance of capital as a social relation transforms the social order in such a way that all relations are subsumed under the capital relation as the basis of the valorisation process.
> (Burnham 1991: 78).

Rather than treating all factors as equal, he argues that the social relations of production must be attributed primary importance. It is not ideas and organic intellectuals which determine economic policy and state strategies more generally, but 'the contradictions of the capital relation and the nature of competition in the world market' (Burnham 1991: 83). A crisis is resolved via the sacrifice of inefficient capitals.

Undoubtedly, the social relations of production must be the starting-point of a neo-Gramscian investigation, because only this makes it possible to comprehend that the apparent separation of the political and economic spheres is not a transhistorical fact but the result of the development of specific social relations of production (Burnham: 1994). In this respect, Burnham is right in saying that a crisis in the accumulation regime is solved via the sacrifice of inefficient capitals. However, the end of one accumulation regime does not imply that there is only one automatic alternative accumulation regime, which will take its place. There is no logical result to which capital-in-general will automatically be driven via market forces. On the contrary, there are always various possible courses of action in times of structural change.

Which course of action is chosen is not determined by the market but depends on which historical bloc is able to establish its strategy as the one generally accepted as best. And it is here that ideology plays a decisive role as a part of the new hegemonic project. As Gramsci points out, 'it is on the level of ideologies that men become conscious of conflicts in the world of the economy' (Gramsci 1971: 162). Consequently, ideas represent an independent force, but only in so far as they are rooted in the economic sphere, going beyond it at the same time; that is to say they are in a dialectical relationship with the material properties of the sphere of production. Only such ideas can be regarded as 'organic ideas'. They 'organise human masses, and create the terrain on which men move, acquire consciousness of their position, struggle, etc.' (Gramsci 1971: 377).

Similarly, not every intellectual is an 'organic intellectual'. According to Gramsci, there is the traditional, vulgarised type of intellectual, which 'can be defined as the expression of that social utopia by which the intellectuals think of themselves as "independent", autonomous, endowed with a character of their own etc.' (Gramsci 1971: 8–9). Organic intellectuals, by contrast, are regarded as the true representatives of a particular social group, generated by the sphere of production.

To conclude, the fact that organic ideas and organic intellectuals are rooted in the material structure demonstrates the primacy attached to the sphere of production by neo-Gramscian perspectives. It is the concept of a historical bloc, consisting of ideas and material circumstances, which best shows that ideas and other aspects of the superstructure are not autonomous factors of analysis, but have to be understood in their dialectical relationship with the economic structure. They need to be rooted in the economic structure, directly or via their carriers, the organic intellectuals, in order to be of importance. Organic ideas and organic intellectuals are most likely to have an impact in times of crisis, that is, the end of an accumulation regime. Such a crisis occurred in the early 1970s, when the Fordist accumulation regime broke apart and the structural change of globalisation ensued.

The next chapter looks at globalisation and the struggle over a successor regime to Fordism in more detail. It considers how and to what extent globalisation has affected Austria and Sweden. Chapter three of the book deals with the processes leading to the Austrian and Swedish application, while chapter four concentrates on the struggles over the referenda on membership in both countries. Chapter five then examines the impact that the end of the Cold War and the changing security structure had on the two countries' move towards membership. Even before Austria and Sweden actually acceded to the EU, several countries from Central and Eastern Europe had already applied for membership. Chapter six briefly assesses the prospects of these applications by looking more closely at the cases of Poland, the Czech Republic and Hungary. It evaluates the extent to which the neo-Gramscian perspective, employed in the analysis of Austria's and Sweden's accession to the EU, may be used for the investigation of other instances of enlargement. Finally, the conclusion attempts to identify those social forces, which may be able to provide the basis for a project of transformation away from neo-liberal capitalism. As Devetak maintains, 'the knowledge critical . . . theory seeks is not neutral; it is politically and ethically charged by an interest in social and political transformation' (Devetak 1996: 151).

The discussion and construction of an emancipatory project is beyond the scope of this book. It is hoped, however, that the analysis of the configuration of the Austrian and Swedish, and to a lesser extent Polish, Czech and Hungarian, social forces on EU membership provides a starting-point for further analyses of the prospects for overcoming neo-liberal capitalism on a national and European level.

2 Austria and Sweden in an era of global structural change

The post-war international economic order in the Western world was a compromise between the principles of economic liberalism and national interventionism, labelled 'embedded liberalism' (Ruggie 1982: 393). On the one hand, it consisted of the acceptance of the principles of multilateralism and tariff reductions, which led to several consecutive GATT negotiation rounds furthering international free trade. On the other hand, the right of national governments to maintain capital controls and to intervene in their own economy in order to ensure domestic stability via economic growth and social security was generally accepted. This hegemonic world order rested on the Fordist accumulation regime, a specific organisation of the social relations of production at the national level. Its core features were the mass production of consumer goods and mass consumption (Holman 1996: 16). The corresponding form of state was the Keynesian welfare state, characterised by interventionism, a policy of full employment via budget deficit spending, the mixed economy and an expansive welfare system (Gill and Law 1988: 79–80).

At the end of the 1960s, the Fordist accumulation regime showed its technical limitations within the capitalist core countries in the form of stagnating productivity and a decline in the rate of profit (Holloway 1995: 24). The attempt to overcome these problems within Fordism led to social unrest. 'Labour increasingly [resisted] management's efforts to expand its control and step up the work pace' (Oberhauser 1990: 215). Additionally, faced with an inflationary surge due to the Vietnam war effort and President Johnson's 'Great Society' programme (Gill and Law 1988: 173), the USA was no longer prepared to sustain the international economic system. In 1971, President Nixon decided to ease the inflationary strain on the American economy through running a bigger balance of payments deficit and cutting the link between the dollar and gold. While this eliminated the US current account deficit by transferring the adjustment burden overseas (Helleiner 1994: 112–13), Nixon sounded the death-knell of 'embedded liberalism' in general and of the Bretton Woods system of fixed exchange rates in particular. In the following years, globalisation led to a fundamental transnational restructuring of social relations.

The first section of this chapter looks more closely at the processes of globalisation and their impact on governance at the national and global level. It is, however, only by empirical studies of individual countries that the impact of globalisation can be evaluated. Hence, after providing an outline of the Austrian and Swedish post-war economic and political systems, the chapter analyses how both countries have been affected by global structural change. The last section identifies the configuration of social forces in Austria and Sweden by looking at the countries' production structure.

The processes of globalisation

'Globalisation' as a concept has entered the general academic debate in social sciences and is increasingly regarded as a multi-dimensional phenomenon. It is partly defined, for example, as 'the rise of global cultural flows and "deterritorialized" signs, meanings, and identities' (Amin and Thrift 1994: 4).[1] Although these processes are not without importance, globalisation is here mainly understood from a political economy perspective. Most importantly, it is characterised by two inter-linked processes, the transnationalisation of finance and production at the material level, and a shift from Keynesianism to neo-liberalism at the ideological level (Cox 1992: 30; Cox 1993: 259–60 and 266–7).[2] Within the political economy perspective, some authors regard new technological developments in microelectronics and telecommunications as a driving force of globalisation and, therefore, as an additional important dimension (e.g. Agnew and Corbridge 1995: 178–85; Strange 1994a: 119–38). Here, however, technology is not treated as an independent force and core feature of globalisation. Rather, the way it is used depends on those who hold social power (Cox 1987: 21). While new technologies have facilitated the transnationalisation of production and finance (e.g. Higgott 1997: 12), they could also have been used to strengthen national controls and regulations and, therefore, to prevent transnationalisation.

Structural change at the material and ideological level

The transnationalisation of finance

Since the early 1970s, the transnationalisation of finance has led to the emergence of a fully-fledged global financial market. The first component of this process was the rise of financial offshore markets. 'It was first in evidence in the 1960s when Britain and the United States strongly supported growth of the Euromarket in London' (Helleiner 1994: 8). While the USA did not control the overseas business of US financial institutions and banks, Britain refused to regulate dollar trading in London. As a consequence, 'the Eurodollar loan became a new unregulated growth point in the international financial system; and the faster US corporations moved to Europe, the faster their bankers followed to London, and later to other European cities' (Strange 1994a: 106). As non-national money markets, they offered a regulation-free environment for the trading of financial assets and, therefore, facilitated expansion (Gill and Law 1988: 165, 174–6). Between 1973 and 1984, there was a dramatic rise in the offshore markets to $1,000 billion, from levels of only $3 billion and $75 billion in 1960 and 1970 respectively (Strange 1994a: 107).

The second component of the transnationalisation of finance goes hand in hand with the support of financial offshore markets. Instead of responding with more regulation, 'the United States from the mid-1970s led the way to more deregulation of money markets and financial operators' (Strange 1994a: 110). Due to competitive pressure, the other two major financial centres followed swiftly. In 1979, the British government abolished its forty-year-old system of capital controls overnight, and Japan followed in the first half of the 1980s (Helleiner 1994: 149–56). Then, the EU as a whole, New Zealand, Australia and the Scandinavian countries followed the same path (Helleiner 1994: 156–66). Eventually, due to the deregulation of national financial markets, the differences between them and offshore markets disappeared and an integrated global financial market emerged. This had not been inevitable, but was the result of conscious governmental decisions. Helleiner demonstrates how it could have been stopped, if not reversed at four historical points: Britain in 1976, the United States in both 1978–9 and 1979–80 and France in 1983 (Helleiner 1994: 124).

The transnationalisation of production

The transnationalisation of production 'signifies the integration of production processes on a transnational scale, with different phases of a single process being carried out in different countries' (Cox 1981: 146). The growth of TNCs in numbers and in size drives the transnational organisation of production. They are 'the agents that integrate trade, technology transfer and financial flows for the purpose of [transnational] production in the context of the firms' strategy' (UN 1991: 83). The rise in foreign direct investment (FDI) is a good indicator of the rising importance of TNCs. 'Since FDI, by definition involves the establishment of lasting managerial control, it creates networks of ongoing relationships between parent firms and foreign affiliates and, increasingly, among foreign affiliates' (UN 1992: 252). Outflows of FDI rose from $88 billion to $225 billion, which is an annual increase of 26 per cent between 1986 and 1990 (UN 1992: 14). There was a downturn in FDI in 1991 and 1992, mainly due to recessions in the biggest economies, but it picked up again from 1993 onwards up to $424 billion in 1997 (UN 1998: 2). The significance of FDI demonstrates the close connection between the transnationalisation of production and finance. The deregulation of national currency control systems was a precondition for the free movement of capital, making an increased level of FDI possible.

The increase in FDI on its own, however, does not indicate the overall importance of TNCs in the global economy. One way of doing this is to compare FDI with world exports and world output. Between 1983 and 1989, outflows in FDI increased about three times faster than world exports and roughly four times faster than world output (UN 1991: 4). This is further confirmed by the indicator of the global sales of foreign affiliates in host countries, which is better suited for the comparison with trade flows, since it includes the value of output of TNCs' activities in contrast to FDI. Including world exports of commercial services and excluding intra-firm trade, global sales of foreign affiliates were $4.4 trillion in comparison to world exports of $2.5 trillion in 1989. Thus, 'global sales of affiliates are considerably more important than exports in delivering goods and services to markets world-wide, which underlines the importance of TNCs in structuring international economic relations' (UN 1992: 54).

Hirst and Thompson reject the idea of globalisation based on the transnationalisation of production. They argue that the international economy was more open in the pre-1914 period than in the period from the 1970s onwards. 'International trade and capital flows . . . were more important relative to GDP levels before the First World War than they probably are today' (Hirst and Thompson 1996: 31). They overlook, however, the fact that FDI flows are not of a similar nature to trade flows because FDI does not end with the initial transaction. It is an indicator for the establishment of transnational production units, that is, longer lasting links between economic agents across borders. A study of TNCs by the United Nations concludes that 'the growth of cross-national production networks of goods and services of some 35,000 transnational corporations and their more than 150,000 foreign affiliates is beginning to give rise to a [transnational] production system, organized and managed by transnational corporations' (UN 1992: 5). These figures further increased to 53,607 parent corporations and 448,917 foreign affiliates by 1997 (UN 1998: 4).

In their rejection of globalisation, Hirst and Thompson further point out that FDI is not globally spread in an equal way, but concentrated on the Triad of North America, Japan and the European Economic Area in respect of both the originators and destination for FDI (Hirst and Thompson 1996: 51–75). Finally, they stress the fact that there are only few 'real' TNCs without the identification of a home region or country, an internationalised management and the willingness to invest in the world, wherever the highest and/or most secure returns are to be expected. Instead, the international economy is characterised by multinational corporations, which are still predominantly concentrated on a home region or country with reference to their assets and sales (Hirst and Thompson 1996: 76–98).

It is not argued here that the transnationalisation of production has led to a borderless global economy, a level playing field with truly global firms as the prime movers. Nevertheless, in contrast to Hirst and Thompson, it is realised that the growth in size and numbers of TNCs with a regional home base, indicated by the concentration of FDI in the Triad, is also part of the globalisation process. As Higgott outlines, regionalisation and globalisation are not necessarily contradictory phenomena. Rather, regional integration may be 'an important dimension of the evolving world order in an era of globalisation' (Higgott 1997: 16). TNCs are predominantly characterised by a home region or country. Even with production units in only two countries, however, a TNC gains the ability of moving or threatening to move production units between countries, and thereby achieves some degree of leverage over national regulations. This led Strange and Stopford to argue that states no longer bargain only with other states, but that a 'triangular diplomacy' is emerging, in which states must also negotiate with TNCs (Stopford and Strange 1991).

The change at the ideological level

The structural changes at the material level were accompanied and supported by a change in the dominant economic paradigm (Cox 1993: 266–7; Helleiner 1996: 194). A neo-liberal, monetarist policy replaced Keynesianism from the mid-1970s onwards, when it had become clear that the latter's expansionary response to the economic crisis of the early 1970s had failed. 'The importance of monetarism is the rejection of the commitment to a policy of full employment in favour of the subordination of social relations to so-called market freedom' (Bonefeld 1995: 37). Efficiency and price stability are the new priorities, the privatisation of the state-controlled enterprises and the liberalisation and deregulation of the economy at the national level are advocated, social peace is imposed rather than negotiated and there is no commitment to redistribution or social reform. Globalisation, consequently, is not only a material reality, but also provides 'a powerful ideological framework within which big business pushes for a redistribution of income, wealth and power towards economic elites' (Radice 1997: 16). This shift can be observed in all three major instances of regionalism: the EU, the North American Free Trade Area and the Asia Pacific Economic Co-operation (Gamble and Payne 1996). Although it is not clear for how long it will last, neo-liberalism also triumphed in the developing world during the 1980s (Biersteker 1995: 174–80), indicating the truly global nature of the spread of neo-liberalism. The changes at the material level and ideological level are closely interlinked. Helleiner points out that the decisions to follow the USA in deregulating financial markets were not only the result of competitive pressure. They also reflected 'the policy shift from embedded liberal [Keynesian] to neo-liberal frameworks of thought' (Helleiner 1994: 167).

Globalisation and the restructuring of the state

There are different conceptualisations of the state's role in the global economy. Globalists such as Ohmae regard globalisation as moving inevitably to a borderless world, an economic level playing field, on which truly global companies are the primary actors. There is little or no role left to states beyond the provision of infrastructure and public goods required by business (Ohmae 1990; 1995). Similarly, Strange talks about an increasing hollowness of state authority, or a 'retreat of the state' (Strange 1996). Conversely, internationalists consider states to be still the main actors in international economics and politics. Hirst and Thompson argue that the economy is predominantly international, not global, and that, therefore, states, although in a slightly different way, still play a central role in its governance (Hirst and Thompson 1996: 178–89). In this perspective, the changes are termed internationalisation, not globalisation, and are defined as a drastic rise in cross-border flows of goods, capital and services (Keohane and Milner 1996). It is argued here that neither of the two extreme positions adequately conceptualises the role of states in globalisation. Globalisation should not be counterpoised to the state. The role of the state has not diminished, it has changed and the state has been restructured 'from the proto-socialist aspirations of welfarism and the pursuit of full employment, towards wholehearted support for private capital accumulation' (Radice 1997: 4).[3]

On the one hand, national autonomy and sovereignty in economic policy-making has been restricted. Although large, developed countries are more able to counter the loss of autonomy than small and developing ones, 'even the autonomy of the United States, Japan, and the European Union is constrained in matters of macroeconomic policy by the globalisation of finance and production' (Gill 1995: 412–13). It is, for example, increasingly difficult for governments 'to tax capital, which has tended to shift the fiscal burden on to other factors of production, notably labour, and/or erode the tax base' (Oman 1995: 11). Furthermore, governments have to adapt their performance to criteria acceptable to global production in order to attract investment from TNCs and to global finance in order to obtain good credit ratings. Hence, governments need to adjust their policies to the requirements of rating agencies, as these agencies allocate the credit ratings, which are so crucial in the increasingly important securities market (Sinclair 1994a; 1994b). Cox concludes that states have been, 'by and large, reduced to the role of adjusting national economies to the dynamics of an unregulated global economy' (Cox 1994: 105). This 'internationalisation of the state gives precedence to certain state agencies – notably ministries of finance and prime ministers' offices – which are key points in the adjustment of domestic to international economic policy' (Cox 1981: 146).

This is, however, a very one-sided perception of the role of the state, which only grants states the ability to adapt to globalisation, which is perceived to be an external force. In contrast, Panitch points out that 'capitalist globalisation is a process which also takes place in, through, and under the aegis of states; it is encoded by them and in important respects even authored by them' (Panitch 1994: 64). Thus, states not only respond to, but also bring about globalisation. In more detail, retaining the notion of the internationalisation of the state, officials of those state institutions which are linked to the global economy are likely to play an active role in the drive towards globalisation. Helleiner, for example, points out that officials of finance ministries and central banks 'were often the most enthusiastic advocates of financial liberalization' (Helleiner 1996: 194). Ministries linked to national problems (such as labour ministries, social affairs ministries), on the other hand, are frequently sidelined and overruled in the neo-liberal restructuring of the state.

Globalisation, thus, implies the reorganisation of state–society relations. In general, 'the neo-liberal concept projected a transition away from the welfare, social compromise state towards the night-watchman state of classical liberalism' (van der Pijl 1989: 66). The institutions linked to the global economy have become dominant within the 'political society' and transnational social forces dominate important parts of the 'civil society' such as political parties, trade unions and so on. Nationalised industry is privatised, the economy in general liberalised and deregulated, including the labour market, and the welfare system cut back. The goal of full employment is replaced by low inflation and price stability.

Of course, not all states were welfare states to the same extent and not all states have moved to an extreme form of night-watchman. The historical reality of national political and social relations implies that neo-liberal restructuring has had a different face in every country. However, the character of neo-liberalism is transnational (Overbeek 1993: XI) and, on a continuum which has the welfare state and the neo-liberal night-watchman state as ideal types at opposite extremes, a general move in the direction towards the latter can be identified throughout the developed world (see the analysis of Austria and Sweden in this chapter).

Globalisation and the emergence of a transnational historical bloc

The transnationalisation of production and finance broke apart the organisation of production at the national level and split both capital and labour into several fractions. The hierarchy of capital 'can be plotted as (1) those who control the big corporations operating on a world scale, (2) those who control big nation-based enterprises and industrial groups, and (3) locally based petty capitalists' (Cox 1987: 358). The third group has increasingly come under the dominance of the first through 'franchise' mechanisms, but there is room for a possible conflict between national and transnational capital. The latter strongly supports an open global economy, whereas the former may seek national or regional protectionism against global competition. Furthermore, 'it can be seen that cumulatively [the changes in the production structure] have been destructive of labor's autonomous collective social power' (Cox 1987: 336).

Cox identifies two main lines of separation within the working class. First, there is a rift between workers of transnational companies and those of national companies, shadowing the conflict within capital. Second, while some few, highly skilled workers in core plants enjoy a high status and job security, the overall number of established workers has declined during the course of industrial restructuring and a rift between established and non-established workers has opened up (Cox 1981: 235).

Due to transnational production and finance, 'it becomes increasingly pertinent to think in terms of a global class structure alongside or superimposed upon national class structures' (Cox 1981: 147). Thus, Cox 'has noted that . . . there may be an emerging transnational historic[al] bloc' (Gill and Law 1988: 65). Transnational capital of TNCs in manufacturing and services and of global financial management, the driving force behind the transnationalisation of production and finance, is at the apex of this historical bloc. Small and middle-sized businesses, such as contractors or suppliers, import–export businesses, and service companies, such as stockbrokers and accountants, all linked to TNCs and, thereby, the global economy also form a part of it (Gill 1995: 400–1). Moreover, 'the established workers in the sector of [transnational] production are potential allies of [transnational] capital' (Cox 1981: 148). The system of 'enterprise corporatism', which closely links core workers to their particular company via special benefits and secure employment, may provide the basis for an alliance of this type (Cox 1987: 70–4). They are supported by elements from the state apparatuses of the Group of Seven countries, most importantly officials of those national ministries and institutions which are linked to the global economy through the internationalisation of the state such as finance ministries, prime ministers' offices and central banks. Finally, this order is further sustained by institutions such as the Organisation for Economic Co-operation and Development (OECD), the International Monetary Fund (IMF) and the World Bank, which contribute to the spread of neo-liberal economic ideas.

Neo-liberalism has been the hegemonic project of the transnational historical bloc's bid for hegemony (Overbeek and van der Pijl 1993: 2, 14–16). In particular two neo-liberal offensives were organised by organic intellectuals in networks such as the Mont Pèlerin Society. The first was the propagation of a neo-liberal, deregulatory economic programme to replace the Keynesian welfare state from the early 1970s onwards. The second had the goal of starting a world-wide offensive against Communism, forcing the Soviet Union to the wall economically in an intensified and highly technological arms race, in the late 1970s, early 1980s (van der Pijl 1995: 122–4). This does not mean that these intellectuals and their neo-liberal offensives were directly responsible for the various policy outputs. It implies, however, that they contributed to the setting of the agenda for a new, global hegemonic order based on the ideas of neo-liberal economics and strict anti-Communism.

Nevertheless, as in every truly dialectical process, there are also opposing social forces, pointing to alternative forms of development, to other possible hegemonic orders. The crisis due to the break-up of the hegemonic order of 'embedded liberalism' is 'a crisis of representation: one historic[al] bloc is dissolving, another has not taken its place' (Cox 1987: 285). So far, the transnational historical bloc outlined above enjoys a position of supremacy. It is dominant within the current world order, but has not gained hegemony yet (Gill 1995: 400). The achievement of the latter is doubtful for two reasons. First, internal contradictions may break the transnational historical bloc apart, unless new international regulatory mechanisms are established. There are tensions between 'short-term-thinking' transnational finance, causing insecurity in the financial markets, and 'long-term-thinking' TNCs in manufacturing. Transnational capital is not a homogeneous class fraction.[4] Furthermore, the neo-liberal economic logic itself contains a contradiction. 'If all countries compete to prove their monetary soundness, their deflationary policies will have negative multiplier effects. World recession is the natural outcome if all countries deflate simultaneously' (Gill and Law 1989: 494).

Second, alternative historical blocs may arise with their own hegemonic project and endanger the transnational bloc's supremacy. For example, a neo-mercantilist class alliance consisting of national industries, dependent on protectionism and state subsidies, their employees and those ministries which are concerned with national problems such as unemployment is a possible alternative. 'The hegemonic concepts within this type of bloc are those of national security and territorial sovereignty' (Gill and Law 1988: 105). So far, the transnational historical bloc has gained supremacy and may eventually win hegemony over the neo-mercantilist national social forces, but the opposite development remains possible too.

To sum up, since the early 1970s, we have experienced a structural change called globalisation. 'The new reality is that the system of states is overlaid by a highly integrated, incompletely regulated, rapidly growing – but consequently somewhat unstable – [global] economy' (Strange 1994b: 212). This has implied the restructuring of states as well as the re-configuration of social forces. Global in its nature, this structural change has not left the EU unaffected. As elsewhere, globalisation has led to a transnational restructuring of social relations. The deregulation of national financial markets was institutionalised in the Internal Market programme, which stated that all remaining capital controls of member states had to be abolished by 1 July 1990. Only Greece and Portugal were given an extension of this period until the end of 1995. The significance of Euro-companies has increased drastically in economic and employment terms since the 1980s. The transnationalisation of production has not only affected countries such as the UK and the

Netherlands, which were always characterised by the presence of TNCs, but also France and Germany (Marginson and Sisson 1994: 18–23).

Finally, as indicated in chapter one, the shift towards neo-liberalism was expressed by the very nature of the Internal Market programme and EMU. Gill infers that 'an assessment of the recomposition of social structures and political arrangements during the 1960s, 1970s and 1980s is crucial to understanding the complexities of the "new" Europe' (Gill 1992: 159; see also Holman and van der Pijl 1996: 65–6). Hence, the revived process of European integration since the mid-1980s and, by extension, the Austrian and Swedish accession as a part of it have to be analysed against the background of globalisation.

The post-war economic and political systems in Austria and Sweden

According to Katzenstein, similar to other countries with small, open and vulnerable economies, Austria and Sweden, 'while letting international markets force economic adjustments, [chose] a variety of economic and social policies that [prevented] the costs of change from causing political eruptions' (Katzenstein 1985: 24). An active investment and employment policy, restraints on wage and price increases and the maintenance of a large public sector were among their most important domestic policies. In both countries, these policies were conducted within a corporatist system. Corporatism signifies an institutional set-up in which the organised co-option of interest associations in the policy-making process exists parallel to the party system. Lehmbruch's definition of corporatism contains the following three dimensions (Lehmbruch 1982: 5–6). First, interest groups are co-opted into the decision-making process of the government, and particular groups are closely linked to particular parties and participate in policy formulation and implementation in their specific area. Second, interest associations are hierarchically organised with compulsory membership and, enjoying a monopoly in their specific area, do not have to compete with other associations. Finally, industrial relations are characterised by a strong concertation of labour and capital with the government at the national level.[5]

The Austrian economic and political system: 'Austrokeynesianism'

The Austrian economic system

In the post-war era, the Austrian government made full employment its primary economic target. Hence, it first promoted investment through tax incentives and cheap credit. Second, the restraint of wage and price increases was achieved within the corporatist system of Economic and Social Partnership (ESP) (see p. 29). Third, the large publicly owned companies were expected to conform to government policy. They were export-oriented, but subsidies were used to ensure full employment. Overall, they employed 'about one-quarter of the Austrian labour force and [generated] about one-third of net production and almost half of all investment' (Marin 1985: 121).[6] The exposure of industrial sectors to international competition was further counterbalanced by a large sheltered sector encompassing areas such as agriculture and the food processing industry. Estimates indicate that up to 50 per cent of the market may have been part of the sheltered sector (Luif 1994: 26). Moreover, a Keynesian policy of budget deficit spending during economic recession, practised during the 1970s in particular (Lauber 1996: 133–4), was flanked by a hard currency policy through linking the Austrian Schilling (AS) to the German Mark (DM) (Dörfel *et al.* 1993).[7] The combination of these policy instruments gave the Austrian system the name 'Austrokeynesianism' (Lauber 1992: 163).

From a theoretical perspective, this unorthodox policy mix cannot work. A hard currency policy usually endangers jobs linked to the export industry, because the products of a country become more expensive abroad, thereby undermining the policy of full employment. Nevertheless, in the Austrian case, full employment 'was secured via expansive budget deficits, via one-off improvements in efficiency and productivity gains or via the extension of export and investment support schemes' (Winkler 1988: 226, author's translation). Kurzer further points out that 'the Austrian establishment could get away with this contradictory arrangement because the financial integration of the Austrian economy into the world economy was moderate' (Kurzer 1993: 190). This was to change in the course of the 1980s and Austria's integration in the emerging global financial market.

The Austrian political system: institutionalised corporatism

The Austrian party system has long been dominated by two big parties, the Austrian People's Party (ÖVP) and the Social Democratic Party (SPÖ). Between 1945 and 1966, they governed Austria together in a grand coalition, a situation which has been repeated since 1987. From 1966 to 1970, the ÖVP formed a government by itself; between 1970 and 1983 it was the SPÖ's turn to do the same. Only between 1983 and 1986 did a small party share power, when there was a coalition of one of the two big parties, the SPÖ, with the small Austrian Freedom Party (FPÖ). The joint predominance of the ÖVP and SPÖ is most clearly expressed in their combined share of the vote. Although this figure declined steadily from the early 1970s onwards, it was not before the general elections of 1994 that they lost their two-third majority, only to regain it in the elections in the following year (see Table 2.1).[8] In 1986, the Green Alternative Party (GA) entered parliament as the fourth party and in 1993, five MPs left the FPÖ to establish the Liberal Forum (Müller

Table 2.1 Elections to the Austrian Parliament, 1945–95 (% of votes)

Election year	ÖVP	SPÖ	FPÖ	GA	LibFo	Combined shares of SPÖ and ÖVP
1945	49.79	44.59	—	—	—	94.4
1949	44.03	38.71	11.66	—	—	82.7
1953	41.25	42.10	10.94	—	—	83.4
1956	45.95	43.04	6.52	—	—	89.0
1959	44.19	44.78	7.70	—	—	89.0
1962	45.43	43.99	7.04	—	—	89.4
1966	48.34	42.56	5.35	—	—	90.9
1970	44.69	48.42	5.52	—	—	93.1
1971	43.11	50.03	5.45	—	—	93.2
1975	42.94	50.42	5.40	—	—	94.0
1979	41.90	51.02	6.06	—	—	92.9
1983	43.22	47.65	4.98	—	—	90.8
1986	41.29	43.12	9.73	4.80	—	84.4
1990	32.06	42.80	16.63	4.78	—	74.9
1994	27.67	34.92	22.50	7.31	5.97	62.6
1995	28.30	38.32	22.08	4.57	5.28	66.6

Source: Müller 1996b: 74 (1945-94 elections); Lauber 1996: 277 (1995 elections); Dachs 1991: 266 (GA result for 1986); Dachs 1991: 273 (GA result for 1990); Müller 1996b: 91 (combined shares of SPÖ and ÖVP)

Notes
ÖVP   Austrian People's Party
SPÖ   Austrian Social Democratic Party
FPÖ   Austrian Freedom Party
GA   Green Alternative Party
LibFo Liberal Forum
Other parties are not included in this table
Percentages given are for valid votes cast

1996b). The fact that the SPÖ formed a single party government from 1970 to 1983 does not mean that it enjoyed a hegemonic position within the Austrian party system. Austria's federal structure always gave the ÖVP a governmental role in several of the *Länder*.

Even more importantly, the ÖVP was guaranteed direct impact on policy-making in the corporatist institutional set-up, the Economic and Social Partnership (ESP). Historically, the Austrian corporatist system was established after the Second World War as a response to the experience of civil war in 1934, repression, defeat in war and foreign occupation (Katzenstein 1985: 188). Additionally, Marin makes clear that the success of corporatism depended on its correspondence to the underlying socio-economic structure. The nationalised industry allowed for a certain governmental control of the means of production, and the absence of a powerful financial and industrial bourgeoisie further added to the balance of power between capital and labour (Marin 1985: 121–2). Austrian corporatism comes very close to Lehmbruch's ideal type definition. As for the first dimension, the four main interest associations, the social partners, comprising the Chamber of Labour (AK), the Chamber of Commerce (BWK), the Chamber of Agriculture (LK) and the Austrian Federation of Trade Unions (ÖGB), are co-opted into governmental decision-making through the key institution Parity Commission. The social partners are closely linked to the government/party politics level through intensive mutual inter-penetration, multiple activities of functionaries (*Personalunion/ Ämterkumulierung*) and staff-sharing (Marin 1985: 101). Many of the social partners' 'leaders sit in Parliament, occupying important party functions. Holders of ministerial portfolios for economic and social matters are recruited among them' (Lehmbruch 1982: 17). In general, the AK and the ÖGB are controlled by the SPÖ, while the ÖVP dominates the BWK and the LK (Tálos 1996: 108).

In the second dimension of corporatism, the three Chambers are hierarchically structured and membership is obligatory. They are strongly centralised bodies, which enjoy a monopoly in their sphere. Only the ÖGB is based on voluntary membership, but it is also extremely centralised and the degree of unionisation is high in Austria with more than 60 per cent of blue- and white-collar workers (Tálos 1996: 105).

In the third dimension, the concertation of industrial relations takes place within the Parity Commission, which consists of members of the Chambers, the ÖGB and two members of government. It has three main functions represented by three sub-committees. The price sub-committee used to regulate about one third of all prices until 1992, when its role was changed into competition policy. The wages sub-committee 'decides on the timing of autonomous collective bargaining and ratifies its results, which are not valid without its consent' (Marin 1985: 108). Finally, the Economic and Social Advisory Board develops 'concepts and proposals for decision-making in economic policy and middle-term planning based on scientific information' (Marin 1985: 108–9).

To sum up, the policy of 'Austrokeynesianism', managing an economy with a competitive sector, open to world free trade, a large export-oriented, but subsidised industrial public sector, and a sheltered sector, protected against international competition, was based on a system of institutionalised corporatism which attributed clear policy functions to interest associations.

> Essentially, it obliged the social partners to monitor incomes policy in a way that was consistent with a hard currency stance, in return for an obligation by the government to take fiscal action if full employment and/or business income was endangered.
>
> (Wieser and Kitzmantel 1990: 434–5)

The economic and political system in Sweden: the 'Swedish Model'

The Swedish economic system

A sophisticated economic model, developed by the Swedish Trade Union Confederation (LO) theorists Gösta Rehn and Rudolf Meidner at the beginning of the 1950s, allowed Sweden to combine a policy of full employment with low inflation. The solidaristic wage principle was its core feature. The wage rate was not set according to the ability of an individual firm to pay, but as a 'just' wage across all sectors. For inefficient firms, exposed to international competition, this wage was often too high and they, consequently, went bankrupt and set labour free. Efficient, competitive firms, though, were able to reap large profits, as the set wage was lower than what they were able to pay. Together, higher profits and the labour supply of bankrupt companies were strong incentives for expansion in the dynamic sectors of the economy (Ryner 1994: 400–1). Additionally, the state supported the transfer of labour from declining to expanding industrial sectors via an active manpower policy which included education, job training, information, generous grants for families to move and the creation of some sheltered employment (Esping-Andersen 1985: 229–31). This active manpower policy together with the solidaristic wage principle made wage restraint acceptable to Swedish trade unions.

The Swedish public sector is of a different nature from the Austrian. Between 1978 and 1980, state-owned enterprises accounted for about 6 per cent of Sweden's GDP. Except for the Netherlands, this was the smallest share in Western Europe (Parris *et al.* 1987: 27). The public sector is responsible for the provision of education, health care, day nurseries, pre-school educational facilities and (although less so) housing, all areas which are not exposed to international competition. Public spending in these areas rose from roughly 30 per cent of the GNP in 1960 to 66 per cent by 1980. In addition to being a tool for constant social reform, the expansion of the public sector was used to safeguard full employment. In the 1970s, expanding industrial sectors were less and less able to absorb labour shed by declining industries. Almost 90 per cent of job growth took place in public social services during this time to take up the slack (Heclo and Madsen 1987: 165–6).

Luif, furthermore, points out that 'in addition to the huge sheltered sector, there was an . . . encompassing regulation of the financial markets in the corporatist EFTA-countries' (Luif 1994: 26, author's translation). Through their control of currency transactions these governments, including Austria and Sweden, were in a strong position to manage their national economy. While Austria chose to adopt a hard currency policy, the regulation of national financial markets allowed Sweden to pursue its policy of full employment via repeated devaluations. In 1977, it left the 'Snake', a predecessor of the European Monetary System (EMS), and devalued the Swedish Krona (SKr) by 10 per cent the following day, having already devalued in April 1977 by 6 per cent. Another devaluation of 10 per cent followed on 14 September 1981 (Moses 1995: 413–19).

The Swedish political system

The Swedish party system has been characterised by social democratic hegemony. 'Between 1932 and 1976 Sweden was governed uninterruptedly for 44 years by a Social Democratic prime minister' (Bergström 1991: 8). Only between 1976 and 1982 and from 1991 to 1994, was the SAP out of office. There have traditionally been three parties on the right of the party system: the Liberal Party (FP), the conservative Moderate Party (MS) and the Centre Party (CP), the former Agrarian Party. Additionally, in 1991, the Christian Democratic Party and the right-wing populist party New Democracy gained seats in the Riksdag, the Swedish parliament. While the former just managed to hang on in 1994, the latter dropped out again three years later (Madeley 1995: 425).[9] These two parties do not feature highly here due to this short-lived and unstable electoral success. On the left, there have additionally been the VP and, since 1988, the Green Party (GP). The latter did not gain parliamentary seats in 1991, but was re-elected in 1994.

The social democratic hegemony has not been expressed in its share of the electoral votes. Table 2.2 shows that the SAP has gained 40 per cent and more most of the time, but it never received a decisive majority, except in 1940. The SAP often formed a minority government and relied on the tacit support of the CP and/or VP and also the GP in the 1990s. Castles points out that the split of the right into three parties has been as important for the SAP's dominant position as its own electoral strength. It 'made it very difficult to find the necessary cohesion to offer a credible alternative to Social Democratic rule' (Castles 1978: 23; see also 131–42). More importantly, however, hegemony was ensured via the SAP's immense organisational power in terms of members, active campaign workers and close links to the Swedish Trade Union Confederation (LO) and other mass membership organisations. The SAP had a long tradition of programmatic renewal (Sainsbury 1993: 42) and its regular new programmes, developed together with the LO, were generally accompanied by a range of educational materials, study circles and local conferences. 'Contemporary Swedes have been taught to comprehend their present as the result of a largely coherent sequence of Social Democratic plans and therefore have become inclined to look to the Social Democrats for workable future solutions' (Heclo and Madsen 1987: 44).

The Swedish corporatist system was established in the 1930s in response to the Great Depression. Its political basis, the alliance between farmers and workers, was formed in 1933 in a crisis agreement. Its cementing of 1936 in the form of a formal coalition 'paved the way to industrial peace in

Table 2.2 Elections to the Swedish Riksdag, 1932–98 (% of votes)

Election year	SAP	VP	GP	MS	FP	CP
1932	41.7	8.3	—	23.5	11.7	14.1
1936	45.9	7.7	—	17.6	12.9	14.3
1940	53.8	4.2	—	18.0	12.0	12.0
1944	46.7	10.3	—	15.9	12.9	13.6
1948	46.1	6.3	—	12.3	22.8	12.4
1952	46.1	4.3	—	14.4	24.4	10.7
1956	44.6	5.0	—	17.1	23.8	9.4
1958	46.2	3.4	—	19.5	18.2	12.7
1960	47.8	4.5	—	16.5	17.5	13.6
1964	47.3	5.2	—	13.7	17.0	13.2
1968	50.1	3.0	—	12.9	14.3	15.7
1970	45.3	4.8	—	11.5	16.2	19.9
1973	43.6	5.3	—	14.3	9.4	25.1
1976	42.7	4.8	—	15.6	11.1	24.1
1979	43.2	5.6	—	20.3	10.6	18.1
1982	45.6	5.6	1.7	23.6	5.9	15.5
1985	44.7	5.4	1.5	21.3	14.2	9.8
1988	43.2	5.8	5.5	18.3	12.2	11.3
1991	37.7	4.5	3.4	21.9	9.1	8.5
1994	45.3	6.2	5.0	22.4	7.2	7.7
1998	36.4	12.0	4.5	22.9	4.7	5.1

Source: Petersson 1994: 226 (1932–94); Swedish Embassy/London for 1998

Notes
SAP Social Democratic Party
VP Left Party
GP Green Party
MS Moderate Party
FP Liberal Party
CP Centre Party
Data for 1932–1968 refers to elections to the Lower House
Other parties are not included in this table
Percentages given are for valid votes cast

the 1938 Saltsjöbaden agreement, concluded between the central organization of business and the labour movement' (Katzenstein 1985: 141, see also Esping-Andersen 1985: 86–7). The unions acquiesced in the continuation of private control over property and capital markets, openness to the world economy, and offered industrial peace. In exchange, the employers accepted higher labour costs, a relatively expansive fiscal policy and the growth of welfare services. The SAP government supported the agreement through its commitment to full employment, its active manpower policy and the maintenance of a large public sector.

As for the first dimension of Lehmbruch's definition of corporatism, the interest associations enjoyed a strong influence on policy-making and implementation until the early 1990s. They were represented on the lay boards of about thirty state agencies such as the Labour Market Board and on state commissions, which had the task of preparing major social reforms. They also considered the reports of these state commissions and participated in local government tasks such as the administration of unemployment insurance. Finally, they participated through general agreements, of which the agreement in Saltsjöbaden of 1938 was the first (Lewin 1994: 67–8).

The SAP has strong links with the LO via collective affiliation, phased out between 1987 and 1990, and 'overlapping membership of the LO leadership in the executive bodies of the party' (Sainsbury 1991: 40). Leaders of the Swedish Confederation of Professional Employees (TCO) have frequently been members of the SAP (Bergström 1991: 8). There are also strong links between the CP and the Federation of Swedish Farmers (LRF). At the end of the 1970s, about 65 per cent of LRF members were members of the CP. This figure has decreased since then, but it is estimated to be still over 50 per cent. Between 20 and 25 per cent of LRF members are members of the MS (Interview no. 50; Stockholm, 14 November 1996). 'Large business interests and upper-income groups traditionally have been associated with [the MS]' (Heclo and Madsen 1987: 17). Their links to bourgeois parties are, however, less strong. They had often withdrawn from partisan politics, because they were quite satisfied with the social democratic government's economic policy (Swenson 1991a: 536–7). In parliament, these links implied that between 1971 and 1979 35 per cent of MPs were members of the LO, 29 per cent of the TCO, and 15 per cent of the Swedish Confederation of Professional Associations (SACO), while 9 per cent were members of employers' associations (Gustafsson 1986: 40).

In the second dimension, the degree of unionisation at about 85 per cent of the total workforce is very high and the Confederation of Swedish Employers (SAF) 'represents 40,000 firms in private industry, including all of the largest firms' (Ahlén 1989: 331).[10] In contrast to Austria, however, there is no compulsory membership, more rank and file autonomy, and no individual peak trade union or employers' association enjoys a representational monopoly. The LO organises blue-collar and the lower-paid non-manual workers and is the main trade union, with over 2 million members. The TCO, however, with over one million white-collar members, as well as SACO) which mainly represents university-trained professionals and has roughly 350,000 members, also enjoy an independent voice.[11] On the employers' side, there are two big associations, which work as partners in the promotion of business, the Federation of Swedish Industries (SI) and the SAF. While the former lobbies the government on policies, advises constituent firms and trade associations and informs the public about these issues, the latter was until the early 1990s responsible for collective bargaining with the trade unions (Milner 1989: 87). *Företagarna*, the Federation of Private Enterprises, mainly represents small and medium-sized enterprises, for which it fulfils the same function as the SI for its members (Interview no. 69; Stockholm, 3 December 1996).

Within the various associations, there was a strong hierarchy and predominance of the central organisations over their affiliated unions or member associations. During the 1980s, however, this hierarchy was undermined and the principle of collective wage-negotiations came under pressure (see p. 46). Finally, the LRF represents agricultural interests. The fact that it organises farmers and the food processing industry at the same time makes it a powerful interest association (Milner 1989: 76). It is the only association, which enjoys a representational monopoly.

Considering the third dimension of corporatism, unlike in Austria, the concertation of industrial relations has not been institutionalised, but it became a regular feature of Swedish politics via the repetition of collective central wage-bargaining year after year. In the 1950s and 1960s, the SAF–LO negotiations in the private sector provided the unchallenged guidance for other negotiations. This was to change in the late 1960s and 1970s. As a result of a rapid expansion of the service sector, the public sector unions within the LO gained in importance. Additionally, the TCO and the SACO played an increasingly independent role. A new model was devised at the end of the 1960s by the SAF and LO together with the TCO, but this did not prevent the emergence of additional collective wage-bargaining rounds. In the private sector, the Federation of Salaried Employees in Industry and Services was formed as a negotiation cartel by unions affiliated to the TCO and SACO. It bargained in parallel to the LO–SAF negotiations (Ahlén 1989: 331–2).

In the public sector, affiliated unions of all three major trade union organisations formed two negotiation cartels, one for state employees and one for local government employees. Overall, however, even without a central institution to co-ordinate the negotiations (as did the wages sub-committee of the Parity Commission in Austria), the main trade union confederations LO, TCO and SACO enjoyed a strong position in relation to their affiliated unions until the early 1980s, as did the SAF towards its member federations (Milner 1989: 86–91; The Swedish Institute 1994).

In sum, corporatism and the SAP hegemony within the party system provided the political structure for the economic policies of full employment, solidaristic wages, active manpower, large public sector and generous welfare provisions. Together, this is often referred to as 'the Swedish Model'. A final component of this model is the emphasis on gender equality to be achieved via equality in the labour market and economic independence for women. Especially the rapidly expanding public sector absorbed female labour in the 1970s and 1980s (Eduards 1991). As in Austria with 'Austrokeynesianism', the Swedish Model was based on the compromise of 'embedded liberalism' at the international level (Ryner 1999: 51). Its break-up and the onset of globalisation in the early 1970s put the Swedish Model under strain.

The impact of the processes of globalisation on Austria and Sweden

According to the characteristics of globalisation, the transnationalisation of finance and production and the change in the economic paradigm from Keynesianism to neo-liberalism, three primary indicators can be identified. First, the transnationalisation of finance implies that a country's financial markets have been integrated into the global financial market. The clearest indicator for this is whether Austria's and Sweden's financial markets have become deregulated and liberalised, since this has been identified as one of the components of the transnationalisation of finance.

The second indicator relates to the transnationalisation of production. It has to be investigated whether there has been a change in the countries' production structure since the early 1970s and, if so, in what way. Considering the crucial role of TNCs and FDI, the degree of the transnationalisation of production is assessed here, initially through the number of TNCs and the scale of their activities in the production system of Austria and Sweden. The percentage of employment and turnover abroad indicates their general orientation. Furthermore, changes in FDI flows indicate an increasing or decreasing degree of transnationalisation.

Third, the extent to which neo-liberalism has taken root in Austria and Sweden needs to be examined. This can be identified in the expression of a conflict between neo-liberal and Keynesian ideas about issues such as deregulation, privatisation and cut-backs in the welfare system, which are all points on the neo-liberal agenda. In order to ascertain the influence of neo-liberalism, a change should, however, also be noticed in the two countries' actual policies. In other words, it is necessary to investigate whether a shift from the welfare state in the direction of the neo-liberal night-watchman state has occurred.

The impact of globalisation on Austria

The transnationalisation of Austrian finance

The real power in the post-war Austrian financial system rested with the joint-stock commercial banks, not the Austrian National Bank (ANB), Austria's central bank. Public control over these banks and, thereby, over the financial system had been the result of pre-war developments, when the government had nationalised several banks to rescue them from bankruptcy (Kurzer 1993: 38). As a result, of the three most important joint-stock commercial banks, the Creditanstalt Bankverein and the Österreichische Länderbank were in public ownership. Only the Österreichische Kontrollbank was privately owned. The ANB was jointly owned and controlled by the government and the social partners, each holding 50 per cent of the shares. In general, the financial system was oriented towards the domestic market. 'Neither commercial banks nor specialized credit institutions were driven by international ambitions, nor were they at the forefront of financial innovations' (Kurzer 1993: 168). Integration into the global financial market was achieved in a different way.

The Austrian preference for low inflation and a hard currency has to be seen in the light of Austria's monetary history since the 1920s (Dörfel *et al.* 1993: 116). Having experienced hyperinflation between 1920 and 1922, a currency crisis in 1931 and turbulent times directly after the Second World War, a hard currency policy became a legal obligation for the ANB. Consequently, from 1971 onwards, but especially after 1973 and the final break-up of the Bretton Woods system of fixed exchange rates, the AS was first pegged to a currency basket and then, in 1977, solely to the DM as the only remaining strong currency within the basket. When it became clear that the 1979 EMS had the goals of low inflation and stable exchange rates, Austria followed EU policy more closely. The ANB decided to shadow the EMS autonomously and, in order to achieve credibility for its hard currency policy, openly declared the pegging of the AS to the DM in 1981. When the SEA included the free movement of capital, Austrian decision-makers followed. The gradual liberalisation of Austrian financial markets started in 1986 and 'culminated in the abolition of the last exchange restrictions in November 1991' (Dörfel *et al.* 1993: 118).

In conclusion, Austria gave up an autonomous monetary policy by pegging the AS to the DM. It thereby voluntarily accepted restrictions on its national policy autonomy in the 1970s. Although international pressure through the processes of globalisation was felt in Austria (Interview no. 16; Vienna, 18 May 1995), the integration of Austrian financial markets into the global financial market was the logical consequence of the hard currency policy adopted previously. As argued earlier, states not only have to adapt to the global economy, they also play an active role in the processes of globalisation.

The transnationalisation of Austrian production

Austria's post-war production structure has been predominantly characterised by small-scale industry. In 1992, of the 2.19 million working population, 55 per cent were employed in small-sized companies with less than 100 employees, and 28 per cent in medium-sized companies with less than 1,000 employees. This is a relatively high percentage in international terms. In general, these companies contribute only between one and two thirds to the overall national employment (Breit and Rössl 1992: 191).

Siegel identified twenty-one Austrian TNCs, but only one of them, Austrian Industries, lived up to international standards in 1990 (Siegel 1992). It was formed as a state-owned holding company in 1987, when the public industry sector was restructured, but the experiment to create an Austrian TNC of international significance failed in 1992. The company was split up and sold off in parts. The production structures of the twenty-one TNCs were concentrated mainly in Austria, employing only 20 per cent of their workforce abroad (Siegel 1992: 167). In short, the low number of TNCs and their focus on Austria signals a low degree of the transnationalisation of production.

Nevertheless, this does not mean that Austria has been totally unaffected by globalisation. Although still modest in overall terms, both inward and outward FDI rose during the second half of the 1980s. During the crucial years for the debate about Austrian EU membership, outward FDI increased from US$ 66 million in 1985 to US$ 1,601 million in 1990 and inward FDI from US$ 164 million to US$ 557 million during the same period (see Table 2.3). This tendency was underlined by the growth of the foreign private sector in Austria, where employment rose by 16 per cent between 1970 and 1985 (Pichl 1989: 164). It indicates an increasing, albeit overall small, presence of foreign TNCs in Austria.

In general, however, Austria is linked to the global economy mainly via the traditional route of exports and imports in goods. In 1990, outward FDI accounted for only 3.9 per cent of the export in goods and inward FDI for only 1.3 per cent of the import in goods despite the general increase in FDI, outlined earlier (Bellak 1992: 31–2). Furthermore, the quantity of outward and inward FDI is small in comparison with total domestic investment. For example, inward FDI made up only 4.4 per cent of domestic investment in 1990 (Bellak 1992: 30–1). This is in stark contrast to the Swedish situation, where outward FDI in 1989 was larger than total domestic investment (as discussed later in this chapter). To conclude, the degree of the transnationalisation of production increased in the 1970s and 1980s only slowly. Austria is still linked to the global economy via cross-border flows with an emphasis on trade. Globalisation has been felt as increasing internationalisation, not transnationalisation of production.

Table 2.3 Austrian outward and inward FDI (in million US $), 1982–90

	Outward FDI	Inward FDI
1982	148	203
1983	162	217
1984	67	109
1985	66	164
1986	243	162
1987	389	376
1988	186	404
1989	672	550
1990	1601	557

Source: EFTA 1991: 43–4

The restructuring of the Austrian state

The ideological debate between Keynesian and neo-liberal ideas started in Austria in 1982 against the background of severe economic difficulties. Economic growth slowed down, and was even negative in 1981 at minus 0.3 per cent, while unemployment reached a level of more than 3 per cent, unheard of in a country which had been used to a level of around 1 per cent throughout the 1970s. At the same time, inflation increased to above 6 per cent in 1980 and 1981 and the budget deficit, apart from not achieving stronger economic growth and full employment, could not be turned around (see Table 2.4, page 40).

In this situation, the ÖVP adopted a neo-liberal strategy, which included demands for budgetary cuts, tax reform, flexibility, deregulation and privatisation, as an alternative to the SPÖ's Keynesianism (Meth-Cohn and Müller 1994: 162–3). Significant parts of the SPÖ also started supporting the change in economic policy and, although slightly later than the ÖVP but before both parties formed a coalition government in 1987, took up neo-liberal ideas. On the one hand, against the background of the devastating economic situation in general and the huge deficits of the public sector industries in particular, the belief that a social democratic manager is morally better than a capitalist one vanished (Interview no. 15; Vienna, 17 May 1995). On the other hand, Franz Vranitzky, a former bank manager who was Finance Minister from 1983 onwards, became the new SPÖ chancellor in 1986. He approached the economic problems as a business man, and his 'team abandoned [the] policy of relying on the nationalised industries, interventionist industrial policies, and stimulative fiscal deficits to secure full employment' (Schultz 1992: 189). Instead, together with the ÖVP as coalition partner since early 1987, 'it now emphasised budget consolidation, profitability and privatisation for the public sector' (Lauber 1992: 157). Subsidies for the public sector should, consequently, be allocated according to the principle of efficiency, not in order to maintain full employment. The coalition agreement between the ÖVP and the SPÖ of 16 January 1987 further spelled out that the open sector of the economy could no longer be alone responsible for structural adjustment. The new task is 'to expose, step by step, more areas of the sheltered sector to international competition. The orientation towards regulation will have to give way to the market' (*Arbeitsübereinkommen* 1987: 652, author's translation).

This change in economic ideas prepared the ground for political action. Once neo-liberalism had got hold of both governing coalition parties, policies of this type appeared to be the only possible option in view of Austria's economic problems. The new coalition government announced the consolidation of the budget through a period of austerity in 1987. This was not always successful during the following years (Lauber 1996: 137–8), but the intention to pursue austerity policies indicated a change in practical politics. Moreover, in general

Table 2.4 Austrian economic data, 1970–97

	Economic growth	Unemployment	Budget deficit	Inflation
1970	6.4	1.1	+1.2	4.4
1971	5.1	1.0	+1.5	4.7
1972	6.2	1.0	+2.0	6.3
1973	4.9	0.9	+1.3	7.6
1974	3.9	1.1	+1.3	9.5
1975	-0.4	1.5	-2.5	8.4
1976	4.6	1.5	-3.7	7.3
1977	4.5	1.4	-2.4	5.5
1978	0.1	1.7	-2.8	3.6
1979	4.7	1.7	-2.4	3.7
1980	2.9	1.5	-1.7	6.3
1981	-0.3	2.1	-1.8	6.8
1982	1.9	3.2	-3.4	5.4
1983	2.8	3.8	-4.0	3.3
1984	0.3	3.9	-2.7	5.7
1985	2.2	4.2	-2.6	3.2
1986	2.3	4.5	-3.8	1.7
1987	1.7	4.9	-4.4	1.4
1988	3.2	4.7	-3.3	1.9
1989	4.2	4.3	-3.1	2.6
1990	4.6	4.7	-2.4	3.3
1991	3.4	5.2	-2.7	3.3
1992	1.3	5.3	-1.9	4.0
1993	0.5	6.1	-4.2	3.6
1994	2.5	5.9	-5.0	3.0
1995	2.1	5.9	-5.1	2.2
1996	1.6	6.3	-3.7	1.9
1997	2.5	6.4	-1.9	1.3

Notes

Economic growth: Real GDP (percentage change from previous period). Source: OECD 1990: 181 (1970–81); OECD 1998: 191 (1982–97)

Unemployment rate: Commonly used definition. Source: OECD 1990: 199 (1970–81); OECD 1998: 211 (1982–97)

Budget deficit: General government financial balances (surplus (+) or deficit (-) as a percentage of nominal GDP). Source: OECD 1990: 194 (1970–81); OECD 1998: 220 (1982–97)

Inflation: Consumer prices (percentage change from previous period). Source: OECD 1985: 181 (1970–78); OECD 1998: 206 (1979–97)

terms the state withdrew from the market and the nationalised sector was restructured. Politicians left the boards of directors of companies, while managers from the private sector took over. Non-competitive firms were closed down, and their employees given early retirement or made redundant (Interview no. 8; Vienna, 11 May 1995). Parts of the public sector were privatised between 1987 and 1990. This policy was reinforced, when 'in November 1993 the coalition parties signed a new agreement on the nationalised sector which [meant] nothing less than the abolition of what was once relatively the most important state-owned industrial sector in Western Europe' (Meth-Cohn and Müller 1994: 174). Two tax reforms, in 1989 and in 1994, were also carried out as supply-side measures, making Austria 'a country with remarkably low business taxation' (Lauber 1996: 139). Finally, as noted above, the financial markets were fully liberalised.

The impact of globalisation on Sweden

The transnationalisation of Swedish finance

Foreign exchange controls and other forms of capital market regulations had been introduced in Sweden at the outbreak of the Second World War. During the 1950s, they were strengthened even further. These regulations, including lending ceilings, liquidity ratios, cash ratios, investment ratios, bond issue control and interest rate regulations, were administered by the Riksbank, the Swedish central bank (Jonung 1986: 109–11; Kurzer 1993: 176). The Riksbank is directly responsible to the Swedish parliament. Six of its seven directors are elected by parliament, the seventh director, who is also the chairman, is appointed by the government. As a consequence, 'the Riksbank functioned as an agency affiliated with the Ministry of Finance' (Kurzer 1993: 175). As the governing party, the SAP made control over the Riksbank and the financial market regulations a cornerstone of their full employment policy. Control of the financial markets separated the domestic from the international financial markets and provided the necessary economic autonomy for a counter-cyclical Keynesian economic policy.

From 1974 onwards, but especially after the SAP had returned to power in 1982, the financial market regulations were removed step by step. Among other measures, the liquidity ratio requirements for banks were abolished in 1983 and the ceiling on lending by banks removed in 1985 (Jonung 1986: 111). There are several reasons for the eventual deregulation of the financial markets. First, against the background of the severe economic crisis, the government had run up a budget deficit of 7 per cent by 1982 (see Table 2.6, page 49). In order to service these debts, it had to devise new forms of finance, often via finance houses outside the regulated markets. Additionally, 'the Swedish government was forced to start borrowing from abroad which contributed to a reduction in Sweden's financial isolation' (Jonung 1986: 113). Thus, the government's influence over monetary, credit and exchange rate policies started to decline. Second, the regulations themselves had been an incentive to the formation of finance houses. They grew rapidly in numbers in the 1970s and 1980s. 'Almost half of them were subsidiaries created by the large commercial banks in order to evade the restrictions imposed by the Riksbank' (Olsen 1991: 128).

The TNCs also participated in this development. In order to reduce exchange-rate uncertainty, but also to gain greater autonomy *vis-à-vis* the financial market regulations, TNCs like Volvo and Asea set up internal financial companies. From the early 1980s onwards, attempts were made to regulate these finance houses, but new ways of financing were developed with every new regulation, while the *de facto* control of Swedish banks was disturbed. Eventually, the government opted for deregulation (Notermans 1993: 145–6). It was considered to be better to abolish all regulations than to have regulations which did not work (Interview no. 37; Stockholm, 7 November 1996). In 1986, foreign banks were allowed to open branches in Sweden and, three years later, the SAP government took the final step and abolished foreign exchange controls.

Overall, Swedish financial markets have become integrated into the global financial system. This to a large extent deprived the SAP government of its monetary and economic policy autonomy. Although this was predominantly a response to outside pressure, however, (Jonung 1986: 116; Olsen 1991: 128), there was also a voluntary element to it. As outlined in the next section, the SAP adopted a hard currency policy in 1982. The liberalisation of the financial markets increased the costs of pursuing a flexible exchange rate and, thereby, gave more credibility to the policy of stable exchange rates.

The transnationalisation of Swedish production

Sweden has fostered an impressive number of large TNCs and important parts of production have, thus, always been transnationalised (Andersson *et al.* 1996: 27–47; Braunerhjelm *et al.* 1996: 2). Due to a wave of mergers since the end of the 1960s and a trend towards cross-ownership since the late 1970s, four main ownership groups emerged in a dominant position in the Swedish production structure by the mid-1980s: the Wallenberg empire, the closely linked Volvo and Skanska spheres, and Industrivarden-Svenska Handelsbank (Olsen 1991: 117–19).

The degree of transnationalisation increased dramatically in the second half of the 1980s, when there was a drastic upturn in outward FDI. Table 2.5 shows that while inward FDI had only risen from US$ 396 million in 1985 to US$ 2,328 million in 1990, outward FDI increased from US$ 1,783 million to US$ 14,136 million during the same period. This is even more dramatic, if one takes into account that 'in 1989 for the first time ever, Sweden invested more abroad than at home' (Kurzer 1993: 133). The increasing transnationalisation of Swedish production is also expressed in the change in the Swedish and foreign share of TNCs' employees and production. In 1965, TNCs employed 33.9 per cent of their employees abroad, where they achieved 25.9 per cent of their turnover. By 1990, the situation had drastically changed. Now, 60.6 per cent of the workforce was employed in production abroad, accounting for 51.4 per cent of the turnover. This increased emphasis on production abroad was especially

Table 2.5 Swedish outward and inward FDI (in million US $), 1982–90

	Outward FDI	Inward FDI
1982	1226	359
1983	1462	238
1984	1509	294
1985	1783	396
1986	3707	938
1987	4496	583
1988	7231	1497
1989	9683	1523
1990	14136	2328

Source: EFTA 1991: 43–4

apparent between 1986 and 1990. The percentage of employees abroad rose by 11.4 per cent, representing 42.7 per cent of the overall increase between 1965 and 1990, and the percentage of turnover abroad by 9.1 per cent, which is 35.7 per cent of the overall increase between 1965 and 1990 (Braunerhjelm *et al.* 1996: 10). Initially, foreign production by Swedish TNCs led to increased exports by these companies and, therefore, had no negative effect on the Swedish economy (Swedenborg 1979: 223). From the mid-1980s onwards, however, increased investment abroad substituted expansion at home and implied the transfer of production units (Andersson *et al.* 1996: 126). In some instances, this even included the transfer of headquarters. Asea Brown Boveri moved to Zürich in Switzerland and Tetra Pak and IKEA to locations in the EU.

The restructuring of the Swedish state

The SAP could not overlook the rising budget deficits and general economic crisis in the late 1970s and early 1980s. Economic growth had come to a halt in 1981, unemployment rose to over 3 per cent in 1982, which is high in a country used to full employment, the budget deficit reached a record high of 7 per cent and inflation was in double figures, at 13.7 and 12.1 per cent in 1980 and 1981 respectively (see Table 2.6, page 44).

On its return to power in 1982, the SAP implemented its so-called 'third way' strategy, supposed to be an alternative situated between traditional Keynesianism and neo-liberalism (Ryner 1994: 387–99). A 16 per cent devaluation of the SKr was carried out to ensure export-led growth and the recovery of the Swedish economy. This time, however, the devaluation was the start of a new monetary policy, not the continuation of the past, and 'the Big Bang's yield was to be insured with a new commitment to a fixed exchange rate regime' (Moses 1995: 313). Credibility for this hard currency policy with the goal of getting inflation under control was achieved not by linking the SKr

Table 2.6 Swedish economic data, 1970–97

	Economic growth	Unemploy- ment	Budget deficit	Inflation
1970	6.7	1.2	+4.6	7.0
1971	0.6	2.1	+5.3	7.4
1972	2.4	2.2	+4.4	6.0
1973	4.2	2.0	+4.1	6.7
1974	3.2	1.6	+2.0	9.9
1975	2.7	1.3	+2.8	9.8
1976	0.4	1.3	+4.7	10.3
1977	-1.5	1.5	+1.7	11.4
1978	2.0	1.8	-0.5	10.0
1979	4.0	1.7	-3.0	7.2
1980	1.4	1.6	-4.0	13.7
1981	0.0	2.1	-5.3	12.1
1982	1.0	3.2	-7.0	8.6
1983	1.8	3.5	-5.0	8.9
1984	4.0	3.1	-2.9	8.0
1985	1.9	2.8	-3.8	7.4
1986	2.3	2.5	-1.2	4.2
1987	3.1	2.1	+4.2	4.2
1988	2.3	1.7	+3.5	6.1
1989	2.4	1.5	+5.4	6.6
1990	1.4	1.6	+4.2	10.4
1991	-1.1	3.0	-1.1	9.7
1992	-1.4	5.3	-7.8	2.6
1993	-2.2	8.2	-12.3	4.7
1994	3.3	7.9	-10.3	2.4
1995	3.9	7.7	-7.0	2.9
1996	1.3	8.1	-3.5	0.8
1997	1.8	8.0	-0.8	0.9

Notes

Economic growth: Real GDP (percentage change from previous period). Source: OECD 1990: 181 (1970–81); OECD 1998: 191 (1982–97)

Unemployment rate: Commonly used definition. Source: OECD 1990: 199 (1970–81); OECD 1998: 211 (1982–97)

Budget deficit: General government financial balances (surplus (+) or deficit (-) as a percentage of nominal GDP). Source: OECD 1990: 194 (1970–81); OECD 1998: 220 (1982–97)

Inflation: Consumer prices (percentage change from previous period). Source: OECD 1985: 181 (1970–78); OECD 1998: 206 (1979–97)

to the DM, but by the Riksbank's action in the market place. In 1985 and 1990, it did not float the currency to relieve the pressure building up on the Swedish reserves. 'Instead, both times, it preferred to hike its overnight interest rates rather than devalue' (Moses 1995: 318). The liberalisation of the financial markets gave further credibility to the hard currency policy, since it made a flexible exchange rate policy more expensive.

The original success of the 'third way' strategy was impressive. Sweden maintained one of the lowest unemployment rates of the OECD countries, at less than 2 per cent between 1988 and 1990, and a 7 per cent budget deficit in 1982 was transformed into a 5.4 per cent surplus in 1989 (see Table 2.6). At the beginning of the 1990s, however, the economy faced the same problems as at the beginning of the previous decade. Economic growth slowed down and turned negative from 1991 onwards and the budget deficit again became negative in 1991, reaching 7.8 per cent in 1992 (see Table 2.6). As it turned out, while the macroeconomic balance had been restored, the structural problems of the Swedish economy had not been solved by the 'third way' strategy. Consequently, 'productivity growth increased only slightly between 1982 and 1990 to an average annual increase of 1 percent' (Ryner 1994: 396). While unemployment had successfully been checked, inflation had not been brought under control by the one-sided adoption of a hard currency regime. At an average of 8.6 per cent, it was significantly higher than the German rate of 3 per cent (Notermans 1993: 139). 'In February 1990, the government put forward a drastic action programme which among other things included a statutory pay freeze and a ban on strikes' (Bergström 1991: 15). This was defeated in parliament due to an outcry by the rank and file of trade unions.

After a new currency crisis in October 1990, the government, this time successfully, put forward another emergency package, including among other measures a partial privatisation of the Swedish state sector (including the telecommunications system and the electricity network) and a cut in the level of sickness benefits (Luif 1996: 215). It was further concluded that a general expansive fiscal policy in order to counter rising unemployment was no longer possible. 'Social Democrats eventually saw no other way than to abandon their central policy goal [of full employment] and institute a policy regime which consciously created unemployment in order to restore price stability' (Notermans 1993: 148).

According to Wilks, the change in economic policy was due to a change in the strategy of capital. 'What undermined the model was the rejection of the 50 year old historical compromise by Swedish business' (Wilks 1996: 94). Transnational capital had started dominating Swedish capital in general in the mid-1970s and its members took over key leadership positions in the employers' associations (Olsen: 1991: 131). When Asea's Curt Nicolin became the SAF's new executive director in 1978, the association not only changed its policies towards neo-liberalism but also the nature of its activities. The SAF attempted 'to shape intellectual and popular discourse and the terrain of contestability in civil society in a market friendly direction' (Ryner 1999: 59). In other words, it started transforming itself from a wage-bargaining institution into an ideologically-motivated think tank, which offered the platform for organic intellectuals to spread the neo-liberal message. It 'expanded into the political arena, where it ventured into "the marketing of capitalism" by establishing a range of publishing houses and by organising campaigns aimed at selected target groups to promote pro-capitalist ideology, particularly amongst the young'

(Whyman and Burkitt 1993: 607). The SAF's efforts were at first directed against the wage earner funds, which would have given workers the control over investment.[12] Then, the attack went against the solidaristic wage policy, corporatism and the welfare state (Olsen 1991: 131–6). In the spring of 1990, the SAF left the system of central wage-bargaining. 'The following winter, it withdrew from the system of corporatist representation on government bodies' (Pontusson 1994: 39). Simultaneously, as outlined earlier, Swedish TNCs directed their investment abroad. In sum, the advance by Swedish capital consisted of two parallel offensives. On the one hand, it mobilised ideologically via the SAF; on the other, it applied structural pressure by shifting production units abroad.

Nevertheless, the offensive by capital is only one part of the story. As indicated earlier, states not only adapt to globalisation, they also bring it about voluntarily. The SAP also contributed to the change in economic policy. By incorporating some principles of neo-liberalism in its 'third way' strategy, it sowed the seeds of the demise of the Swedish Model. For example, the SAP consciously decided in favour of the fixed exchange rate regime and liberalised capital markets. This 'undermined what little monetary autonomy might have remained in the hands of [Swedish] policy-makers' (Moses 1995: 342). When the economic crisis of 1989–90 hit Sweden, the country had to adapt to the global economy, concentrating on price stability via austerity measures in order to stem the flight of capital. By opening itself up to transnational capital through the deregulation of foreign exchange controls, it effectively foreclosed the option of pursuing a full employment policy.

Similarly in 1981, the SAP, still in opposition, participated in a compromise on tax reforms together with the CP and FP, which lowered the marginal rates of national income tax in general and for the highest rates from 85 per cent to 50 per cent. Then, in another drastic reform, national income tax was abolished for around 85 per cent of the taxpayers in 1990–91. These reforms, with cuts that were higher for the well-off than for the poorly paid groups, implied 'a departure from earlier SAP tax policies, which emphasised income taxation as a key instrument of redistribution' (Sainsbury 1991: 37).

Finally, in order to reduce the budget deficit, the payroll cost in the public sector had to be restrained. Hence, the SAP government supported the separate wage-negotiations deal between the engineering employers and the Metal Workers' Union in 1983 and, thus, successfully delinked wage increases in the private sector from the public sector (Swenson 1991b: 383–87). In doing this, however, the SAP undermined the central wage-negotiations in general and clearly contributed to their eventual abolition in 1990. Thus, the demise of the Swedish Model and the replacement of full employment by price stability and low inflation as economic priorities were partly a SAP response to pressures of globalisation, expressed in Sweden especially by the increasing transnationalisation of Swedish production and the SAF's push towards neo-liberalism. Partly, though, it was also due to an incremental turn of the SAP towards neo-liberalism.

To conclude, in both Austria and Sweden, the three indicators of globalisation – changes in the production structure, the finance structure and the dominant frameworks of thought – can be noticed. Production has been increasingly internationalised in Austria and transnationalised in Sweden, the financial markets have been deregulated in both countries and are, thus, integrated into the global financial market. Moreover, a shift took place from Keynesianism to neo-liberal economics in theory and in practice, moving both countries towards the neo-liberal night-watchman state. Consequently, the two countries' accession to the EU has to be analysed against the background of structural change. The final part of this chapter identifies the relevant Austrian and Swedish social forces in this struggle.

Globalisation and the configuration of social forces in Austria and Sweden

As argued in chapter one, a basic distinction can be made between transnational and national social forces of capital and labour. Additionally, the geographical orientation as expressed in the trading patterns of companies has to be taken into account as a factor relevant for the formation of collective actors. When considering capitalist fractions, Holman (1992: 16) suggests a fourfold classification:

1 Import-competing producers of tradable goods for the domestic market
2 Import-competing producers of tradable goods for the European market
3 Export-competing producers of tradable goods for the world market;
4 Globally operating financial institutions.

These categories do not necessarily exhaust all possibilities. For example, considering the distinction between national and transnational production, globally operating TNCs are a further group. This is of no concern here, because the focus is on the configuration of social forces at the national level. It implies, however, that the social forces based on national production can be divided into nationally-oriented social forces, engendered by national production that produces for the domestic market, and internationally-oriented social forces, stemming from national production that produces for export, be it for the European or the world market. Globally operating TNCs and financial institutions are part of the transnational social forces.

Transnational social forces, be they capital or labour, are likely to be in favour of a neo-liberal, deregulatory economic policy, because they favour a world without borders and national regulations, which represent barriers for their business. They are probably supported by internationally-oriented social forces, for which borders also constitute barriers for their exports.[13] Nationally-oriented capital and labour, on the other hand, tend to oppose neo-liberalism, because they may depend on state protectionism against international competition.

Austrian social forces

Considering the Austrian production structure as outlined in this chapter, the main line of potential conflict is between nationally-oriented and internationally-oriented forces. The few transnational social forces from TNCs can be treated as forming an alliance with the latter. The trade unions are mainly organised according to the industrial principle, whereby employees belong to national unions determined by the economic sector within which they work. Consequently, the individual unions as parts of the AK and ÖGB can be analysed in relation to their particular economic sector, whether it is export-oriented or produces for the domestic market. The BWK is divided into six sectors at the national level: the '*Gewerbe*' sector (family business, crafts), the trade sector, the industry sector, the sector for money, credit and insurance, the transport sector and the tourism sector. With the exception of the internationally-oriented industry sector and the sector for money, credit and insurance, they do not correspond to the separation of nationally- and internationally-oriented economic sectors and, therefore, do not serve as an analytical unit. In other words, both internationally- and nationally-oriented social forces must be expected in these sectors. None the less, there are some employers' associations, which can be clearly identified, such as the internationally-oriented Association of the Austrian Textile Industry. The LK is more likely to be a homogeneous, nationally-oriented actor as the whole agricultural sector was protected against foreign competition.

There is one institutional exception in the area of interest associations. The Federation of Austrian Industrialists (VÖI) can be treated as a homogeneous organisation, as it represents the interests of internationally-oriented and transnational capital. In 1979, the VÖI was relatively weak in structural terms. Nearly all important industrial firms belonged to the public sector and were, therefore, out of the reach of the VÖI, which organises only private capital (Lehmbruch 1979: 159). This has since changed. Between 1979 and 1988, public ownership, calculated according to the percentage of employees in Austria's 100 largest firms, declined by about 15 per cent, while private ownership, be it national or foreign, increased by approximately 14.5 per cent (Karazman-Morawetz and Pleschiutschnig 1991: 382; own calculations). This trend towards private ownership accelerated from 1989 onwards due to the ongoing process of privatisation. Being privatised, these companies are now eligible for VÖI membership and, indeed, some have already joined (Interview no. 18; Vienna, 22 May 1995). The VÖI has, thus, become a powerful actor in structural terms. It should not, thereby, be viewed as a social actor in its own right, but rather as a potential organisational expression of a class force, the structural power of which transcends that of any individual actor. The VÖI is based on voluntary membership, but forms at the same time part of the ESP. In practice, it represents the sector of industry within the BWK and, therefore, enjoys excellent access to policy-making.

It is difficult to distinguish internationally- and nationally-oriented social forces within parties, since they are the expression of social forces and not related to particular economic sectors. The two big parties in Austria can, however, be divided according to their internal leagues and the possible different ideological outlook of these leagues. Conflicts between classes and fractions of classes are not only expressed by different organisations and/or orientations of economic sectors, but also by different ideologies, which are related to different parts of production. The ÖVP consists of three leagues: the Business League (ÖWB), the Farmers' League (ÖBB) and the League of Blue and White Collar Workers (ÖAAB) (Lehmbruch 1979: 179). There is frequently a rivalry between the ÖAAB, the social wing of the party, and the ÖWB, its economic wing. 'Despite greater emphasis under the new grand coalition governments since 1986 upon deregulation and the market, ideological dissent within the Catholic-conservative Lager has if anything intensified' (Luther 1992: 62). It is no surprise that under these circumstances an unequivocal stance on EU membership may have been difficult to forge. The SPÖ is also divided into leagues, but they do not play an important role within the party (Müller 1996b: 78). However, it has to be investigated at the ideological level whether there was a group opposed to the free market minded team around Chancellor Vranitzky.

It is more difficult to operationalise small parties from a neo-Gramscian perspective. Because of their size, they generally have to be treated as the institutional expression of a particular fraction of social forces instead of an institutional framework, within which social forces struggle for dominance. The ideological outlook of the party may give the clearest indicator of the social forces represented. The FPÖ has two opposing directions, a liberal one oriented towards the free market economy and a nationalist one based on its origin, the old German-national Lager with ex-Nazis as its members (Luther 1991a: 254–9). In the 1970s and especially in the early 1980s, the liberal, market-oriented view dominated over the nationalist tradition. This has changed slowly but significantly since 1986 and the arrival of Haider as the new party chairman. The anti-immigration policy expressed in the slogan 'Austria first' has featured widely in the party's public appeal ever since. Its electoral success, however, must also be credited to its relentless criticism of Austria's corporatist arrangement for being undemocratic and corrupt. This helped the FPÖ to attract many protest voters who were dissatisfied with the unchanging and rigid institutional structure (Riedlsperger 1992). In 1993, when five MPs left the FPÖ parliamentary fraction and formed the Liberal Forum, the liberal part of the party had largely abandoned the FPÖ in protest against its nationalist outlook.

The Green Alternative Party (GA) places great emphasis on the environment and regards the capitalist economy as the cause of environmental disaster. In order to achieve an ecological modernisation of the capitalist production system, the party maintains that the primacy of politics over economics has to be established and new aims need to be developed in opposition to the logic of growth. This should be complemented with a focus on the redistribution of wealth. The democratisation of all aspects of society is a further point of the GA agenda, to be accomplished partly via the decentralisation of the decision-making process to the local level (Dachs 1991: 269–73). As outlined in chapter one, parties such as the FPÖ and the GA represent forces, which are, in completely different ways, engaged in a class struggle against further capitalist exploitation of the social and natural sphere of reproduction.

Finally, national institutions also need to be taken into account by relating them to their place in the global mode of production. Officials of the Chancellor's Office, the Finance and Economic Ministries and the ANB, linked to transnational production and finance, have to be viewed differently from the Ministries for Labour and Social Affairs, for the Nationalised Industry and of Agriculture, dealing with merely national problems.

Swedish social forces

Given Sweden's production structure, a strong group of transnational social forces can be expected due to the TNCs. A group of national social forces mainly to be found in the large public sector is also likely. Internationally-oriented social forces play a secondary role. The trade unions in Sweden are characterised by an early dominance of industrial unionism. The LO especially, but also the TCO are primarily organised according to this principle. These trade unions can, consequently, be analysed according to whether the production in their economic sector is organised on a transnational or national basis. The unions affiliated to the SACO are structured according to the craft principle. Nevertheless, even in this case, it is possible to distinguish unions representing workers of national sectors from unions in transnational sectors. Sometimes, individual unions may represent national and transnational social forces. In this case, the unit of the individual union has to be divided further into the various sections of the workers the union represents. The member associations of the SAF and SI are also predominantly organised according to different economic sectors, and it can, therefore, be distinguished between national and transnational associations.

As for political parties, it has first to be investigated whether a group has formed in the SAP to oppose the rise of the neo-liberal wing since the early

1980s and, if so, whether this had an impact during the debate on EU membership. The CP, although only a small party with less than 10 per cent of the electoral vote, does exhibit internal divisions. The agricultural wing is grouped around the LRF, while the environmentalist wing is rooted in the party's Youth League (The Swedish Institute 1996a: 2). Its endorsement of a free market economy is, consequently, less clear-cut. Social justice and measures to improve the environment also feature highly on its agenda (Taylor 1991: 6). Thus, it represents agricultural interests, and here in general the smaller farmers in the North of Sweden and forestry farmers in the South, and environmentally concerned social groups.

The other parties can be treated more or less as homogeneous actors according to their ideological outlook. The VP mainly attracts workers from the public sector, especially in the health service, education and welfare (Petersson 1994: 144). It has often been claimed that the VP is mainly supported by white-collar workers, but it has always extended its appeal to blue-collar workers, and recently even more so (Interview no. 38; Stockholm, 8 November 1996). The party favours redistributive policies and opposes neo-liberal economics. It therefore mainly represents parts of those social forces, which are in favour of maintaining the Swedish Model with its strong emphasis on full employment, generous welfare provisions and a large public sector.

The GP gives the highest priority to environmental questions. It argues that economic policy must be subordinated to these concerns and 'an economy based on ecocycles must be introduced, meaning that finite natural resources will not be exhausted and natural assets will not be consumed faster than they are renewed' (The Swedish Institute 1996a: 3). The party rejects neo-liberal economic policy based on economic growth and advocates redistribution policies. Overall, the party represents social forces opposed to neo-liberalism and increased exploitation of the reproduction sphere.

The MS has pursued a consistent defence of neo-liberal economic policies, which was also reflected in its government policies from 1991 to 1994, when it headed a four-party coalition. The FP, although always with a certain emphasis on the need for social policies to accompany free market forces, has supported the MS in this drive and both parties formulated a joint economic programme in April 1991. This included a strong emphasis on the promotion of a market economy, tax reductions, slimming of the public sector, privatisation and a more flexible and cost effective labour market (Taylor 1991: 5–6). Both parties, thus, represent transnational social forces of capital.

As in the case of Austria, a distinction has to be made between national institutions according to their relation to the global economy. On the one hand, there is the Prime Minister's Office and the Ministries of Finance, of Trade and of Industry, but also the Riksbank, which in general deal with international issues. On the other, the Ministries of Labour and of Social Affairs mainly deal with national issues and are, therefore, more closely attached to national forces.

Conclusion

Overall, the Austrian and Swedish economic and political systems have to be seen as institutional structures within which social forces operate and try to make their ideas and interests into those of the general Austrian and Swedish national interest. It is not argued here that other policy-making theories are unable to treat parties and interest associations in such a way. A neo-Gramscian perspective, however, has the advantage that it provides a clearer method to identify the relevant actors by pointing to the sphere of production. Moreover, the analysis of particular events and actors is linked to the surrounding structure via an overall theoretical framework.

To have different groups of social forces within parties and/or social partners does not mean that there has actually been a split over the question of EU membership. It only points to possible divisions, which have to be examined. By the same token, to have identified a single ideological outlook of a party does not mean that internal splits are impossible. In short, analysis of the production structure is not sufficient to identify and explain the emergence of a successful alliance of social forces. It only shows the range of potential collective actors and points to likely alliances. The actual position of forces on EU membership still has to be empirically examined. Additionally, in accordance with the dialectical view of structure and superstructure, it is necessary to investigate which organic intellectuals of which social group managed to form a hegemonic project allowing the successful establishment of a historical bloc in favour of EU membership in Austria and Sweden. In other words, the analysis has to go beyond mere economic issues and needs to include the other ideas which were part of the successful historical blocs' content. It is also important to consider whether there were rival historical blocs with a rival hegemonic project and, if so, why they did not succeed. Overall, only empirical analysis gives the final answer about which social forces were in favour and which opposed accession to the EU. Consequently, the following chapters first analyse the struggles within the countries leading to application (chapter three) and then investigate the contests over the referenda (chapter four).

3   Social forces and the struggle for application in Austria and Sweden

The bilateral Free Trade Agreements (FTAs) of 1 January 1973 between the EU on the one hand, and Austria and Sweden on the other, had been satisfactory for the majority of forces in both countries. There was little discussion on European integration in Austria and Sweden until the mid-1980s (Jerneck 1993: 25; Schultz 1992: 187). This was to change in 1985 with the EU's Internal Market programme, which removed internal trade barriers between the member states and implied higher barriers to countries from the outside. Hence, EU companies gained a competitive advantage over their Austrian and Swedish competitors. The achievements of the FTAs were questioned (Luif 1988: 167). Both countries, consequently, had to respond.

Nevertheless, although a response was required, this did not imply that membership was the only option. Far-reaching participation in the Internal Market short of full membership could also have been a course of action (Traxler 1992: 200–3). In fact, forces opposed to membership argued along this line in both countries (as described later). Hence, in contrast to intergovernmental analyses, application to the EU was not the inevitable result of economic necessity, but the outcome of an open-ended struggle between different social forces.

The first section of this chapter deals with the struggle over the decision on application in Austria and the second investigates the situation in Sweden. The conclusion compares both cases. While the final decision to apply was the same in both countries, the way it came about, and its timing, was quite different.

The struggle over the Austrian application to the EU

The Internal Market initiative by the EU in 1985 was the starting-point of the discussion in Austria (Kramer 1996: 171; Leitner 1993: 87; Luif 1994: 21–2; Schneider 1990: 85–6; Schultz 1992: 187; Traxler 1992: 204). As outlined in chapter two, Austria was linked to the global economy predominantly via trade. A breakup in the shares of main areas of trade shows that this link was concentrated at the regional European level.

Austria's share of exports and imports with the EU had steadily risen over the years and reached 68.6 per cent of imports and 65.2 per cent of exports in 1990 (see Table 3.1).

Although less important for Austria's link with the global economy, the distribution of FDI represents a similar picture. 48 per cent of outward FDI went to the EU in 1988–90 and 79.4 per cent of inward FDI came from the EU in 1989–90 (see Tables 3.2 and 3.3). In this situation, it was realised that Austria had to respond quickly to the Internal Market programme in one way or another.

Initiating the debate: the VÖI and the formation of a hegemonic project

The main actor initiating the discussion about full membership was the VÖI. As the representative of internationally-oriented and foreign transnational capital, it was deeply concerned about possible new trade barriers. On 14 May 1987, it published a statement and asked the government 'to do everything possible for Austria to become a full member of the [EU] as soon as possible' (VÖI 1987a: 42, author's translation). Only membership, it was argued, would guarantee participation, including co-decision making power, in the dynamic integration process of the EU (VÖI 1987a: 32). The Internal Market would, moreover, require the dismantling of Austria's sheltered sectors, thereby bringing about restructuring and increased competitiveness (VÖI 1987a: 38). In spring 1989, the VÖI prepared the Austro-Cecchini

Table 3.1 Shares of main areas and countries in Austria's total trade (%), 1981–90

		EU*	EFTA**	Germany	USA
1981	Imp.	58.6	7.5	38.7	4.1
	Exp.	52.2	11.9	28.7	2.6
1985	Imp.	62.1	7.6	40.9	3.7
	Exp.	56.1	10.5	30.1	4.7
1986	Imp.	66.9	7.7	44.0	3.2
	Exp.	60.1	11.8	32.7	4.0
1987	Imp.	68.0	7.8	44.2	3.5
	Exp.	63.4	11.1	34.8	3.6
1989	Imp.	68.3	7.1	44.1	3.6
	Exp.	65.1	10.7	35.8	3.5
1990	Imp.	68.6	7.1	44.0	3.6
	Exp.	65.2	10.1	37.4	3.2

Source: Luif 1988: 161 (1981-87); EFTA 1991: 62, 69 (1989–90)

Notes
*   EU: ten members including Greece in 1981; plus Spain and Portugal in 1985–90
** EFTA: 1981: Finland, Iceland, Norway, Austria, Portugal, Sweden and Switzerland; 1985–90: without Portugal

Table 3.2 Regional distribution of outward FDI in Austria (%), 1982–90

	EFTA	EU	North America	Other	Total
1982–1985	12.0	32.5	37.2	18.3	100
1986–1988	21.4	44.8	32.8	1.0	100
1988–1990	17.7	48.0	11.0	23.2	100

Source: EFTA 1991: 27

Table 3.3 Regional distribution of inward FDI in Austria (%), 1982–90

	EFTA	EU	North America	Other	Total
1982–1988	19.0	64.8	5.6	10.6	100
1989–1990	8.7	79.4	1.5	10.4	100

Source: EFTA 1991: 29

report, in which the economic benefits of EU membership as opposed to non-membership were outlined (VÖI 1989).

Although the main drive was of a neo-liberal economic nature, the VÖI soon realised that Austria's neutrality could be the main argument against EU membership. Hence, in 1987, it commissioned an investigation by Hummer and Schweitzer, two experts in international law, which came to the conclusion that EU membership and neutrality were compatible under certain conditions (Hummer and Schweitzer 1987) (see chapter five). Two more publications covering the economic and the constitutional aspects of membership followed in 1988 (Breuss and Stankovsky 1988; Öhlinger 1988). The goal of these publications, supported by media statements and brochures, was to establish a basis for discussion on membership, which had not existed before (Interview no. 18; Vienna, 22 May 1995). This did not directly lead to the eventual application, but it changed the frameworks of thought in such a way that EU membership could be discussed. Membership now appeared a possible course of action to both the political elite and the wider public in response to the Internal Market programme. As outlined in chapter one, ideas as a part of the structure not only constrain or reinforce actors' strategies, but may also be changed by agency. Finally, the VÖI made EU membership a question of Austrian identity. The quest for accession was 'also the expression of a clear commitment to the West and to the basic values of the Free World' (VÖI 1987b: 495, translation by the author). The VÖI had perceived the receptiveness of the Austrian population for a confirmation of their national identity, which had been shaken up during the international outrage about the national socialist past of its new President Kurt Waldheim in 1986.

In addition to this public campaign, the VÖI used all its political channels to achieve an application to the EU for full membership. It raised the question within the ESP and used its close connections with the political sphere. The economic wing of the ÖVP was lobbied, as were individual ministers including the Foreign Minister Alois Mock. Close contacts were also maintained with the Economic Ministry and the Foreign Ministry (Interview no. 18; Vienna, 22 May 1995). Taking all this into account, it becomes clear that the officials of the VÖI can be viewed as organic intellectuals of internationally-oriented capital. Stemming from the same industrial sectors, they used the VÖI as an institutional platform in order to formulate for their social group a pro-membership hegemonic project, which went beyond mere economic issues by including neutrality, constitutional problems and the question of Austrian identity.

Some argue that it was more the ÖVP itself which took the initiative, and especially the Foreign Minister and ÖVP chairman (Parteiobman) Mock (Interview no. 12; Vienna, 12 May 1995). Partly due to the ÖVP, the new coalition government of SPÖ and ÖVP stated in its government declaration on 16 January 1987 that 'participation in the further development of the process of European integration is of primary importance to Austria' (*Arbeitsübereinkommen*: 1987: 652, author's translation). This, however, did not necessarily signify EU membership, as the unilateral adoption of all new EU legislation (*autonomer Nachvollzug*) and the so-called global approach, consisting of participation in the Internal Market short of full membership, were debated as alternative options. It was not before 1 December 1987 that Mock spoke about the possibility of full membership in a presentation to the cabinet: if full participation in the Internal Market was only possible via membership, 'the option of [EU] membership, in consideration of the requirements of permanent neutrality, should not be excluded for the future' (Mock 1987: 28, author's translation). Then, in January 1988, the ÖVP leadership decided at its annual meeting in Maria Plain to pursue membership while respecting Austria's neutrality as its official party policy (ÖVP 1988: 245). The economic wing of the party, the ÖWB, the members of which are often members of the VÖI or have close ties with it, played a crucial role in the coming about of this decision (Interview no. 25; Vienna, 26 June 1996).

The *Landeshauptmännerkonferenz's* (Conference of Land Governors) decision of November 1987 to follow the VÖI and demand full membership (*Landeshauptmännerkonferenz*: 1987: 514) played a similarly important role in the ÖVP internal debate. In contrast to Germany or Switzerland, the *Länder* hardly enjoy any power in the Austrian constitution (Luther 1991b). Nevertheless, it is the extra-constitutional governors' conference via which the *Länder* exert significant influence. Each governor enjoys a strong position within his/her respective party, 'which will not normally enact legislation at federal level against the will of their Land party organisations' (Müller 1992: 125). Within the governors' conference, it had been the ÖVP governor of the *Land* Salzburg, pressed by the export-oriented industry of his *Land* – between 70 and 75 per cent of the exports of Salzburg go to the EU – who had taken the initiative (Laireiter *et al.* 1994: 77). Similar pressure to demand full membership was applied on the ÖVP governors of the Western *Länder* Oberösterreich and Vorarlberg by their export-oriented industries (Schaller 1994a: 74). It was these governors who spoke out in favour of membership at Maria Plain and governor Martin Purtscher of Vorarlberg was appointed head of the ÖVP's Commission on Europe (Schneider 1990: 201).

Despite the leadership decision in January 1988, the agricultural wing of the ÖVP remained sceptical (Leitner 1993: 103). In a resolution, the ÖBB demanded financial restructuring help and a transition period for the adaptation to the agricultural regulations in the EU (Österreichischer Bauernbund 1988: 273–5). Progress was slow until October 1988, when the ÖVP chairman Mock offered the farmers a party agreement on Europe, which included financial restructuring help. The ÖVP was, finally, united in favour of membership. Overall, the ÖVP soon followed the VÖI in demanding EU membership, but had to take into account its hesitant agricultural wing. The forces for membership originated in the economic wing of the ÖVP, and from the ÖVP governors of the Western *Länder*, who were pressed by their predominantly export-oriented industries. In the party's manifesto of April 1988, the reasons for the membership course were spelled out. It was argued that membership implied a dynamic push towards the necessary restructuring measures of the Austrian economy. To discontinue the liberalisation drive by remaining outside the EU, on the other hand, would lead to stagnation and recession, a decrease in competitiveness and higher unemployment (Schneider 1990: 203–4).

The FPÖ, dominated by its liberal wing until 1986, also played a role in putting membership on the agenda. In its party manifesto of 1985, it argued that EU membership was possible and necessary, provided that Austria retained its status of neutrality (FPÖ 1985: 321). Only this would guarantee participation in the economic dynamic of European integration and co-decision making in the EU institutions. The adoption of EU legislation was regarded as a method of getting rid of Austria's highly regulated and protected sectors (Interview no. 26; Vienna, 25 April 1996). Unhappy about the vacillations of the government coalition, the FPÖ put forward a formal motion in parliament in November 1987, in which the start of negotiations on membership was demanded (FPÖ 1987: 328).

Overall, however, the role of the FPÖ should not be overestimated. It had barely gained 10 per cent of the votes in the general elections of 1986 and faced a governing coalition of the SPÖ and ÖVP which had a comfortable two-thirds majority in parliament (see Table 2.1). While the VÖI supported the FPÖ with some minor financial donations for its pro-EU stance (Interview no. 34; Vienna, 10 May 1996), it concentrated its efforts on the more influential ÖVP and BWK in order to achieve full membership.

The formation of a pro-EU historical bloc

The position of capital

The BWK demanded EU membership at its annual general conference on 9 December 1987. If this was not achieved, it was argued, full participation in the Internal Market would not be guaranteed (BWK 1987: 458). Membership was regarded as a good way of restructuring the sheltered sector. The fight against unemployment was deemed necessary, but this should be maintained via a prospering economy through private initiatives in a free market economy, not through Keynesian budget deficit spending, be that at the national or European level (Interview no. 5; Vienna, 10 May 1995).

The decision, however, was not as clear cut as it may seem at first sight and it was no surprise that it came after that of the VÖI. The capital fractions linked to the export sector, for example the textile industry, had demanded EU membership even earlier (Kunnert 1993: 91). The textile industry had suffered under the outward processing regulations of the EU. These stated that textile products processed in countries such as Algeria, Morocco and Tunisia that enjoyed special bilateral arrangements with the EU could be re-imported tax-free into the Union, provided the original material was of EU origin. Consequently, when selecting textiles to be processed in these countries, EU producers chose material originating from within the Union rather than material from non-EU countries such as Austria to which the tax-free regulation did not apply (Bundessektion Industrie 1989: 29–30). In order to underline the urgency of their demand for full membership, which would solve this problem at once, some textile employers even threatened to transfer production units to EU countries (Interview, No.24; Vienna, 24 April 1996). Moreover, globalisation had affected textiles more than other sectors since the early 1970s. Thus, the access to a bigger 'home market' was of vital importance (Interview, No.22; Vienna, 23 April 1996).

Capital fractions linked to the nationally-oriented, protected industrial sectors, in contrast, were very hesitant. In particular the largest parts of the food processing industry such as dairy factories, mills, and the sectors linked to meat, cattle and grain production were raising their voices against application to the EU. They had worked in a completely sheltered and regulated sector with guaranteed prices, supply and markets and were worried about the negative consequences of trade liberalisation (Interview no. 5; Vienna, 10 May 1995; Interview no. 19; Vienna, 23 May 1995). The trade and transport sector, having achieved its profit from the import and export of goods, was also not happy about a possible membership, where foreign companies could directly penetrate the Austrian market (Interview no. 18; Vienna, 22 May 1995).

In the end, the social forces linked to the export sector won over their opponents for several reasons. First, nationally-oriented capital was badly organised, as for example the mill owners (Interview no. 12; Vienna, 12 May

1995). Second, the industry sector enjoyed a near-dominant position within the BWK due to its larger financial contribution and the capability to employ more staff to carry out research. It was, thus, in a good position to influence the debate decisively (Interview no. 24; Vienna, 24 April 1996). Finally, some people in the sheltered sectors accepted the argument that, overall, the Austrian economy would benefit from accession and that a restructuring of the sheltered sectors was necessary in order to regain competitiveness (Interview no. 5; Vienna, 10 May 1995). Thus even in the BWK's *'Gewerbe'* sector (family business, crafts), where most of the sceptic forces were organised, there was no majority against membership (Interview no. 21; Vienna, 23 April 1996).

The position of labour

The debate within the AK and ÖGB took longer, but went along similar lines. The support for application, expressed by the ÖGB in its *'Europa-Memorandum'* of December 1988 (ÖGB 1988) and by the AK in its *'Europa Stellungnahme'* of January 1989 (AK 1989), was initially more or less a decision by leading officials (Interview no. 1; Vienna, 8 May 95). During high-ranking talks within the institutions of the ESP, it had become clear that the trade unionists did not have an alternative way to offer the same increase in general welfare that EU membership, put forward by capital, promised to yield. Against the background of global restructuring and Austria's difficult economic situation, the opening of the sheltered sectors seemed to be the only way forward and EU membership was the best way of bringing this about. In other words, the trade union representatives agreed that membership was necessary for the revival of the Austrian economy, as were privatisation, tax reforms and a new focus on efficiency (Interview no. 13; Vienna, 12 May 1995). Globalisation and the limitations of state autonomy were accepted as economic facts, and national Keynesian solutions were ruled out as a possibility in this new international environment (Interview no. 1; Vienna, 8 May 1995). Experts such as Heinz Zourek of the AK realised the problems for the sheltered Austrian sectors in the event of accession, but pointed out that this would lead to lower prices for consumers and for inputs of the export-oriented industries and, thereby, improve the overall economic situation (Zourek 1989: 189).

Once the Cold War had come to an end in 1989, the ÖGB leaders additionally had to take into account the prospect of new competitors in Eastern Europe. Therefore, these high-ranking officials accepted the bid for membership while focusing on a 'just' distribution of the expected welfare gains (Interview no. 13; Vienna, 12 May 1995). Overall, it was argued that, due to economic imperatives, full participation in the Internal Market should be the aim. As membership seemed to be the EU's precondition for full participation, Austria's accession to the EU could not be excluded (ÖGB-Rednerdienst 1988: 7).

The results of the inter-ministerial 'Working Group for European Integration', established by the new coalition government of SPÖ and ÖVP in February 1987, had been crucial for both associations. Together with representatives of all ministries and the Austrian *Länder*, the social partners participated in the evaluation of the consequences of the various options for Austria. Implicitly, the working group argued in favour of membership during the presentation of its results in June 1988. Participation in the Internal Market would cause no problems for Austria. This, however, implied an automatic adoption of EU legislation, which was not satisfactory to a country unable to participate in the shaping and passing of this legislation. Moreover, there was no guarantee that the EU accepted this kind of unilateral participation (Leitner 1993: 93). Consequently, full participation in the Internal Market was only considered to be possible via membership, and this position was reiterated by the ÖGB and the AK.

The *Europa-Memorandum* of December 1988 by the ÖGB laid out the conditions for its support for membership. First, Austria's neutral status must be maintained (ÖGB 1988: 2–3). Second, the economic benefits must be used to improve the income, employment and welfare of the general population with a commitment to full employment as the priority of economic and social policy. Third, decision-making in social policy must remain at the national level (ÖGB 1988: 3), and the right of the ÖGB and AK to participate in all spheres of the decision-making process related to European integration and Austria's possible EU membership must be guaranteed (ÖGB 1988: 4). The ÖGB's position was echoed by the AK (1989).

Both the ÖGB and the AK strongly emphasised the importance of a European social dimension in addition to economic integration and demanded that the Austrian government worked towards this in case of membership (ÖGB 1988: 2; AK 1989: 5). The opinion of Jacques Delors, President of the European Commission, that a European social dimension was a necessary complementary part of the Internal Market helped leading Austrian trade unionists in their support for membership (Interview no. 22; Vienna, 23 April 1996). In view of the loss of national policy autonomy due to globalisation, exemplified by the French failure of Keynesian policies between 1981 and 1983, the EU with its social dimension, it was pointed out, offered some compensation at the European level and provided better possibilities for the control of TNCs (Vogler 1991: 179).

At first, opposition arose across all industrial sectors against this position. Nevertheless, the trade unions linked to the export sectors soon offered their support, while the trade unions of the sheltered sectors remained opposed. It was the Union for Textile, Clothes and Leather, arguing in a similar way to the employers in the textile industry (as discussed earlier), which was the driving force within the ÖGB. Its president Harald Ettl became the head of the ÖGB Integration Committee set up in late 1987 (Interview no. 22; Vienna, 23 April 196). Industrial unions such as the Chemical and the Metal Workers' Unions also supported participation in the

Internal Market. However, the Rail, Postal and Public Workers' Unions, as well as construction and wood workers opposed such a move (Schaller 1994a: 94). The Gewerkschaft der Privatangestellten (White Collar Workers' Union, GPA), which was the strongest individual union within the ÖGB, representing the white-collar workers in industry, crafts, money and credit, trade, social insurances, insurances, agriculture and forestry was never positive about EU membership. The sheltered and regulated areas of transport companies and the food processing industry in particular opposed accession because of the likely job losses. Information relating to this was published by the GPA (Interview no. 35; Vienna, 14 May 1996). The executive board of the Food Processing Union accepted that the maintenance of the sheltered position was unfair on the consumers, who had to pay for it via high prices. It was also realised that the GATT Uruguay Round would lead to further free trade and, therefore, undermine the sheltered sectors anyway. Consequently, the union did not oppose membership but demanded financial restructuring help for the food processing industry before accession and the setting-up of so-called 'work-foundations' with the goal to retrain workers, who had lost their job in the course of restructuring (Interview no. 20; Vienna, 22 April 1996). Nevertheless, in a conference on the EU by the extended executive board in March 1988, dissenting voices were raised. Representatives of the tinned food and the tobacco industries opposed membership, arguing that this would push Austrian products out of the market in their sectors and lead to job cuts (Food Processing Trade Union 1988a: 8). Additionally, representatives of the dairy and sugar industries rejected restructuring of their sectors via the closing down of production units. Some employers misused the EU argument, it was alleged, for their rationalisation programmes, which could be avoided. Furthermore, consumer prices could also be lowered by paying farmers less for their agricultural products (Food Processing Trade Union 1988b, comments by Kollege Huber, Kollege Krcal and Kollege Uhl).

Eventually, the pro-EU decision triumphed within the ÖGB, but a long campaign until 1992 was needed in order to convince the members and work-council officials at the company level (Interview no. 1; Vienna, 8 May 1995). Objections and doubts were partly removed by the central organisation through the promise of financial restructuring help and retraining programmes (Interview no. 22; Vienna, 23 April 1996).

The position of the agricultural sector

Apart from some limited exports to the EU in the area of cattle, agriculture was a totally nationally-oriented sector. Austrian production prices were higher than in the EU partly due to a different agricultural structure based on small and middle-sized farms with a strong emphasis on ecological factors, in contrast to large-scale agricultural production in the EU which focused on efficiency. Furthermore, Austrian farmers had to cope with weaknesses in the related food processing industry (Kunnert 1993: 82–3). Overall, it was feared that many farmers would be made bankrupt. Unsurprisingly, leading officials of the Austrian agricultural complex such as the President of the LK Alois Derfler and the Agricultural Minister Josef Riegler, both members of the ÖVP, rejected full membership throughout 1987 (Kunnert 1993: 80–1). A turning-point was the ÖVP's decision in January 1988 to demand full membership. Riegler and Derfler are likely to have bowed to pressure from the economic wing of their party (Schaller 1994a: 100).

Similarly important was the presence at Maria Plain of the President of the *Raiffeisenverband* Dr. Kleiss, member of the ÖVP and the ÖBB. The *Raiffeisenverband*, originally a network of local self-help organisations of farmers, had developed into a huge industrial enterprise with a market-dominating position in the agricultural supply and processing industry and, even more important, a financial sector with international links. Dr. Kleiss agreed that membership was absolutely necessary and arranged a positive statement by the *Raiffeisenverband* in the wake of the ÖVP's decision (Interview no. 28; Vienna, 3 May 1996). In particular, the financial sector of the *Raiffeisenverband*, comprising internationally-oriented social forces, sought to gain unhindered access to European financial markets and, therefore, strongly supported membership (Krammer 1991: 372). As the presidential conference of the LK consisted of representatives of the *Land* organisations and the *Raiffeisenverband*, the latter's positive opinion on membership was crucial in the internal decision of the LK (Interview no. 28; Vienna, 3 May 1996).

From this point onwards, the political elite of the LK supported the EU application. It was argued that the situation would worsen anyway for farmers due to the GATT negotiations of the Uruguay Round. Switzerland was cited as an example of a state having to restructure its agricultural sector despite its decision against closer ties with the EU. Moreover, Austrian farmers would have to accept the EU guidelines in any case, if they wanted to export to the EU. Membership would guarantee the right of co-decision making in drawing up these guidelines (Interview no. 17; Vienna, 18 May 95). The LK's *Memorandum zur Europäischen Integration* of February 1989 supported membership, but demanded financial help before and during membership in order to maintain Austria's agricultural structure and environmental standards (LK 1989). A transition period for the agri-cultural sector in the adaptation to EU regulations and restructuring help for the closely attached food processing sector were requested (Interview no. 28; Vienna, 3 May 1996). Many farmers, however, disagreed with the LK's positive opinion and felt that they were passed over or even sacrificed by their political leadership (Leitner 1993: 106). This resistance could not completely be overcome despite an intensive campaign of hundreds of information meetings organised by the LK throughout the country (Interview no. 17; Vienna, 18 May 1995).

Eventually, in March 1989, the social partners supported application to the EU in their joint declaration *Österreich und die Europäische Integration*, as only membership would guarantee full participation in the Internal Market (Sozialpartnerstellungnahme 1989: 11). The increased competition and economies of scale in the Internal Market would lead to higher economic growth. Provided this was accompanied by certain political measures, higher standards of living, a reduction in unemployment and the creation of new jobs would result. Considering the loss of national economic policy autonomy due to the world-wide liberalisation in the trade of goods and services, Austria would have to restructure parts of its industry anyway. Rather than implying a further loss of national sovereignty, the EU offered in this situation some kind of compensation, as the 'the loss of autonomy can be balanced through possibilities of co-shaping and co-decision making at the international level' (Sozialpartnerstellungnahme 1989: 9, author's translation).

The SPÖ's slow turn towards application

The joint declaration of the social partners was crucial for the opinion of the SPÖ, which had waited for the decision of the ÖGB and the AK (Interview no. 1; Vienna, 8 May 1995). The process leading to the pro-membership decision of 3 April 1989, when the national committee voted with a clear majority of fifty to four in favour of membership, was even more painstaking than the one of the ÖVP. From about 1986 onwards, the economic wing of the party around Chancellor Vranitzky, Finance Minister Lacina, Harald Ettl and Brigitte Ederer was convinced that it was necessary to guarantee Austria's full participation in the Internal Market, as this was likely to lead to new barriers for non-member countries. Some within the party even looked to the EU as a way of restructuring Austria's sheltered sectors, which was very difficult to achieve without pressure from outside (Interview no. 32; Vienna, 8 May 1996). Nevertheless, the global approach was the primary aim at this time, as it was for the ÖVP. Only in the wake of the ÖVP's move towards full membership in 1988 and the results of the 'Working Group for European Integration' in the summer of the same year, was accession to the EU carefully considered as an option by this group (Leitner 1993: 101).

However, opposition grew within the party and many linked their criticism of membership to a critique of capitalism in general, echoing the position of large sections of the party in the 1960s. The socially disadvantaged and female party members in particular argued that the capitalist dominated EU would threaten the social achievements in Austria. They were represented by Hans Hatzl, member of the city council in Vienna, and by Herbert Suko, President of the AK in the *Land* Salzburg (Interview no. 32; Vienna, 8 May 1996). Another, even more important group, divided into two sub-groups, rallied around the principle of neutrality. The first sub-group rejected the notion that membership and neutrality were compatible. The second, of which the former Foreign Minister Lanc was a member, argued that the EU had not been integrated deeply enough yet in order to raise the issue of neutrality. Nevertheless, it was apparent in the late 1980s that the EU had the general goal of political union, which might include a common foreign and security policy. Hence, it was not clear whether the EU would develop in a direction where Austria as a member would have to drop its neutrality. Consequently, this group decided to wait and observe whether future EU development questioned neutrality (Interview no. 23; Vienna, 24 April 1996).

In view of this opposition, Vranitzky waited before he gave a clear sign for membership and stated at the SPÖ congress on Europe in October 1988 that neutrality would never be questioned or negotiated for the sake of membership (Vranitzky 1988: 179–80). The official report by the international law office in the Foreign Ministry about the question of the compatibility of EU membership and neutrality was published in November. It concluded that 'Austria's EU membership under the viewpoint of retaining the status of neutrality would be in principal possible' (Völkerrechtsbüro 1988: 40, author's translation). Some clarifications, however, needed to be made with reference to Articles 223 and 224 of the Treaty of Rome, ensuring the right to use them to maintain neutrality. Furthermore, Austria's status of neutrality should be written into the application for membership. This strengthened the pro-EU camp within the SPÖ and was the basis of its clear victory in the national committee. Only Hatzl, Lanc and two leading functionaries of SPÖ youth organisations voted against the motion put forward by Vranitzky (Schneider 1990: 215). Membership was, however, linked to several conditions. In his presentation to the national committee, Vranitzky outlined the requirements for his party's support: neutrality was not negotiable, Austrian social and environmental standards had to be maintained, special provisions were needed for the agricultural sector in order to soften the impact of accession and a solution of the transit problem was required before the establishment of the Internal Market in 1992 (Vranitzky 1989: 194–8).

In sum, it was the economic wing within the SPÖ, led by Chancellor Vranitzky, which moved the SPÖ towards a pro-EU position. It had to overcome fierce opposition, especially rallying around the principle of neutrality. The clear success of the pro-EU group was partly due to the lack of an alternative concept by the opponents, which went beyond the issue of neutrality (Interview no. 23; Vienna, 24 April 1996).

State institutions linked to the global economy

The Finance Ministry, linked to global finance through its concern for Austria's international credit rating, strongly supported EU membership. Austerity and a consolidated budget were regarded as necessary in times of free capital movement in order to maintain a good credit rating on the global financial market. Membership was considered to be a good way of attaining these objectives (Interview no. 7; Vienna, 11 May 1995). The ANB kept itself out of the discussion in order to avoid the Austrian hard currency policy becoming an object of the debate. None the less, it supported the historical bloc in favour of EU membership through its actions. It shadowed the EMS policy and started liberalising its financial markets when the EU members decided on this move in 1986. The aim was to have a monetary and exchange rate policy compatible with present and future goals of the EU. Moreover, it acquired the status of 'Other-Holder', conferring the right to hold and use official European currency units (ECUs), and it published an official daily exchange-rate for the ECU (Dörfel *et al.* 1993: 121–2; Interview no. 16; Vienna, 18 May 1995). Finally, the Economic Ministry strongly pressed the point that EU membership was a good method of achieving higher efficiency via stronger competition in the Internal Market, forcing Austria's protected sectors to restructure themselves (Interview no. 10; Vienna, 12 May 1995).

To sum up, the initiative was taken by organic intellectuals of the internationally-oriented social forces of capital. They formed an alliance with the social forces of labour also attached to these sectors, and were supported by the ministries and institutions linked to the global economy. Their main arguments were of an economic nature. However, by dealing with other issues such as neutrality too, it was possible to formulate a hegemonic project in favour of EU membership, which went beyond mere economic interests and led to the control over the two governing parties and the social partners. Nevertheless, in order to attract other social forces and obtain at least the acquiescence of some nationally-oriented social forces, concessions such as the maintenance of neutrality and social and environmental standards, special provisions for agriculture and financial restructuring help for disadvantaged industrial sectors had to be made.

The discourse of membership demonstrates two things. First, the arguments of all pro-EU forces were underwritten by neo-liberal ideas, for example that efficiency via higher competition, to be achieved through membership and participation in the Internal Market, guaranteed a healthy economy, which would eventually lead to the creation of more wealth and jobs. The social purpose of membership was the neo-liberal restructuring of the Austrian state–society relations. EU membership was realised as a continuation of the change in economic policy at the national level, being especially crucial for the opening up of the sheltered sectors to international competition. Trade unionists may have pointed to the importance of a social dimension at the European level, but they did not challenge the neo-liberal logic as such. Second, the reference to globalisation as making this neo-liberal policy necessary shows that globalisation had not only acquired an existence at the material level, but also at the level of ideas.

Forces against membership

Nationally-oriented capital and labour

Both capital and labour related to the protected sectors rejected membership. This included mainly the food processing industry, customs officials, transport companies and the agricultural sector. Some of the employers and trade unions in these sectors worked together in individual instances and tried to influence their respective Chamber. They raised their voices of opposition whenever they could, but were eventually outnumbered (Interview no. 19; Vienna, 23 May 1995). Their position was weakened internally, since not all sectors within the food processing industry were negatively affected. On the one hand, there were severe problems for dairy companies, mills and the sugar industry. On the other, the so-called 'protocol II' industries, those affected by a special bilateral agreement between Austria and the EU in 1972 such as breweries, soft drinks companies and cattle exporters, could expect gains from accession (Food Processing Trade Union 1988a: 6). Consequently, they were less inclined towards a negative position. A small section of the social forces of capital in the food processing industry, moreover, sided with the majority, arguing that a restructuring of the sheltered sectors was necessary anyway. They even threatened to transfer production units to Eastern European countries in the event of non-membership (Interview no. 1; Vienna, 8 May 1995).

Political parties against application

The GA was the only significant party, which opposed membership from the very beginning. In March 1987, the leader of the GA fraction in parliament, Freda Blau-Meissner, rejected the view that neutrality was compatible with membership. On the contrary, membership would endanger Austrian independence (and her role as mediator between East and West), not least through the sell-out of the Austrian economy (Blau-Meissner 1987: 345–6). In February 1989, the party published a detailed manifesto on Europe. The Internal Market programme was accused of merely aiming at economic-industrial expansion. Its liberalisation would not only make reforms in environmental and social standards impossible, but would threaten standards already achieved without solving the problem of unemployment. Additionally, the GA criticised the EU's democratic deficit and perceived military component. In this situation, instead of applying to the EU, Austria should, on the one hand, pursue a strategy of international co-operation with the goal of an improved environment, social justice, democratic renewal and international peace. Next to the EU, these efforts should also incorporate Central and Eastern Europe and the other European neutrals. On the other hand, Austria had to concentrate on reforms at the national level, which would have a stronger impact on the EU than Austria could ever hope to achieve as a member (GA 1989: 348–52).

Shortly before the decision in parliament, the GA supported the newly founded initiative *Kritische Europainformationen* (Critical Europe Information) in its organisation of a bus tour through Austria with the aim of disseminating information against application (Interview no. 27; Vienna, 2 May 1996). Nevertheless, the decision on application was ultimately taken in parliament in June 1989, and there the GA fraction was the only one to vote against application. With roughly 5 per cent of the votes in the 1986 general elections (see Table 2.1) and eight MPs, this was a lost battle from the beginning.

Resistance in the extra-institutional environment

After the social partners and the two governing parties had decided on application, there was only the extra-institutional environment left to mobilise resistance against the EU membership course. In 1988, publications appeared which criticised the argument that membership was a natural necessity and pointed to alternative strategies. Morawetz outlined the undemocratic nature of the EU and the dominant structural position of 'big capital' lobby groups within it. Labour could only lose in this situation, in terms of its influence in general and the prevailing social standards in particular (Morawetz 1988). Scherb, while acknowledging the objective tendency in the economy towards transnationalisation, rejected the one-sided orientation towards the EU. As an alternative, she urged a diversified transnationalisation strategy and retention of the status of an independent neutral able to mediate between East and West (Scherb 1988: 69–70). Althaler *et al.* pointed to a range of alternative strategies such as a further development of the 1973 FTA or association. As these strategies promised similar economic gains, membership would be everything but a must for Austria (Althaler *et al.* 1988: 44–5).

These publications helped EU opponents to formulate their arguments (Schaller 1994a: 112–13). In November 1988, the *Initiative Österreich und Europa* was established with the SPÖ's former Foreign Minister, Lanc, as one of its most prominent co-founders. It was a loose association of individuals including former ambassadors (Bielka, Thalberg) and university professors (such as Hagen, Pelinka and Weinzierl) (Leitner 1993: 107). Its aim was to initiate a broad public debate on EU membership in general and the question of its compatibility with neutrality in particular (Interview no. 23; Vienna, 24 April 1996). Together with the *Institut für Staats- und Politikwissenschaft*, it organised a symposium *Österreich – EG – Europa* on 30 and 31 January 1989. Amongst others, Lanc argued that a European Economic Area combined with a diversified transnationalisation strategy was economically sufficient (Lanc 1989: 257). Bielka pointed out that the process of transnationalisation including the take-over of Austrian companies by foreign TNCs had already been undermining Austria's independence. Membership would increase this tendency and threaten neutrality. It would also imply participation in the European Political Co-operation, the forerunner of the CFSP, and, therefore, undermine Austria's role as a neutral mediator in international politics (Bielka 1989: 259). Thalberg suggested that the further internal development of the EU should be monitored before a decision on application was taken (Thalberg 1989: 264). More than a hundred similar public information meetings were organised all over Austria (Interview no. 23; Vienna, 24 April 1996). This intensified public debate was not without consequences. Shortly before the parliamentary debate on application at the end of June 1989, several demonstrations took place, which demanded that application to Brussels should not be made (Schaller 1994a: 247).[1]

Reasons for the failure of the anti-EU groups

A range of social forces opposed membership, but it turned out to be impossible for them to form a successful alliance against application. For a start, they did not have a clear common agenda apart from their opposition to membership. For example, within the *Initiative Österreich und Europa,* membership was rejected because of neutrality, social, environmental, agri-cultural, regional, and democratic-political considerations without arranging these points in a coherent programme (Leitner 1993: 107). The attempt by the GA to organise an anti-EU campaign before the *Land* eletions of spring 1989 was rejected by the *Initiative Österreich und Europa* (Schaller 1994a: 150) as was the attempt to form a new party. According to Lanc, the opponents were generally focusing on small and local issues, which affected them directly such as the anti-transit movements in some *Länder* or some local SPÖ or ÖVP mayors, who feared for their re-election. The GA was considered to be merely a sectoral party. For the successful establishment of a new party, however, a comprehensive programme would have been necessary. More importantly, it had never been the aim of the *Initiative* to form an anti-EU movement in the first place. It wanted to start a public debate on the pros and cons of EU membership and, consequently, had always invited pro-EU speakers to its conferences, too. When this target had been achieved, the *Initiative* was dissolved in 1991 (Interview no. 23; Vienna, 24 April 1996). In short, neither the GA nor the *Initiative Österreich und Europa* could provide the platform for organic intellectuals.

Another factor was the lack of any support from ministries linked to national problems, such as the Ministry of Agriculture, the Ministry for Labour and Social Affairs and the Ministry for the Nationalised Industry (Interview no. 14; Vienna, 17 May 1995). As all decisions were taken on a consensus basis within the cabinet, the Agriculture Minister could theoreti-cally have vetoed the decision on application (Interview no. 25; Vienna, 25

April 1996). In practice, however, because of internal pressure within the ÖVP, such extreme opposition was unlikely. The Agriculture Minister together with the ÖBB and the LK, however, made it very difficult for the pro-application forces and successfully demanded many concessions (Interview no. 36; Vienna, 15 May 1996). The Ministry for Labour and Social Affairs did not oppose the quest for membership either. The need for application was accepted in view of the overall economic gains membership promised to yield. Job losses would have to be dealt with, as a restructuring process of the protected sectors was on the agenda in any case, and the Austrian work and social standards even had to be raised to Community levels in some areas (Interview no. 1; Vienna, 8 May 1995). Eventually, the ministry only demanded that Austria's participation in the structural funds of the EU and a transition period with reference to women's nightwork were part of the negotiation position (Interview no. 30; Vienna, 6 May 1996).

At first sight, one might assume that the Austrian Ministry for the Nationalised Industry would oppose EU membership fiercely, as a large public sector was hardly compatible with the liberalisation drive of the Internal Market accompanied by a wave of privatisation across the EU. Nevertheless, considering that privatisation and the restructuring of the Austrian nation-alised industry had already been accepted and started in 1987, membership offered a good way of continuing this process and was, therefore, welcomed rather than opposed (Interview no. 31; Vienna, 7 May 1996).

Furthermore, the opposing social forces were outside the corporatist system and in a minority position within parliament. Once they had lost the struggle within the governing parties and the social partners, there was no institution left which would have allowed them to influence policy-making. Finally, the importance of the change in ideas from Keynesianism to neo-liberalism, part of the processes of globalisation, should not be forgotten. This contributed to a situation in which nationally-oriented social forces of capital and labour found it impossible to consider alterna-tives to participation in the Internal Market, despite the obvious disadvantages for their sectors. Similarly, a critique of this new type of economic policy and the suggestions of alternative development strategies as presented by the GA and individual intellectuals had little chance to be accepted by a wider audience in this ideological environment.

To conclude, social forces linked to the national, protected industrial sectors opposed EU membership. None the less, the breaking of the ranks by some social forces of capital, the lack of uniformity in the issues priori-tised to oppose membership, the unsupportive attitude by ministries linked to national problems and the exclusion from the corporatist policy-making institutions prevented these social forces from forming a successful historical bloc against membership. Alternatives to membership based on a different economic policy were more or less precluded in a structural environment, which was partly constituted by neo-liberalism in the form of intersubjective meanings.

Sweden and social democratic hegemony: the struggle postponed

The new dynamics of the EU in the mid-1980s triggered a rethinking of Sweden's integration policy (Luif 1996: 204). In contrast to Austria, however, membership was not discussed as an option, since the governing SAP had repeatedly made it clear that neutrality prevented such a step, before it suddenly announced its intention to apply to the EU in October 1990. Nevertheless, to some extent the different positions of various social forces can already be detected at this stage.

Labour, capital and agriculture: membership is not on the agenda

The position of labour

There was not much discussion of the 1985 Internal Market initiative within the LO until 1987–8. The Swedish Model was considered to be beyond debate (Interview no. 46; Stockholm, 13 November 1996; Interview no. 56; Stockholm, 21 November 1996). None the less, from 1987 onwards, unions in the transnational production sector started to point out that some kind of response was necessary (Interview no. 46; Stockholm, 13 November 1996). In particular the Metal Workers' Union, representing a sector which is charac- terised by TNCs such as Ericsson, Electrolux and Volvo and which exports more than 50 per cent of its products, became aware of the possible negative impact of the Internal Market on economic competitiveness and, thereby, employment in its sector. The TNCs had made this clear in discussions with local union branches, which, in turn, demanded some action from their central organisation. The central union then used its close contacts with the SAP and pressed for an initiative. This contributed, at least partially, to the eventual government bill on 'Sweden and West European Integration' of December 1987, which outlined the new approach (Interview no. 66; Stockholm, 29 November 1996).

In 1987–8, the first ideas about the new relationship between Sweden and the EU were aired mainly by the peak organisation LO and the affiliated Metal Workers' Union.[2] It was stressed that the Internal Market programme was going to affect Sweden and that, therefore, a response was required.

> Whatever we in Sweden may think about all this, we will be affected by what is now happening. All other considerations aside, it has to do with the coordination of a market with about 320 million inhabitants. Half our total exports go to these countries.
>
> (Molin 1988: 10).

Although increased co-operation with the EU was deemed to be necessary in this situation, all contributors agreed that membership was not on the agenda for Swedish trade unions. It was important 'to keep national self-determination in certain important economic, social and security policies' (Dahlström 1987: 6). It was also made clear 'that Sweden's nonalignment policy should, of course, remain in place' (Molin 1988: 11). Participation in the EMS in order to obtain a hard currency policy was the furthest suggestion with respect to integration (Olsson 1988a: 6). Closer co-operation was to be achieved via the formation and strengthening of common EFTA-positions (Dahlström 1987: 7) and via active participation in the discussions within the European Trade Union Confederation (ETUC) and the Council of Nordic Trade Unions (Olsson 1988a: 6; Molin 1988: 11).

These contributions in favour of closer co-operation, though not integration with the EU, already deployed those arguments which would become so important to the pro-EU side of the labour movement in later stages of the debate on membership. First, the failure of the Keynesian, 'old social democratic' way in France between 1981 and 1983 was pointed out. The labour movement, consequently, would require a European vision beyond the national level (Olsson 1988a: 5; Olsson 1988b: 8). Second, it was argued that a greater degree of international trade union co-operation was necessary to counter TNCs' structural power and to balance the concentration of transnational capital, which was especially represented in Europe through the emergence of 'Eurocapitalism' (Olsson 1988a: 6; Olsson: 1988b: 9). European co-operation would likewise be necessary in order to strengthen Europe's competitiveness *vis-à-vis* the USA and Japan and, thereby, secure Europe's economic well-being (Olsson 1988b: 9; Molin 1988: 10). Other international issues such as pollution, employment and peace would also require international solutions and, therefore, international co-operation (Olsson 1988a: 5). Great emphasis was, furthermore, put on the necessity of a continuing development of the social dimension complementing the Internal Market (Molin 1988: 11). While a transnational, European level was identified as the crucial level of policy-making, Swedish achievements were not discarded. Rather, it was pointed out that Sweden could contribute positively to European co-operation. 'For example, full employment, the social welfare safety net and the pivotal role of strong trade unions in the structure of Swedish society are of interest in a broader European perspective' (Olsson 1988a: 6).

In 1988, the LO Committee on relations with the EU was established. It consisted of about thirty members. Each affiliated union was represented by one member except for the Municipal Workers' Union, which had two representatives; the other members came from the central organisation (Interview no. 57; Stockholm, 21 November 96). By 1988, it had become clear that participation in the Internal Market was crucial for Swedish economic development and exports, and the Committee, consequently, unanimously supported closer co-operation short of full membership and the eventual EEA. This was intended to allow Sweden participation in the Internal Market without having to become an EU member (see chapter four). Full membership, however, was only discussed after the SAP decision. It should be noted that the Committee was not a decision-making body, but an expert group to give advice to the LO (Interview no. 59; Stockholm, 26 November 1996). Issues such as labour laws, health and safety regulations related to the adaptation to EU law under an EEA-type agreement had been the main concerns (Interview no. 58; Stockholm, 26 November 1996).

The TCO sensed as early as 1986 that the Internal Market programme implied threats to the Swedish economy. Nevertheless, the EEA , rather than membership, appeared to be the solution and was never regarded as a mere stepping-stone to full membership. The SAP's turnaround in October 1990 came as a total surprise to the union (Interview no. 40; Stockholm, 11 November 1996). The SACO hardly engaged in the debate. Relations with the EU were considered an issue of foreign policy, not a trade union matter (Interview no. 41; Stockholm, 11 November 1996). None the less, in May 1990 the Swedish Association of Graduate Engineers, an affiliate of the SACO, became the first trade union to demand membership (Luif 1996: 112). Its members often occupied high positions within the transnational sector industry and therefore represented transnational forces. They argued that in case of non-membership many jobs would be lost and followed the line of the SAF in general (Interview no. 41; Stockholm, 11 November 1996). Overall, the influence of this particular union should not be overestimated. As for the SACO in general, it had no direct links with political parties, and therefore was not crucial for the SAP position. The demand does, however, indicate that transnational labour supported the move towards closer co-operation and, eventually, integration with the EU.

To summarise the position of trade unions up to October 1990, it was transnational sector unions which first raised the demand for a response to the Internal Market programme in 1987, a demand which was in general accepted by both transnational and national labour in 1988. From then onwards, especially the LO discussed the possible impact resulting from participation in the Internal Market short of membership. Membership itself, however, was not on the agenda except for the SACO affiliate the Swedish Association of Graduate Engineers, and this not before May 1990.[3] Finally, it must be noted that some parts of the labour movement in the public sector feared the possible negative impact of closer ties with the EU on the Swedish Model and welfare system even before membership was on the agenda (Hamilton and Stålvant 1989: 20). This line of division within the trade unions became sharper after the SAP's decision to apply for membership.

The position of capital

Initially, the Internal Market programme did not capture the attention of Swedish capital. Peter Wallenberg for example, President of the SI, was still focusing on the USA in 1986 (Interview no. 52; Stockholm, 15 November 1996). This complacency has to be seen against the background of the stagflation in European economies. Middle-sized companies in particular favoured expanding in the USA rather than investing in the EU (Interview no. 51; Stockholm, 15 November 1996). In 1987, the picture changed. Wallenberg spoke out openly in favour of membership in December and other business leaders also made this point via formal and informal political channels (Interview no. 61; Stockholm, 26 November 1996). The SI and SAF took care, however, when arguing the case that they did not drive the trade unions into a hostile position. Membership was perceived as the ultimate goal at the time, but it was considered impossible, since the SAP had stated its incompatibility with the policy of neutrality. It was, instead, argued that everything should be done to ensure that Swedish companies would be able to compete on equal terms with their EU counterparts in the Internal Market. How this might be achieved was considered to be a political question, and thus the responsibility of the government (Interview no. 43; Stockholm, 12 November 1996). The SI feared the loss of markets and companies, which transferred production units and sometimes even their headquarters to the EU. Membership was considered as the best remedy for this danger in informal discussions with government politicians before 1989, but the pressure was not very strong. It was clear that the SAP would have to make the eventual decision (Interview no. 54; Stockholm, 19 November 1996).

In sum, and in contrast to Austria, there was no institution of capital within which organic intellectuals formulated a pro-membership hege-monic project. The relative political inactivity should not, however, be interpreted as inactivity as such. Swedish industry did react towards the Internal Market programme. Swedish TNCs realised that they must be part of the Internal Market to avoid possible discrimination and to be geographically closer to the consumers of their products. As outlined in chapter two, there had been a drastic rise in outward FDI between 1985 and 1990 (see Table 2.5). Table 3.4 shows that this increase in FDI went predominantly to the Union. Whereas between 1982 and 1985 only 29.9 per cent of outward FDI went to EU countries, the average share between 1988 and 1990 had risen to 62.1 per cent. In contrast, FDI to North America declined from 22 per cent in 1982–85 to only 7 per cent in 1988–90, indicating a re-direction of investment from the USA to the EU.

Table 3.4 Regional distribution of outward FDI in Sweden (%), 1982–90

	EFTA	EU	North America	Other	Total
1982–1985	8.2	29.9	22.0	39.9	100
1986–1988	14.0	40.7	16.8	28.4	100
1988–1990	6.7	62.1	7.0	24.1	100

Source: EFTA 1991: 27

While other factors contributed to the increase of Swedish FDI in the EU, there is a strong indication that 'a major cause for this shift was uncertainty about a future Swedish Union membership and a fear of Fortress Europe' (Braunerhjelm and Oxelheim 1996: 114). Increased investment abroad did not complement but substituted for expansion at home, indicating a shift of production to the EU. Especially in the knowledge-intensive industries, except for chemicals and pharmaceuticals, investment at home was substituted by FDI (Andersson *et al.* 1996: 126, 135; Braunerhjelm and Oxelheim 1996: 114). In comparison with other countries outside the EU, Swedish companies were the most aggressive ones in the relocation of production (Interview no. 65; Stockholm, 28 November 1996).

A report on the consequences of the Internal Market programme for the Swedish economy in general, and the Swedish manufacturing industry in particular, commissioned in February 1987 by the SI, had already spelled out the possible need for Swedish companies to transfer production units to the EU. It was made clear that the impact of changes in the economic structure due to the Internal Market did not affect only trade in goods and services. The focus also had to be on long-term structural implications (Ohlsson 1988: 12–13). For example, participation in the EU's R&D policy, the education and training programmes and special support schemes for small and medium-sized companies was considered to be crucial for the structural renewal of the Swedish economy (Ohlsson 1988: 34–44). The same argument was put forward for the importance of access to the efficient EU capital markets (Ohlsson 1988: 44–50) and skilled labour of the Internal Market (Ohlsson 1988: 50–3). The report did not demand membership, but implied that it was absolutely necessary. This was underlined by the threat that production units might be transferred to the EU. The report pointed out that in the run-up to 1992 necessary actions by Swedish companies might include company acquisitions, mergers, joint ventures and other strategic investments in the EU (Ohlsson 1988: 15). The threat was even more direct in the case of the government procurement market within the EU (equipment for transport, water supply, energy production and distribution, and telecommunications). 'The strategic decisions large companies will have to make during this period will tend to shift their production base into the EU' (Ohlsson 1988: 33). Eventually, the high level of FDI in the EU by transnational capital became a political statement, since no country can afford sustained capital flight (Interview no. 67; Stockholm, 29 November 1996).

The position of the agricultural sector

The internal debate of the LRF started in 1988–9. It was realised that EU membership would come sooner or later. Consequently a competitiveness study was commissioned in order to evaluate the opportunities for Swedish farmers within the EU. The overvalued SKr and excessive cost levels due to taxation were identified as problems. Apart from that, however, the level of education, skill, technology and productivity in Sweden implied that Swedish agriculture was competitive with the most advanced agricultural nations such as Britain and the Netherlands. Equal conditions, however, could only be obtained via membership (Interview no. 50; Stockholm, 14 November 1996).

Simultaneously, the regulated agricultural market in Sweden itself had come under criticism. It had been established in 1932 in a deal between the CP, then the Agrarian Party, and the SAP. The former accepted unemployment benefit in exchange for a guaranteed higher price per litre of milk, an arrangement which had also been accepted by the other parties later on. During the 1980s, however, the Liberal Party left the party consensus and demanded deregulation and the introduction of market principles. When the SAP also started to move in this direction, the LRF recognised that deregulation was on the agenda. It responded with a twofold strategy. On the one hand, it accepted deregulation but asked for a five-year transition period; on the other, it strongly argued in favour of EU membership.

In 1990, the Swedish parliament passed a law on agricultural reform. 'A major feature of the new policy was to subject the agricultural sector to the free play of market forces' (The Swedish Institute 1995: 2). In practice, this meant that all subsidies were supposed to be phased out between 1991 and 1994. In June 1990, the LRF adopted a decision in favour of membership, which was to be reiterated each following year (Interview no. 50; Stockholm, 14 November 1996). The EU's Common Agriculture Policy (CAP) suddenly offered not only a larger market but also higher subsidies than the deregulated Swedish market (Interview no. 51; Stockholm, 15 November 1996). It cannot be said that this decision influenced the SAP. The LRF did not engage in political lobbying at this time due to the taboo on discussing neutrality, and it had no formal ties with the Social Democrats (Interview no. 50; Stockholm, 14 November 1996). With reference to the CP's position on the EU, however, the LRF was to play a crucial role in the years to come.

Close economic co-operation without membership: the SAP maintains its traditional position

The first response to EU-internal discussions about the Internal Market had been the Luxembourg Declaration of the EU and European Free Trade Area (EFTA) in 1984, which included a commitment to intensified EU–EFTA relations and the eventual creation of a European Economic Space (Gstöhl 1996: 49–51). By 1987–8, however, the EFTA-countries realised that the process was slow, inadequate and costly, while the EU itself had moved rapidly towards the completion of the Internal Market with the signing of the SEA in 1986. In an address to a meeting of Swedish ambassadors to Western Europe, Anita Gradin, the Swedish Minister for Foreign Trade, described the situation as follows:

What concerns us, however, is that co-operation is progressing too slowly and is too narrow in scope. So far the [EU–]EFTA negotiations have mainly focused on the free movement of goods, while the other three freedoms have virtually lain fallow as far as the EFTA countries are concerned. And in the mean time, as I have said, the pace of internal [EU] co-operation has been constantly accelerating.

(Gradin 1988: 248).

Against the background of this development, the SAP government decided at the end of 1987 to start a new initiative. This was partly due to pressure by the employer associations and transnational sector trade unions, which feared the negative impact of the Internal Market on their sectors, but it also reflected the SAP's historically positive attitude towards big business. 'What is good for Volvo, is good for Sweden' had always been more than just a saying (Interview no. 52; Stockholm, 15 November 1996). This new policy was designed according to two basic principles:

The Government's policy is oriented towards ensuring that Swedish companies will continue to be able to compete on the [EU] market on equal terms with other West European firms. Second, the Government's position, as in the past, is that membership is not compatible with our policy of neutrality.

(Gradin 1987: 301)[4]

The new approach, first outlined in the government's bill on 'Sweden and West European Integration' of December 1987, included a three-fold strategy: 'We shall further develop the Nordic co-operation, we shall strengthen EFTA at the same time as we extend and deepen the co-operation with the [EU] as far as this is compatible with our policy of neutrality' (Swedish Ministry for Foreign Affairs 1987: 5). It was acknowledged that the deepening of the co-operation with the EU mainly implied the harmonisation of regulations via the adaptation to the Union's existing rules (Swedish Ministry for Foreign Affairs 1987: 28–9).

In spring 1988, the government set up a complex institutional structure based on this bill. A Cabinet Committee on European Affairs was established consisting of the Prime Minister, the Ministers for Foreign Affairs, for Foreign Trade, of Finance and of Industry. This Cabinet Committee was part of the wider Council for European Affairs, which additionally included high-ranking representatives of Swedish business and trade unions, the Governor of the Bank of Sweden and the Chancellor of the Swedish Universities. More than twenty working groups were established, which involved all ministries except for the Ministry of Defence. Where it was considered necessary, advisory groups consisting of interest associations' representatives were attached. Ulf Dinkelspiel was designated as chief negotiator for the negotiations with EFTA and the EU (Swedish

Government 1988b). The main goal of these government committees and commissions was to achieve harmonisation with EU rules wherever possible (Jacobsson 1990: 16). At the international level, Sweden worked for a revival of the multilateral EU–EFTA relations. There are strong indicators that the Swedish and Norwegian social democratic governments devised in late 1988, together with Jacques Delors, the President of the EU Commission, the initiative leading to the EEA (Gstöhl 1996: 55–6; Interview no. 52; Stockholm, 15 November 1996). Overall, the SAP response to the Internal Market initiative resembled the global approach, one of the two alternatives to membership discussed in Austria (Interview no. 61; Vienna, 26 November 1996).

The government's position showed great similarities with the points raised by LO representatives. The first priority was that closer co-operation with the EU should not involve the deterioration of the environment, weakened worker protection or poorer product safety (Gradin 1987: 302). According to Gradin, 'we wish to maintain our level of aspiration as regards workplace safety and health and environmental standards' (Gradin 1990a: 222). Second, increased importance should be attached to the development of the social dimension (Swedish Ministry for Foreign Affairs 1987: 6; Swedish Government 1988a: 225). Prime Minister Carlsson emphasised that 'we shall work together for a policy which secures full employment and social security within the framework of a free labour market' (Carlsson 1988: 231). Gradin admitted that there was, for example, only slow progress within the EU towards employee participation, but she pointed to Delors' initiative of January 1989 for a new form of 'social dialogue' between the Union of Industrial and Employers' Confederations of Europe (UNICE) and ETUC as a positive sign in this area (Gradin 1989: 273). Third, international co-operation by governments and trade unions would be required in order to overview TNCs' activities (Swedish Ministry for Foreign Affairs 1987: 13–14; Gradin 1988: 251). 'Since national economies are already integrated, there needs to be political and trade union coordination if welfare objectives are to be safeguarded' (Gradin 1989: 272). International problems such as pollution also required international solutions (Swedish Ministry for Foreign Affairs 1987: 14). In short, while membership was not on the agenda, the arguments, so important in the section of the SAP favouring membership later on, can already be identified at this stage.

In sum, between 1987 and the announcement of application in October 1990, the SAP pursued a traditional way of co-operation with the EU. Co-operation should be as close as possible in order to guarantee the competitiveness of Swedish companies, but short of membership to secure Sweden's policy of neutrality. While closer economic co-operation was desired, the Swedish Model with its developed public sector and generous welfare system was not to be compromised. On the contrary, it was considered to be a possible positive contribution to West European co-operation (Carlsson 1989: 140).

The political parties in the shadow of Social Democratic hegemony

In spring 1988, the Foreign Policy Committee of the Riksdag discussed the Government bill on 'Sweden and West European Integration'. In contrast to the bill, membership was not excluded as a possibility for all time, but the SAP, FP, MS and CP made clear that it was not a matter to be contemplated immediately in the forthcoming negotiations with the EU. Co-operation with the EU should be deepened and widened as long as this was compatible with neutrality (Luif 1988: 190).

The position of the MS and FP

This compromise, more or less in line with the government's position, further demonstrated the SAP's hegemonic position within Sweden. The MS had traditionally been in favour of close alignment with the EU and it had demanded membership in its Action Programme of November 1984 (Luif 1988: 188). In May 1987, however, Carl Bildt, the party chairman, spelled out why membership was not on the agenda: 'neutrality politics requires us to abstain from taking part in binding foreign policy cooperation' (quoted in Hamilton and Stålvant 1989: 15). Thus, the MS followed the official SAP line in foreign policy. The closest possible relation with the EU short of membership was, consequently, the aim and the EEA initiative by Delors in 1989 was deemed to be a good opportunity. Nevertheless, this policy was not necessarily a matter of conviction. It was rather a careful strategy by Bildt to avoid locking the SAP in a 'no'-position, similar to the SAF's and SI's strategy towards the trade unions (Interview no. 51; Stockholm, 15 November 1996).

The FP similarly perceived that the eventual decision for membership had to come from the hegemonic SAP and, therefore, did not demand membership openly before the fall of the Berlin Wall in November 1989. It also favoured the closest possible relation to the EU short of membership. Some people in the MS but also the FP had argued even before 1989 that membership was compatible with neutrality, but the parties did not officially adopt this position. The SAP had often used such statements to accuse its opponents of being untrustworthy in foreign policy and of neglecting the Swedish 'holy grail' of neutrality. As the majority of the population held neutrality in a similar high esteem, this was an electorally impossible position (Interview no. 55; Stockholm, 19 November 1996; Luif 1996: 141).

This situation, however, changed immediately after the fall of the Berlin Wall in November 1989. Bengt Westerberg, the FP chairman, stated that 'my conclusion as a Social Liberal and internationalist . . . is that it is desirable for Sweden, without abandoning its neutrality policy, to become a full-fledged member of the European Union before the end of this century' (quoted in Lindmarker 1991: 3). This was not only the result of economic concerns, but also the expression of the strong internationalist direction of the FP, which favoured the creation of peace via international co-operation (Interview no. 55; Stockholm, 19 November 1996). In May 1990, Westerberg was even more explicit and demanded that Sweden should apply for membership during the parliamentary period of 1991–94 (Luif 1996: 211). Bildt and the MS followed immediately with the same demand. The MS had already become extremely unhappy with the process of the EEA negotiations in January 1990 as it had realised that the EEA would never provide Sweden with co-decision making powers. Hence, Sweden would eventually have to choose between membership or remaining outside the EU and, thereby, endanger the Swedish TNCs' position. From this point onwards, the EEA was merely seen as a stepping-stone towards eventual full membership (Interview no. 51; Stockholm, 15 November 1996). The change in the European security environment removed all hesitations of the MS and FP to demand application for membership. The final decision, however, still remained with the SAP.

The position of the CP

The CP was also part of the party compromise in spring 1988. It totally accepted the SAP's position that membership was incompatible with neutrality. The Internal Market programme had only initiated a debate about an EEA-type solution and the party compromise promised exactly this (Interview no. 42; Stockholm, 11 November 1996). Furthermore, the CP 'apparently wishing to emphasize an all-European perspective, has criticized the [EU] among other things for maintaining high tariff walls and has focused its attention on alternative European organizations such as the CSCE [Conference on Security and Co-operation in Europe] and the ECE (the UN Economic Commission for Europe)' (Lindmarker 1991: 6). Representing environmental and agricultural interests, it supported the maintenance of a self-sufficient system and environmental and food standards, which it regarded as being endangered by EU membership (Luif 1988: 189–90). On the basis of this position, the party reacted angrily towards the FP and MS suggestion in May 1990 to apply for membership. 'According to the Center Party interpretation, the Moderates and Liberals wished to weaken Sweden's position in the upcoming [EEA] negotiations' (Lindmarker 1991: 6).

The position of the VP and GP

Both the VP and the GP fiercely opposed membership and even closer co-operation with the EU along the lines of the EEA. They rejected the party compromise of spring 1988 and were to maintain their position right through to the referendum in 1994. The VP regarded the EU 'as a capitalist organization, firmly tied to the Western military alliance. Close

Swedish links with the [EU] are therefore incompatible with Swedish neutrality and with the task of ensuring social justice in Swedish society' (Viklund 1989: 41). The main arguments against membership or closer co-operation with the EU were the implied threat to Sweden's welfare system and objective of full employment, the democratic deficit at the EU level and the threat to Sweden's parliamentary sovereignty (Interview no. 38; Stockholm, 8 November 1996). 'As alternatives to Swedish [EU] membership or far-reaching adaptation to [EU] practices, the VP made such suggestions as greater Nordic cooperation, broadening the membership of EFTA and expanding the Council of Europe into "a real European Parliament"' (Lindmarker 1991: 7). In short, national sovereignty should be preserved as much as possible and the country should pursue an independent economic policy with the goal of full employment (Interview no. 38; Stockholm, 8 November 1996).

The GP for its part rejected close co-operation with the EU on several grounds. First was concern over the Union's lower environmental standards; Sweden's were significantly higher, especially in the chemical sector. Second was the EU's democratic deficit; the GP favoured the decentralisation of decision-making to the local level rather than regulation by the supranational institutions in Brussels. The third issue was neutrality, which was considered to be more than merely a Cold War concept. A final concern was the EU's fortress character and its impermeability to countries outside the EU; a tendency, which the party saw enhanced via the internal removal of trade barriers (Interview no. 45; Stockholm, 12 November 1996; Interview no. 70; Stockholm, 3 December 1996). 'At the root of this argument is a hostility to the philosophy of growth' (Lindmarker 1991: 7), which was thought to be incompatible with an environmentally-friendly and sustainable way of life. The 'no' to a closer relation with the EU, however, was not chauvinistic. Instead, the GP looked for some kind of flexible international co-operation beyond the EU and a security regime based on the CSCE, of which the tasks included threats beyond the military sphere such as pollution (Interview no. 70; Stockholm, 3 December 1996). In 1990, the party launched the newspaper *Critical EU Facts*, which provided information about the EU and became later the newspaper of the group 'No to the EU' before and during the referendum campaign (Interview no. 45; Stockholm, 12 November 1996).

Overall, 'the reasons for both parties' anti-EU stances converged and were based around similar concerns for Swedish independence, solidarity with the Third World and scepticism over the future democratic control of the EU structures' (Widfeldt 1996: 113). It should also be noted that the VP in particular had already pointed at this stage of the debate to the possible negative impact of membership on the Swedish Model. This argument was to become important in the later debate on membership.

The SAP's 1990 turn-around

The SAP announcement of its intention to apply for membership in parliament on 26 October 1990 came as a surprise and shock to the other parties, trade unions and employers' associations. It was one point of an economic crisis package and read as follows:

> Swedish membership of the [EU] with continued adherence to Sweden's policy of neutrality is in our national interest . . .; the Government is seeking a new parliamentary decision on European policy which defines more clearly and in more positive terms Sweden's ambitions of becoming a member of the European [Union].
> (Swedish Government 1990: 306).

In the literature, several reasons are identified for the turn-around. First, the traditional economic argument claimed that Sweden had to be a member because of its trade dependence on the EU (Miles 1996: 63). The change in the international security structure after the fall of the Berlin Wall is identified as a second reason. The end of the Cold War increased the freedom of action of neutral countries such as Sweden and, 'suddenly, neutrality was more a hindrance for international influence than an asset' (Pedersen 1994: 124). Third, electoral reasons may have played a role. 'Polls taken in May 1990 indicated a clear majority in favour, with only 21 per cent opposed to membership and 20 per cent undecided' (Huldt 1994: 119). The SAP performed badly in polls and was put under pressure by the FP and MS, which indicated their intention to make application an issue of the 1991 general elections campaign. Moreover, according to Miles, 'the most influential factor in changing Swedish policy was governmental frustration at the slowness of the . . . EEA negotiations and the limitations of any future EEA agreement' (Miles 1996: 64). In particular the lack of influence on decision-making in the EEA is supposed to have pushed the SAP towards application (Gstöhl 1996: 61). Finally, the severe economic crisis, which hit Sweden in early 1990, convinced the SAP leaders that Sweden could not afford to stay outside any longer (Miles 1996: 63).

The first argument about trade dependence, although relevant, is of secondary importance, considering that the transnationalisation of production had increasingly become Sweden's main link with the global economy (see chapter two). Moreover, although imports from the EU increased from 48.2 per cent in 1981 to 55.2 per cent in 1990 and exports to the EU rose from 45.7 per cent to 54.2 per cent during the same period (see Table 3.5, page 82), this change in trade flows was relatively modest and does not indicate why a drastic turn-around was suddenly required in October 1990.

The security argument is dealt with in chapter five in more detail, but it can be stated here that, while it was a necessary background condition to allow the SAP to change its course, it did not push the SAP towards

Table 3.5 Shares of main areas and countries in Sweden's total trade (%), 1981–90

		EU*	EFTA**	Germany	USA
1981	Imp.	48.2	16.7	16.0	8.2
	Exp.	45.7	20.1	11.0	6.1
1985	Imp.	56.0	15.7	17.9	8.4
	Exp.	48.7	19.2	11.5	11.7
1986	Imp.	57.3	16.2	20.5	7.8
	Exp.	50.0	20.7	11.6	11.3
1987	Imp.	57.3	16.5	21.8	6.9
	Exp.	51.0	20.7	11.9	10.7
1989	Imp.	55.5	17.0	20.7	8.2
	Exp.	53.6	19.0	13.1	9.3
1990	Imp.	55.2	18.2	19.8	8.7
	Exp.	54.2	19.0	14.1	8.6

Source: Luif 1988: 163 (1981-87); EFTA 1991: 62, 69 (1989–90)

Notes
*   EU: ten members including Greece in 1981; plus Spain and Portugal in 1985–90
**   EFTA: 1981: Finland, Iceland, Norway, Austria, Portugal, Sweden and Switzerland; 1985–90: without Portugal

application. Limited importance can also be attributed to the argument that the SAP changed its policy for electoral reasons. Undoubtedly, its rating in polls was low and the general elections of 1991 loomed large on the horizon. To jump on the EU bandwagon must have been tempting in order to tap the pro-EU voters. None the less, the possible electoral gain had to be counterbalanced by a possible rift within the party, which actually occurred during the referendum campaign (see chapter four).

The point about dissatisfaction with the lack of influence on policy-making in the EEA treaty has some validity. Delors had twice rejected joint decision-making in January and April 1990 (Luif 1996: 155–7), and interviewees cited this as one of the reasons (Interview no. 44; Stockholm, 12 November 1996; Interview no. 52; 15 November 1996). At the same time, it should not be overestimated. Although there had been discussions between EU and EFTA representatives beforehand, the formal negotiations did not commence before 20 June 1990 and were concluded on 22 October 1991. Consequently, the exact position with reference to co-decision making could not have been known in October 1990. In a report to parliament about the EEA process in January 1990, Gradin did not voice any concern about a possible lack of decision-making influence (Gradin 1990a). In an address to a youth seminar on Europe in September 1990, she pointed to the problem that the EU wanted to retain decision-making autonomy while the EFTA countries sought some kind of participation.

None the less, she still concluded optimistically: 'I am convinced that, given political good will and a little inventiveness, it will be possible to reconcile these two aims' (Gradin 1990b: 266). This was hardly expression of deep disappointment that made a policy change necessary. Gustavsson concludes that 'with better economic prospects . . . the government would have retained its policy of non-[EU] membership, regardless of how the [EU] acted in the EEA negotiations' (Gustavsson 1998: 193). This leads directly to the Swedish economic crisis in the changed transnational structures occasioned by globalisation as the main reason for application.

A tentative reconstruction of the internal SAP process that led to the announcement on application may help to clarify the relevance of this factor. The SAP members were surprised about the turn-around. There had been neither an internal party debate, nor a clear position within the party leadership.[5] The first decisive moment was probably the economic crisis in February 1990 and the defeat of the government's crisis package in parliament (see chapter two). Although a reformed SAP government took office shortly afterwards, this must have left a strong impression. The SAP had lost its confidence that it was able to regulate the Swedish economy. The belief that there was a 'third way' between old-style Keynesianism and conservative neo-liberalism vanished.

As early as 1986, the Finance Ministry had warned that the economy was going to overheat. It failed, however, to convince the other ministers and the Prime Minister that it was necessary to cool the economy via, for example, higher interest rates. The consequence was the crash in the late 1980s, early 1990, which required the February crisis package. Recognising its inability to control the economy, the Finance Ministry pushed strongly within the government for membership, probably from March onwards (Interview no. 49; Stockholm, 14 November 1996; Interview no. 60; Stockholm 26 November 1996). By summer 1990, it is likely that the decision on application was taken.

The eventual timing of application was due to the renewed pressure on the SKr and the rumours about an imminent currency devaluation in October (Interview no. 52; Stockholm, 15 November 1996; Interview no. 61; Stockholm, 26 November 1996). The longer-term reasons were the ongoing capital flight of Swedish TNCs to the EU, the government's loss of economic credibility and rising unemployment (Interview no. 44; Stockholm, 12 November 1996). Application was an attempt to refer a 'sound' economic policy to supranational restrictions and to have a scapegoat for harsh domestic policy measures (Interview no. 49; Stockholm, 14 November 1996). It was a way of regaining economic credibility, stability and budgetary discipline, and achieving a structural reform of the economy. The official position was that Sweden's austerity policy was the result of a sovereign national decision. Nevertheless, there is some truth in the point that application was regarded as a way of introducing greater discipline (Interview no. 68; Stockholm, 2 December 1996).

The idea of application emerged as a joint effort of the Ministry of Finance and the Prime Ministers' Office (Interview no. 68; Stockholm, 2 December 1996; see also Gustavsson 1998: 170–87). This was supported by the Ministries for Foreign Affairs, Foreign Trade, and Agriculture. The Ministries of Labour and of Social Affairs were sceptical, because they feared that membership would restrict the policy-making autonomy of their sectors (Interview no. 49; Stockholm, 14 November 1996). However, they were not asked for their opinion before the announcement in parliament on 26 October 1990 (Interview no. 68; Stockholm, 2 December 1996).

To conclude, the turn-around of the SAP was the result of a perception that the economic problems could only be dealt with through application to the EU. The decision was taken by a very few people within the SAP leadership and government. It did not express the opinion of the SAP as a party, as the later divisions within the party were to prove.

The MS and FP, and also the employers' associations reacted positively. The GP and VP, unsurprisingly, opposed application and voted against it in parliament on 12 December 1990. For the SAP and trade unions, it was the start of their internal debates. They had been totally surprised and there was some disenchantment within the LO that it had not been consulted beforehand, as used to be the case in such fundamental decisions as application (Interview no. 46; Stockholm, 13 November 1996). The CP faced the biggest problems. As was everyone else, the party had been surprised by the SAP's decision and was unhappy that there was no time for an internal party debate. In November 1990, an extended party committee meeting was convened to debate application. It had already become clear at this point that there was a majority in favour of application within the party executive and parliamentary group, while a majority of the members opposed it. Even within the party leadership, however, the situation was not clear-cut. The CP representative voted in favour of the party compromise on application in the parliament's Foreign Affairs Committee on 22 November 1990, but it is doubtful whether there was a proper discussion of this move within the leadership (Interview no. 42; Stockholm, 11 November 1996).

The parliamentary decision of 12 December 1990 was based on this compromise which stated:

> Sweden should strive to become a member of the European [Union], while maintaining its neutrality policy. Only as an [EU] member can our country fully participate in, and influence, European [Union] cooperation. After an overall assessment of foreign and security policy aspects, and after consultation in the Advisory Council on Foreign Affairs, the government should be in a position to submit a Swedish application for membership. In the judgment of the Committee, this can occur during 1991.
>
> (quoted in Lindmarker 1991: 5).

In the parliamentary vote on this report, 287 members of the SAP, MS, FP and CP voted in favour, the forty members of the Green and the Left Party against (Luif 1996: 217). On 1 July 1991, Prime Minister Carlsson submitted the application to the EU in Brussels.

Conclusion

In Austria, a historical bloc in favour of application and membership was firmly established by June 1989. The hegemonic project, devised by organic intellectuals of internationally-oriented capital located in the VÖI, was based on economic neo-liberalism and the idea that neutrality was compatible with membership. It provided the basis for an alliance of internationally-oriented capital and labour, which gained control of the two governing parties and the social partners. Similarly, in Sweden, transnational social forces of capital and labour demanded a closer relationship with the EU and Internal Market initiative. Nevertheless the SAP's decision that membership was incompatible with neutrality prevented any debate on membership between 1987 and 1990. This hegemony was expressed in the SAP's predominant position in parliament, and its leading role in defining the public discourse, but also in the acceptance by the opposition parties and employers' associations that it was the SAP, which ultimately determined whether membership was possible. Consequently, transnational capital represented by the SI, SAF, the MS and FP acquiesced to the EEA solution as the next best option until more was possible. When the SAP eventually decided on application in October 1990, there had been neither time nor effort to form an alliance of social forces. Of course, the representatives of transnational capital immediately supported the move, but there had been no discussions within the labour movement be that within the SAP or the various trade unions. The real struggle was still to come.

Another significant difference was the lack of an institution in Sweden, similar to the Austrian VÖI, which provided the platform for organic intellectuals to form a pro-membership project. The reason, here too, must at least partly be sought in the SAP's hegemonic position. It was difficult to mount a challenge to the predominant view that membership was incompatible with neutrality. Nevertheless, this does not suffice as an explanation. The discussion of the restructuring of the Swedish state–society relations in chapter two demonstrated that capital had succeeded in undermining the Swedish Model in an organised, long-term effort led by the SAF. A similar project could theoretically have been started with reference to EU membership. The Swedish production structure provides an additional factor, why this did not happen.

In contrast to Austria, which was dominated by small and medium-sized firms, Sweden had been characterised by large TNCs. While Austria had participated in globalisation mainly through exports and imports of goods and services, Swedish TNCs played an active part in the transnationalisation of production. These TNCs simply did not have to bother with mounting a political challenge to the SAP's anti-membership course. They had the structural option to transfer investment and production units to the EU and, thereby, counter possible threats of exclusion. The TNCs' continually rising FDI to the EU in 1989 and 1990 showed that they were not convinced of the viability of the SAP's EEA strategy. Eventually, this was one of the major reasons why the SAP decided on application. The flight of capital was no longer endurable. Austria's internationally-oriented capital, in contrast, did not have this option at its disposal due to its domestic production structure. A carefully prepared and carried out political strategy was, therefore, the only way to achieve application.

A third difference was the position of the agricultural sector. Whereas membership was largely opposed in Austria despite its leadership's positive position, the agricultural sector was one of the first in Sweden to demand application. This, again, can be explained by the different production structures. The agricultural sector in Austria was heavily protected against the EU and world markets and, therefore, nationally-oriented. Membership implied deregulation and restructuring. In Sweden, on the other hand, the 1990 agricultural reform signified that the whole sector was in any case going to be deregulated and restructured due to the phasing-out of all subsidies and the concomitant lowering of the price level to world market prices. In this situation, membership and the adjustment to the CAP implied more subsidies and higher prices for Swedish farmers. Consequently, while they were not really internationally-oriented, they could be regarded as European oriented social forces.

Finally, there was a difference in the timing of application. Austria applied two years earlier than Sweden. In the early 1980s, the Austrian economic situation was as bad as the Swedish (see chapter two). In contrast to the SAP, however, the SPÖ and its trade union allies did not have a tradition of developing their own reform programmes. When Keynesianism seemed to have failed, Austrian forces of labour, consequently, were much more receptive to neo-liberal ideas as the new way of capital accumulation and to a hegemonic project of EU membership by internationally-oriented capital, which exactly signified such a neo-liberal restructuring.

In Sweden, by contrast, when the SAP returned to government in 1982, it relied on its hegemonic position and programmatic capacity. It developed a 'third way' strategy as an alternative to traditional Keynesianism and neo-liberalism alike. Thus, the neo-liberal revival of the EU from the mid-1980s onwards did not present a logical continuation of domestic restructuring. Rather, it appeared as a different system, the adoption of which was not tempting in the light of domestic economic success. Only when this strategy ended in another economic recession in 1989–90, did the Swedish SAP government decide on application. It had lost its confidence that it could manage the national economy. It turned away from full employment and adopted price stability as the main concern of economic policy. At this stage, membership suddenly became attractive as a solution for the continuation of capital accumulation after the failure of both Keynesianism and the 'third way'.

The similarities of the two cases, however, should not be overlooked because of these differences. In both countries, internationally-oriented and/or transnational social forces were the driving force behind the bid for application in Austria and close co-operation in Sweden. In Austria, the pro-EU forces were supported by those national institutions, which were liked to the global economy, most notably the Finance Ministry, the Economic Ministry and the ANB. Within the cabinet in Sweden, the Cabinet Committee on European Affairs, established in spring 1988, consisted of the Prime Minister and the Ministers for Foreign Affairs, for Foreign Trade, of Finance and of Industry. In other words, the ministries linked to the global economy were also at the centre of decision-making in Sweden, while ministries such as the Ministries of Labour and of Social Affairs, which deal with national problems, were excluded.

Furthermore, when membership came on the agenda, at least in the inner cabinet circle, it was the Ministry of Finance together with the Prime Ministers' Office, which had initiated the move and were the driving force towards application. In short, despite their different strategies, internationally-oriented and/or transnational capital and labour, together with the national institutions linked to the global economy, pressed for integration and/or closer co-operation with the EU in both countries during the process leading to application.

The formation of opposition to application and, thereby, EU membership was slow in both countries. In Sweden, without a decision on application, there was, of course, nothing to mobilise against. Even in Austria, however, anti-EU forces took until the second half of 1988, early 1989, before first coherent movements had been formed. By then, it had been almost too late to influence the decision-making process within the social partners and governing parties. Nevertheless, the struggles over the referenda to be discussed in the next chapter gave these forces a second chance.

4 The conflict over the EU referenda in Austria and Sweden

In Austria, 'total revisions' of the constitution must be put before the population in a referendum according to Article 44. The outcome is binding for the decision-makers. 'Austria's accession to the EU in 1995 implied a "total revision" of the constitution and thus required a referendum' (Müller 1996a: 25). By the end of 1990, it was decided in Sweden to put the final decision on membership before the population. 'Although referend[a] in Sweden are technically only advisory, the political parties agreed in advance to honor the outcome of the [EU] vote, regardless of their own views' (Berg 1994: 2). Consequently, the social forces against the EU were offered another chance to prevent membership in both countries.

This chapter predominantly deals with the struggles before the referenda in the two countries. Before that, however, the next section provides the background context by examining briefly the impact of the EEA and the Maastricht Treaty. It also presents a short overview of the negotiations and discusses their position within the overall process of accession.

From the EEA via Maastricht and membership negotiations to the referenda

The EEA: a stepping-stone towards membership

In 1988–9, the Commission of the EU's first priority was the completion of the Internal Market, not its enlargement. It was, however, realised that some kind of participation in the Internal Market had to be offered to the EFTA countries. In January 1989, Jacques Delors, President of the Commission, took the initiative and proposed a strengthening of the ties between the EU and the EFTA countries. 'He suggested looking for "a new, more structured partnership with common decision-making and administrative institutions" on the basis of the "two pillars" of the [EU] and a strengthened EFTA' (Gstöhl 1996: 55). The new treaty for an EEA was supposed to allow the EFTA countries participation in the economic gains of the Internal Market without becoming a member of the EU.

Austria participated in the negotiations, although it would have preferred membership negotiations straight away. In Sweden, Delors' initiative was well received. It exactly corresponded to the SAP's position on Europe and indeed there were strong hints that the Swedish social democrats had co-masterminded the new approach. Formal negotiations were opened in June 1990, dragged on until 22 October 1991, and were finally signed in Oporto on 2 May 1992, after some revisions had been made in order to satisfy the ECJ's rejection of a separate EEA Court. Eventually, the EEA came into force on 1 January 1994 (Luif 1996: 151–68).

The results of the treaty confirmed the conviction of the pro-EU Austrian forces that full participation in the Internal Market was only possible via membership. One factor was that the EFTA countries did not obtain co-decision making powers. They 'can only influence the legislative process during the decision-shaping stage' (Laursen 1993: 125). They had no right to initiate legislation, an opt-out of new legislation was possible only through a collective EFTA decision, they gained merely restricted access to EU committees, and the common rules of the EEA were those of the Union's *acquis* (Gstöhl 1994: 358–9). In addition, an EFTA Surveillance Authority and Court of Justice were set up and EEA law gained primacy over national law. In short, EFTA countries lost some degree of national sovereignty without gaining a say at the supranational level.

Furthermore, the EEA also implied significant economic losses in comparison with membership.[1] Full participation in the Internal Market was not obtained, since border controls remained in place between the EU and EFTA, and certificates of origin were still required (Woschnagg 1994: 7). The Common Commercial Policy, the Common Agricultural and Fisheries Policy, Euratom and direct and indirect taxation were not part of the EEA Treaty (Gstöhl 1996: 58). The issue of outward processing, so dear to the Austrian export sectors, had not been resolved. The discriminations led to a decrease in Austrian exports by 5 per cent in 1993 (Interview no. 18; Vienna, 22 May 1995), which amounted to more than 1 per cent of Austrian GDP (VÖI 1994: 29–30). Thus, it is not surprising that the affected sectors, such as the textile industry continued pressing for membership (Interview no. 24; Vienna, 24 April 1996) and that the VÖI and the BWK regarded the EEA only as a transition stage towards full membership (Interview no. 18; Vienna, 22 May 1995; BWK 1992: 468–9; VÖI 1991; 1992). In any case, the EEA had never been an alternative to membership for the pro-EU historical bloc.

In Sweden too, by the time the EEA Treaty had been signed, it was only considered to be a transition arrangement. Ulf Dinkelspiel, the Swedish Minister for European Affairs and Foreign Trade, made this clear in a parliamentary briefing on the EEA agreement on 24 October 1991. 'As far as Sweden is concerned', he stated, 'it will very appreciably strengthen our cooperation with the [EU] and is thus an important step towards Swedish membership of the [Union]' (Dinkelspiel 1991: 269). The lack of political co-decision making power was deplored and economic disadvantages were pointed out. The LRF was unhappy about the exclusion of the agricultural sector (Interview no. 50; Stockholm, 14 November 1996), while the SI rejected the remaining border controls and the exclusion of public procurement. Sweden had several companies in this sector and the EEA did not allow them to participate in the Internal Market (Interview no. 54; Stockholm, 19 November 1996). The SI calculated that membership would imply savings of close to 0.5 per cent of GDP in comparison to the EEA, because it 'abolishes border formalities, certificates of origin, prepayment of VAT, and reduces trade-related compliance costs in firms' (Wijkman 1995: 7). Finally, it was argued by representatives of capital and labour that inward FDI was unlikely to go to Sweden in the case of the EEA, because this did not guarantee complete access to the Internal Market (Interview no. 66; Stockholm, 29 November 1996; Interview no. 67; Stockholm, 29 November 1996; Wijkman 1995: 9–11).

The Treaty of Maastricht: accession business as usual

When the negotiations came finally into sight, the Treaty of Maastricht (signed in December 1991) had changed the EU once more. It now consisted of three pillars: the pillar for justice and home affairs, the pillar for a CFSP, and the one consisting of the original Communities. EMU was incorporated into the latter pillar. At first sight, one might suppose that these changes would make the Austrian and Swedish pro-EU forces rethink their position and restart the debate about membership. In particular the project of a CFSP, further threatening the countries' neutrality, and EMU, forcing them to give up their monetary sovereignty and to adopt a budget policy of austerity via the neo-liberal convergence criteria, were potential causes of concern. None the less, nothing of the kind happened.

In a declaration on the occasion of the signing of the Maastricht Treaty, the Austrian Foreign Minister Mock welcomed the agreement on EMU pointing out that Austria was already fulfilling the convergence criteria and would, thus, contribute to the achievement of this goal. He also confirmed that Austria would 'participate in the common foreign and security policy in an active and solidaristic way' (*Aussenministerium* 1992: 114, author's translation). With reference to the CFSP, the official position of the Foreign Ministry was that it had a purely intergovern-mental nature and was therefore compatible with Austria's neutrality (Interview no. 2; Vienna, 9 May 1995). The SPÖ shared this position (Interview no. 4; Vienna, 9 May 1995; see chapter five).[2] The loss of monetary sovereignty posed no problem, as Austria had given this up long ago by pegging the AS to the DM and by fully liberalising its financial markets. The single currency was favoured by all social forces of the pro-EU alliance, since this would prevent countries such as Italy, which was Austria's second most important trading partner after Germany within the EU, from boosting their exports via devaluations.

The convergence criteria, however, presented a problem. On the one hand, the ANB (Interview no. 16; Vienna, 18 May 1995) and the VÖI (Interview no. 18; Vienna, 22 May 1995) considered the fulfilment of the convergence criteria to be necessary in any case in order to consolidate the budget. The Finance Ministry regarded them as a help for its budget policy of austerity, as it offered the possibility of transferring responsibility for economic and social hardship to Brussels (Interview no. 7; Vienna, 11 May 1995). On the other hand, the employees' associations were disappointed about the missing European social dimension in the convergence criteria and the Maastricht Treaty as a whole. Nevertheless, ÖGB President Verzetnitsch concluded that this made Austria's membership even more urgent, as one could participate in the decision-making process only as a member (ÖGB 1991). Additionally, there were some voices within the AK and the ÖGB, which demanded the adding of an unemployment criterion (Interview no. 1; Vienna, 8 May 1995; Interview no. 22; Vienna, 23 April 1996; Sallmutter 1993: 166). Membership as such, however, was not rejected.

On 11 December 1991, shortly after the conclusion of the Maastricht Treaty, Carl Bildt (MS), the new Swedish Prime Minister, released a statement, in which he welcomed the results of the meeting at Maastricht. In particular, he stated that 'Sweden will actively participate in the foreign policy and security cooperation which has now been decided at Maastricht . . . [and that] . . . Sweden wishes to participate in the task of successively realizing economic and monetary union as soon as possible' (Bildt 1991b: 117). Against the background of the fall of the Berlin Wall and the break-up of the Eastern Bloc, neutrality had not been abandoned, but redefined. Participation in the CFSP was regarded as one way of contributing to the establishment of a post-Cold War European security order (see chapter five). Both peak trade union organisations LO and TCO were disappointed about the neo-liberal convergence criteria of EMU and feared that this would make the fight against unemployment more difficult (as is discussed later). None the less, the pro-EU forces argued during the debate that this was a question to be decided later and that it should, therefore, be treated separately from the issue of EU membership. This strategy was successful and there was no debate about amending the convergence criteria before accession.

The EU's emphasis on deepening integration postponed the start of accession negotiations. Eventually, it was not until the European Council meeting in Edinburgh in December 1992, when the question of the future financing of the Union was settled and it looked as if the Treaty of Maastricht could be ratified soon, that the go-ahead for negotiations was given.

The negotiations in Brussels: bargaining in view of the referenda

The Austrian negotiation position

The EU's negotiations with Austria and Sweden officially opened on 1 February 1993. In a joint report to the cabinet on 21 January 1993, Chancellor Vranitzky and Foreign Minister Mock, who was also Austria's chief negotiator, outlined Austria's negotiation position (*Bundeskanzleramt/ Aussenministerium* 1993). Austria wanted to pay low contributions to the EU and receive some structural fund money. Austria's neutral status was mentioned in combination with a reiteration of its commitment to the CFSP. Moreover, it wanted to retain the right to maintain its higher environmental and social standards and the continuation of the transit agreement with the EU of 1991.[3] In order to keep Austria's particular structure of small and medium-sized farms across the whole country, a transition period in the adaptation to the rules of the Common Agricultural Policy (CAP) and for the closely related food processing industry was requested. Financial restructuring aid from the Union was also sought. Finally, the issue of EU citizens buying secondary residences in Austria was identified as important, especially in rural areas.

These points can be related to the demands of the various groups in favour of membership, but also to the forthcoming referendum. Neutrality was primarily a response to the SPÖ, which had made it a precondition of its support for application four years earlier. However, it also reflected concern about the looming referendum. When opinion polls during the period between October 1988 and May/June 1992 asked whether people would give up neutrality or EU membership if the two proved incompatible, the proportion who answered that they would give up membership rather than neutrality ranged from 64 per cent to 82 per cent (Neuhold 1992: 101–3). Austrian negotiators, consequently, could not drop this requirement. The SPÖ had also demanded the maintenance of environmental standards and the transit agreement. The emphasis on social standards had mainly been a quest by the ÖGB and AK. It was, however, also with an eye to the referendum that Austrian negotiators insisted on the transit agreement, which was considered a great success by the Austrian people and, therefore, could not be abolished (Interview no. 32; Vienna, 8 May 1996). Finally, the agricultural sector and the closely linked question of secondary residencies by EU citizens had been at the heart of the LK and the ÖBB.

The Swedish negotiation position

Between Sweden's application to the EU in July 1991 and the start of negotiations in February 1993, a four-party coalition of the MS, FP, CP and the Christian Democratic Party under Prime Minister Bildt (MS) replaced the country's social democratic government. It was the task of this new government to negotiate in Brussels, and Dinkelspiel, who had become Sweden's chief negotiator, outlined his country's negotiation agenda in his opening statement on 1 February 1993 in Brussels (Dinkelspiel 1993). As stated earlier, Sweden committed itself to become a full and active participant in the CFSP, while maintaining its policy of military non-alignment, and it declared its intention to participate in the EMU. Dinkelspiel pointed out, however, that 'a final Swedish position relating to the transition from the second to the third stage will be taken in the light of future events and in accordance with the provisions of the Treaty' (Dinkelspiel 1993: 31). In other words, Sweden retained the final decision on EMU for its parliament (Interview no. 61; Stockholm, 26 November 1996). The EU never openly acknowledged this, but it did not refute it either. This allowed the pro-EU forces during the debate before the referendum to argue that EMU was not part of the decision on membership.

The crucial (and potentially controversial) issues were higher Swedish environmental standards, alcohol monopolies, Swedish snuff tobacco and, most importantly, the question of budget contributions (Interview no. 49; Stockholm, 14 November 1996). All these issues were vital for the looming referendum. It was inconceivable that there would have been a positive outcome in the referendum, if Sweden had had to lower its environmental standards, give up its alcohol monopolies – part of a long battle against excessive alcohol consumption – and prohibit the consumption of snuff. Finally, it was realised that Sweden with its very high living standard would be a net contributor to the EU. Nevertheless, in view of the catastrophic economic situation at the time, it would have been difficult to sell this to the people from the very beginning. The Swedish negotiators, consequently, sought to have their full contribution to the EU budget phased in over a period of several years (Interview no. 49; Stockholm, 14 November 1996).

Both the TCO and LO had drawn up a list of demands for the negotiations in September 1992 and November 1992 respectively (LO 1994; TCO 1993). Most importantly, it was demanded that EU labour market directives could be enacted, according to the Swedish tradition, via collective agreements between the trade unions and employers' associations rather than through parliamentary legislation as in other member states. The unions also asked for the assurance that foreign companies carrying out work with their own employees in Sweden would be subject to Swedish labour market regulations, in order to avoid social dumping. Finally, the TCO and LO asked for the retention of the right to a national regional policy to continue the support of disadvantaged regions and for maintaining the higher Swedish standards of health and safety regulations at the workplace. These demands became part of Sweden's official negotiation position (Dinkelspiel 1993: 30–2).

The negotiation agenda itself was drawn up in close co-operation with the political parties and main interest associations. It was the government's approach to treat membership as a national question and to give everybody a chance of input. The referendum was unlikely to be won if the SAP opposed it and, therefore, a very close relationship with the social democrats was maintained throughout the negotiations. For example, the opening statement by Dinkelspiel of 1 February 1993 had been discussed with the SAP word by word and several changes were made, some without discussion, others after negotiations. Interest associations such as the SAF, SI, and the trade unions co-operated formally in working groups and advisory boards. The political parties were involved via the parliamentary committee on EU matters. Additionally, Dinkelspiel frequently met trade union leaders to discuss important issues in a more informal way (Interview no. 61; Stockholm, 26 November 1996). In short, the negotiation position was the result of close co-operation between the pro-EU forces. During the negotiations, then, the importance attached to individual issues by the negotiators was the result of an evaluation of their possible effect in the referendum (Interview no. 49; Stockholm, 14 November 1996; Interview no. 61; Stockholm, 26 November 1996).

The membership negotiations

At the end of 1993, the first negotiation chapters were closed. On 21 December 1993, the EU accepted Foreign Minister Mock's oral explanation of Austria's status of neutrality (Interview no. 32; Vienna, 8 May 1996) and Sweden's policy of non-alignment.[4] The applicants and the EU signed a joint declaration, in which their commitment to the Treaty of Maastricht in general and the CFSP in particular was stated (Luif 1996: 310).[5] Common positions were also achieved on EMU. These issues presented no problems during the negotiations (Granell 1995: 132). More importantly, agreement was reached in the area of environmental standards and the health and safety regulations at the workplace, giving the applicants a four-year transition period. 'During this period the [EU] directives would be reviewed and – that was the hope of the applicant countries – be adjusted to the stricter rules in the new member states' (Luif 1996: 311). The problem of alcohol monopolies was solved through a compromise. Sweden agreed to abolish its state monopolies for the import, production and wholesale distribution of alcohol, while it retained the monopoly on retail sales. Finally, it was also accepted that Swedish collective agreements were acceptable for the implementation of labour market directives.

In the case of both environmental standards and alcohol monopolies, Austria and Sweden were far from achieving their negotiation targets. The general impression that these agreements were a victory for the applicants had a great deal to do with the way they were presented with a view to the referenda. There was no guarantee that the two countries would not have to lower their environmental standards after four years and Sweden had, in fact, given up several of its alcohol monopolies (Miles 1994b: 11–12). The agreement on snuff – Sweden was allowed the consumption within the country, while the export of snuff was prohibited – can be seen in the same light. There were strong indicators that the EU dragged this issue out for three months in order to make its concessions appear a success for the Swedish negotiators in the eyes of the public (Interview no. 49; Stockholm, 14 November 1996).

Several difficult issues remained on the agenda after December 1993. In the Austrian case, the issues of transit and secondary residencies were settled in the 'jumbo' ministerial meeting from 26 February to 1 March 1994. Austria gained a ten-year (in reality probably six-year) extension of its transit agreement and a transition period of five years in the area of secondary residencies. Agriculture, however, represented a major problem. According to Foreign Minister Mock, the EU had signalled for a year that it was prepared to accept a transition period for Austria's agricultural sector. Then, it suddenly changed its position and argued that it would permit Austrian national financial aid for the sector instead. Mock was unhappy about that, as it implied an additional burden for Austria's budget, and at one stage, the negotiations were nearly called off (Interview no. 36; Vienna, 15 May 1996). Eventually, Austria accepted on the basis that the EU took over some of the financial aid towards Austrian farmers (Luif 1996: 312).

In the case of Sweden, the budget contributions presented the most difficult hurdle. In the end, a phasing-in of the full amount was impossible for technical reasons, but the Swedish negotiators 'gained a budgetary rebate worth up to ECU 2 billion in the first three years as a farm adjustment payment' (Miles 1994b: 14). The chapter on regional policy was closed with the introduction of Objective Six as a new criterion for structural fund assistance. Sweden was allowed to continue its national regional policy and could even expect EU financial aid for its arctic areas.

This summary of the negotiations demonstrates how they functioned as a link between the agenda-setting process and the struggles in the run up to the referenda and, therefore, played only a secondary role in the Austrian and Swedish accession to the EU. The negotiation teams of both countries had to deliver the compromise of the pro-EU forces, reflected in the negotiation agendas on the one hand, and to achieve satisfactory terms that they could put forward for the referenda on the other.

The referendum struggle in Austria

The pro-EU historical bloc reconfirmed

After the successful completion of the negotiations, the pro-EU forces reconfirmed their unity. On 22 April 1994, the SPÖ and ÖVP passed a 'Europe Treaty', in which the concessions to the various social forces of the bloc were spelled out in detail. Point six outlined the financial restructuring help and the setting-up of work foundations for those industrial sectors which were under pressure due to membership. The food processing industry, transport companies and the suppliers of parts were mentioned in particular (*Parteienvereinbarung* 1994: 2–3). Restructuring payments over four years were planned for the agricultural sector in order to help farmers with the immediate adaptation to EU price levels and opening of the markets (*Parteienvereinbarung* 1994: 8). The employees' associations were satisfied with a common commitment to the establishment of work councils throughout the EU (*Parteienvereinbarung* 1994: 5). Finally, the continuing participation of the social partners in the decision-making process in EU matters at the national and European level was confirmed (*Parteienvereinbarung* 1994: 5–6). The foundation for the referendum campaign was laid.

In December 1991, the government gave the contract for its pro-membership campaign to the advertising agency Demner & Merlicek. From then onwards, with increasing intensity until the referendum itself, the government, individual ministries, the pro-EU parties and the social partners were actively engaged in a campaign with telephone lines, information bus tours, placards, mailings and so forth (Schaller 1994b: 75–9). The VÖI also started a wider campaign. It did not, however, want to be over-prominent, since many people would have viewed this as too one-sided. Therefore, 'independent' EU representatives were identified in companies and provided with information material by the VÖI through the *EuroNews*, covering issues such as the costs of non-membership, transit etc. The Europa-Telegramme, leaflets with short and precise information about EU issues to be pinned on the blackboards of companies, were also distributed. Although drawn up by the VÖI, they were published by the *Österreichische Gesellschaft für Europapolitik* (Austrian Society for European Politics)with the reputation of an independent information institute (as discussed in the next paragraph). The social partners organised together information meetings in companies, during which representatives of VÖI/BWK and AK/ÖGB spoke at the same time. They presented membership as an economic necessity for Austria as a whole, not as the interest of one particular fraction of society (Interview no. 18; Vienna, 22 May 1995). In general, these initiatives reached mainly the particular clientele of a party or social partner.

To achieve a broader appeal, those in favour of membership founded the *Österreichische Gesellschaft für Europapolitik* in November 1991. It was supported by all social partners, the ANB, now more openly involved in the campaign, the financial sector of the *Raiffeisenverband*, but also big companies such as IBM Austria, the Japanese TNC Mita and Alcatel Austria. The *Gesellschaft* did not have the task of developing ideas and positions on the question of membership but of disseminating pro-EU information. The positive stance on membership was its starting point and the arguments in favour of membership had been developed during the process leading to application. Keeping an equal distance from all supporting organisations, the *Gesellschaft* succeeded in establishing a reputation of independence, which greatly enhanced its standing among journalists and the public and, thereby, strengthened the credibility of its pro-EU campaign (Interview no. 29; Vienna, 3 May 1996).

Special brochures financed by individual organisations such as the ÖGB or the Conference of Land Governors, and by Foreign Minister Mock as a private individual, were published under the imprint of the *Gesellschaft*, again in order to give them an independent, objective flavour. In contrast to parties and social partners, the *Gesellschaft* had the opportunity to reach people beyond their direct sphere of influence. Teachers and events in local parishes, fire-brigades and the army were supported with informational material. The *Gesellschaft* produced pages for overhead-projectors, a cartoon book in favour of membership, a school newspaper called *Schule und Europa*, which was distributed to all school speakers, politics teachers and headmasters, and even a Christmas calendar for kindergarten children in order to reach housewives via their offspring. Advertisements, some of them pointing to splits within the GA, were placed in the *Kronenzeitung*, which had a readership of about two million, and pro-EU statements by local functionaries were published in regional newspapers. In order to co-ordinate the campaign, the *Gesellschaft* had a weekly meeting from mid-1993 onwards, in which representatives of the social partners, the *Land* governments, the ANB and various ministries participated (Interview no. 29; Vienna, 3 May 1996). In short, the *Gesellschaft* provided the opportunity for the pro-EU groups to organise their campaign from an independent platform, thereby giving their campaign a higher degree of credibility and allowing the material to reach wider sections of society.

The social forces opposed to membership

The opposing social forces did not remain inactive. Since the application had been a matter for parliament alone, it was only now that they had a real opportunity to react. The situation did not look hopeless. At the beginning of 1994, the supporters and opponents among the Austrian population were more or less equally balanced. A majority in the referendum was possible for either side (Schaller 1994b: 52).

Nationally-oriented capital and labour

Despite the *Europa-Abkommen* between the governing parties, the nationally-oriented social forces had not been completely won over. Some members of the SPÖ did not accept the pro-EU position of their party and tried to forge links with dissatisfied farmers (Interview no. 17; Vienna, 18 May 95).

Moreover, shortly before the referendum, about twenty out of 300 mill owners considered starting an anti-EU media campaign. They even contacted an advertising company but, eventually, the whole scheme came to nothing. Additionally, contacts were made with MPs of the FPÖ, by now in the opposition camp (see pages 99 and 100), but they did not put forward the issues in parliament that the mill owners had hoped for. Finally, there was an attempt to co-ordinate actions with nationally-oriented trade unions, which were, however, constrained by the same adversary circumstances within their own chamber (Interview no. 21; Vienna, 23 April 1996).

A similar degree of resistance amongst nationally-oriented capital was noticeable within the food processing sector of the *Raiffeisenverband*. Some functionaries opposed membership and aligned with either the FPÖ or the GA, which were respectively in favour of a nationalist and environmental agriculture policy (Interview no. 28; Vienna, 3 May 1996). Within the AK and the ÖGB, the fractions close to the GA generally opposed membership (Schaller 1994b: 51). Furthermore, members of the GPA, which had always been negative about EU membership (see chapter three), participated in joint information meetings in companies *and* dared to outline their critical, hesitant position. This was controlled and criticised by ÖGB officials, who put the GPA functionaries under significant psychological pressure and accused them of left extremism. Not surprisingly, the GPA did not attempt to form alliances against membership (Interview no. 35; Vienna, 14 May 1996).

In sum, there was significant resistance within the nationally-oriented economic sectors before the referendum, but the situation within the Chambers made it almost impossible for these forces to voice their opposition. While they were often dissatisfied with the situation, co-operation with either the GA or the FPÖ, the two parties against membership, on a larger scale than outlined earlier was deemed impossible. Both were considered to be too extremist for alliances (Interview no. 19; Vienna, 23 May 1995; Interview no. 21; Vienna, 23 April 1996). In the end, party and association solidarity, so important and firmly established throughout Austria's post-war history, carried greater weight than the question of EU membership.

Political parties opposing membership

The GA had maintained its negative position on EU membership from 1989. It had already opposed the EEA in parliament and a majority of 87 per cent voted for a 'no' recommendation at the party's congress in April 1994. According to Johannes Voggenhuber, spokesperson of the GA on European politics, political integration in Europe might be necessary against the background of instability in Central Europe after the Cold War and the globalisation of markets. Nevertheless, this should not take the form of a federal state, but rather a 'system of confederal co-operation in the whole of Europe' (Voggenhuber 1995: 394). The EU, especially after Maastricht, was criticised for its democratic deficit, which took power away from the people. The neo-liberal economic drive behind the Internal

Market, reinforced by the EMU convergence criteria, moreover, would put downward pressure on environmental and social standards, and increase traffic and, thereby, the need for new roads. It would prevent support for an environmentally friendly system of agriculture. New divisions would be created between the poor and the rich, between East and West, between centre and periphery. Additionally, Maastricht would incorporate the basis of a new military alliance, which made Austria's neutrality impossible.

The Austrian government was criticised for failing to achieve proper conditions for its accession to the EU. Apart from reaching unsatisfactory results in the negotiations, it did not use its leverage to obtain reforms of the EU, such as insisting on social and environmental instead of neo-liberal economic convergence criteria, or demanding an expansive fiscal policy with the goal of full employment. During the referendum campaign, the GA adopted the strategy of a loose network, a non-institutionalised co-operation with other anti-EU initiatives to facilitate the exchange of information (Voggenhuber 1995: 397). Many opposition groups were approached but rarely represented the left, progressive type of policy expected by the GA from their potential allies. The formation of a joint platform, consequently, was not deemed possible (Interview no. 27; Vienna, 2 May 1996).

In the course of the EEA negotiations the FPÖ had, surprisingly, slowly but steadily changed its course and, eventually, voted against the treaty in parliament in September 1992. At a special party congress in May the following year, its new policy was outlined. The FPÖ was in favour of an integrated Europe in the form of a confederation as the basis for a strong European security system. The surrender of sovereignty was rejected as was the idea of a multi-cultural European society (FPÖ 1993: 2–3). Negotiation targets were set including the concession of opt-outs similar to the ones granted to Denmark and the maintenance of Austria's higher environmental and social standards and the transit agreement (FPÖ 1993: 4–6). One year later, the FPÖ evaluated the negotiation results negatively and 85.5 per cent of the delegates at the party congress on 8 April 1994 supported Haider's motion to recommend that the parliamentary fraction should vote 'no' to membership (Interview no. 26; Vienna, 25 April 1996).

The party itself denied that it had changed its policy. On the contrary, it claimed that it was the EU which had changed. The FPÖ had been in favour of free trade and economic integration within the Internal Market, but the Maastricht Treaty with its goal of political union was not acceptable. The party favoured a European confederation of independent states, not a federal state which implied the dropping of the unanimity principle and the loss of sovereignty (Interview no. 26; Vienna, 25 April 1996). Siegfried Dillersberger, FPÖ spokesperson for European questions, pointed out that even the *Salzburger Programm* of 1985, which considered membership to be a necessity, had clearly mentioned a European confederation as the party's goal (Dillersberger 1994: 708). Critics, however, maintained that the FPÖ's negotiation targets had been impossible from the beginning and, thus, constituted only a pretext for rejection (Schaller 1994b: 52). With Haider as the new President, the party had significantly increased its share of the votes by drawing on protest voters (Riedlsperger 1992) and the EU was the perfect issue for such a strategy. Be that as it may, it was important that the FPÖ under Haider's leadership had managed to rise from a marginal party to a strong third, in some places even second, force in Austria. It had increased its share of the votes from about 5 per cent in 1983 to 16.6 per cent in 1990 (see Table 2.1) and seemed likely to rise further. It therefore, posed a strong challenge to the pro-EU bloc. In its anti-membership campaign, the party concentrated on issues such as 'Austria first', anti-immigration, the loss of the AS, the alleged rise in unemployment by 70,000, and the danger of an increase in criminality in a Europe without borders, but also raised questions over transit and agriculture (Schaller 1994b: 80–1). Overall, it attempted to attract all those people who were dissatisfied with the pro-EU policy of the government and social partners.

Initiatives against membership

The anti-EU initiatives were numerous but had only a modest media presence due to their scanty organisational and financial resources (Schaller 1994b: 82). Three exceptions were, however, noticeable. First, the *Kritische Europainformationen* published the magazine *Europa-Kardiogramm* with reports, analyses and comments on European politics, economy and culture (Gmeiner 1996: 259); a special edition in May 1994 had a circulation of 100,000 copies. Second, since the beginning of 1993, the initiative *Arge EU-Nein Danke/Zukunft Europa* had been active in distributing posters, flyers and information-folders. It consisted of intellectuals and scientists, such as the former GA presidential candidate Freda Blau-Meissner and some former members of the *Initiative Österreich und Europa*. It attempted to establish a platform for the co-ordination of the anti-EU social forces. Third, the *Bürgerinitiative gegen den Verkauf Österreichs an die EU* (Initiative against Austria's sell-out to the EU), with about 30,000 members, was of some significance. Between March and May 1994, it sent two mailings to all households supporting a 'no' in the referendum (Schaller 1994b: 83). Together with the GA and FPÖ, these initiatives formed a considerable opposition.

The referendum: a clear 'yes' in favour of membership

The referendum on 12 June 1994 gave a clear majority for accession to the EU. The vote for membership was 66.6 per cent, with only 33.4 per cent against. There are several reasons why the opposition camp was severely weakened. To start with, the two parties themselves did not present an internally united position. In 1993, the Liberal Forum had split away from the FPÖ, partly because of its xenophobic credentials, but partly also because of its negative attitude towards the EU (Schaller 1994b: 52). During the campaign, the

Liberal Forum lobbied strongly for the 'yes' side. Moreover, inside the party, the Liberal Club, a think tank mainly consisting of liberal party members in Vienna, openly opposed the official party line and commissioned a brochure by the *Österreichische Gesellschaft für Europapolitik* in favour of membership. The divisions within the Green camp were also exploited by the *Gesellschaft*, which nominated Herbert Fux as one of the pro-EU representatives for a television debate. Fux had left the GA in 1988 but, having been one of the first Green representatives in local government, he was still widely seen as a standard-bearer for the Green cause among the general population and, therefore, discredited the GA's anti-EU stance (Interview no. 29; Vienna, 3 May 1996).

Even more significant was the ideological split between the GA and the FPÖ. There were many common issues such as the negative evaluation of the negotiation results in the areas of environmental standards and transit. Nevertheless, the ideological distance between the two parties was far too wide for the formation of a common platform. The FPÖ's strategy had a nationalist character concentrating on 'Austria first' slogans and included chauvinist arguments, while the GA focused on the demand for a reformed EU, a different type of European integration which did not discriminate against non-EU citizens. The pro-EU groups used this split and transformed the debate on membership into a fight against Haider, that is pro or contra right-wing extremism (Schaller 1994b: 70). The GA constantly had to distance itself from Haider instead of focusing on its own arguments against the EU (Interview no. 27; Vienna, 2 May 1996). Thus, the FPÖ's shift towards an anti-EU stance was seen as ensuring the success of the 'yes' campaign by other opponents (Interview no. 23; Vienna, 24 April 1996).

The ideological split between the GA and the FPÖ was also reflected in the sphere of initiatives. The *Kritische Europainformationen* opposed the EU because of its dominance by big capital, exploitation of developing countries, neglect of a social dimension, increase in unemployment and continuing environmental pollution. Moreover, the internal security policy against immigrants and the external security policy of moving towards a common security and defence policy around a Euro-army were rejected. The overall goal was a general critique of the EU project 'Fortress Europe' to facilitate a European-wide formation of progressive forces in favour of a just economic policy, solidarity and respect for everybody's human dignity (Gmeiner 1996: 263–72). Meanwhile, the *Bürgerinitiative gegen den Verkauf Österreichs an die EU* followed a nationalist road, warning against a flood of foreigners and the sell-out of Austria's wealth (Gmeiner 1996: 261). Co-operation between these two larger initiatives was no more possible than between the GA and the FPÖ. The *Arge EU-Nein Danke/Zukunft Europa* attempted to remain neutral in its objective of co-ordinating the opposition. Thereby, however, it ended up distributing information by right-wing organisations, which damaged its credibility with the left (Gmeiner 1996: 278).

In addition, the opposition was split between parties on the one hand, and initiatives on the other. For example, the *Arge EU-Nein Danke/Zukunft*

Europa rejected a closer co-operation with the GA, because it wanted to stay independent. Eventually, the positions of the GA and the *Kritische Europainformationen* were the closest and both co-operated in setting up an alternative press agency called 'Euro-Watch-Agency-Report', which published a weekly report in the period before the referendum (Interview no. 27; Vienna, 2 May 1996). The lack of funding, however, limited the success of this undertaking (Gmeiner 1996: 278).

Finally, the pro-EU group could rely on huge financial resources, which allowed it to conduct a massive media campaign (Interview no. 26; Vienna, 25 April 1996; Interview no. 27; Vienna, 2 May 1996). An additional 'angst-campaign' arguing that Austria would either be part of a wealthy Western Europe or part of a poor, underdeveloped Eastern Europe, in the same league as countries like Poland, had an irrational, but effective impact on the population (Interview no. 26; Vienna, 25 April 1996). Membership was presented as yielding direct economic gains for everybody. Slogans such as 'EU membership secures the pension system' were no rarity (Interview no. 26; Vienna, 25 April 1996) and every household was promised it would gain AS 1,000 per month in the case of accession (Interview no. 35; Vienna, 14 May 1996). Overall, the EU opposition was unable to form a joint platform, in contrast to the pro-EU bloc. There were no organic intellectuals who developed a hegemonic project capable of uniting the opposition and offering a credible alternative to membership.

A debate at last: social forces mobilise in Sweden

In 1991, the new Prime Minister Bildt (MS) demanded that all coalition partners sign a declaration which included a commitment to Sweden joining the EU. Consequently, the approach to the EU was a matter of strategy for the government, not a fundamental issue of debate (Interview no. 61; Stockholm, 26 November 1996). Dinkelspiel made each minister responsible for the success of the negotiations in his or her particular area. This tactical manoeuvre ensured every ministry's commitment to membership (Interview no. 51; Stockholm, 15 November 1996). After the September 1994 elections, government changed again and the SAP regained office. Ministers took part on both sides of the campaign, but as individuals, not in their capacity as the chief representative of their particular ministry (Interview no. 47; Stockholm, 13 November 1996). In short, ministries can be discounted during the debate on membership before the referendum.

Labour: EU membership to counter transnational capital

The LO and TCO peak organisations

Both major trade union organisations, the LO and TCO, assessed the question of membership against the background of the changes in the global economy. It was realised that 'capital and ownership have become almost completely mobile in international terms' (TCO 1993: 4). These changes would require a change in trade union strategy. 'Internationalisation in itself means that the Swedish trade unions must cooperate across national borders – primarily in Europe where we have the major part of our economic ties and commitments' (TCO 1994: 5). Representatives in the LO headquarters even argued that there had never been a realistic choice between membership and staying outside. A Keynesian expansive fiscal policy at the national level could not be a possible way forward, as the French example between 1981 and 1983 had demonstrated. Outside the EU, Sweden would be even more in the hands of the global financial market and would, consequently, have to adopt even harsher austerity measures (Interview no. 56; Stockholm, 21 November 1996). Sweden's economy and welfare system depended on a few TNCs, and it would be impossible to remain outside the EU, while the TNCs were part of the Internal Market through their investments (Interview no. 62; Stockholm, 27 November 1996). Thus, membership would support rather than endanger the Swedish welfare system (Interview no. 46; Stockholm, 13 November 1996).

The acknowledgement of the pressures caused by the transnationalisation processes did not, however, imply that the LO and TCO accepted the neo-liberal logic. Competition was regarded as beneficial for economic growth and efficiency, but the importance of regulation at the EU level was stressed. Hence, great emphasis was put on the further development of the social dimension, and the Social Chapter of the Maastricht Treaty was welcomed (Interview no. 56; Stockholm, 21 November 1996). The 'TCO has stressed that European cooperation must have a Social Dimension that counteracts the negative effects of internationalization, free competition and the free movement of capital' (TCO 1993: 9). By the same token, the neo-liberal convergence criteria of EMU were criticised. The LO preferred a less austere monetary policy and wanted to include employment as a criterion for the convergence of European economies. 'A balance is needed between the norms for price stability and for growth and employment' (LO 1994: 6). It was further pointed out by some LO officials that the economy could also be run with 4 or 5 per cent inflation at the European level instead of the 3 per cent envisaged by the Maastricht Treaty. This would allow for more expansive fiscal measures (Interview no. 62; Stockholm, 27 November 1996).

Along the same line, the TCO demanded that 'Sweden should work actively to ensure that economic and monetary co-operation also comprises concrete goals for the reduction of unemployment' (TCO 1993: 18). The latter should be the primary aim. 'The clear political will must be expressed by the convergence criteria being made subordinate to clear employment goals' (TCO 1994: 15). An additional criticism was the lack of democratic control of the ECB (LO 1994: 5; TCO 1993: 18).

Despite this criticism, the LO and TCO were satisfied with the negoti-ation results. Their individual concerns, such as the right to establish EU labour market directives via collective agreements and the maintenance of the higher Swedish health and safety regulations, had been met. Of course, the problem of the convergence criteria remained unresolved, and this was pointed out and criticised:

> [The] TCO is seriously concerned about the fact that the Swedish Government has supported the restrictive economic policy recommended by the EU's Finance Ministers in December 1993 on the basis of the Treaty of Maastricht. This gives the fight against inflation the highest priority and thus hinders the fight against unemployment.
>
> (TCO 1994: 15).

Eventually, however, it was accepted that the convergence criteria had not been up for negotiation. The focus should, therefore, be on future common initiatives for the creation of employment at the European level (Interview no. 40; Stockholm, 11 November 1996). In other words, while the dominant trade union organisations were not entirely happy about neo-liberal policy co-ordination at the European level, in view of the transnationalisation pressures they did not see any viable alternative to membership. Nevertheless, many of their members and affiliated unions were opposed to membership. The LO and TCO, therefore, could not recommend a 'yes' in the referendum. Instead, they decided to adopt a neutral position and to provide members with information to help them make up their minds.

The split within the trade unions over Europe

Within the unions, there was a split between the transnational sector, industrial unions, which were in favour of membership, and the national sector unions opposing it. The LO affiliates the Paper Workers' Union and the Metal Workers' Union played a leading role in the transnational sector. The Paper Workers' Union decided at its congress in autumn 1993 that it would recommend a 'yes' in the referendum on trade union grounds, but leave the final decision to its members whether the consideration of other issues such as security policy still justified an affirmative vote. This decision encouraged the Metal Workers' Union. In early 1994, the union's committee decided that it would not give a recommendation, but it made clear that it was strongly in favour of membership. The argument was threefold. First and most important, considering that the Swedish TNCs had already established themselves on the Internal Market and taking into account the export dependence of the two sectors – the paper sector exported about 80 per cent of its products, the engineering sector more than 50 per cent – remaining outside the EU was economically impossible. Second, the EU regulations had to be accepted anyway due to the EEA. There was, consequently, no reason why the option of participating in the decision-making process via membership should not be taken. Third, the EU was also regarded as a peace project, in which Sweden should take part. Eastern enlargement had already been on the agenda in 1993–94, and it was possible that the EU would bridge the divide between Western and Eastern Europe (Interview no. 66; Stockholm, 29 November 1996).

There were, however, two LO affiliates – the Commercial Workers' Union and the Municipal Workers' Union – which came out heavily against membership, although they did not give a recommendation. Their members' jobs, especially in the public sector, did not depend on exports or transnational production, and the increased structural power of capital consequently played a less significant role. Instead, it was feared that future decisions made in Brussels, with reference to the harmonisation of tax systems for example, could lead to rules, which implied cut-backs in the public sector and, thereby, cause job losses. Moreover, both unions predominantly represented female blue-collar workers, up to 80 per cent in the case of the Municipal Workers' Union. The participation of women in the labour market of the EU members was, with the exception of Denmark, much lower, and these unions were afraid membership would have a negative impact. In short, the Swedish Model with its generous welfare system, full employment policy, large public sector and gender equality via high female participation in the workplace was considered to be endangered by the EU's neo-liberal economic policies (Interview no. 59; Stockholm, 26 November 1996; see also Bjørklund 1996: 26–8).

The Transport Workers' Union, also an LO affiliate, gave a 'no' recommendation to its members in 1994 after conducting an internal referendum, in which 62.3 per cent of the participating members had rejected the EU. There had been technical regulation problems – Swedish lorries are in general larger than EU lorries – as well as the problem of 'cabotage', which implied that EU companies were allowed to set up companies in Sweden to transport goods exclusively in Sweden. Since transport costs were lower in the EU than in Sweden, this implied strong competition and probable job losses (Interview no. 57; Stockholm, 21 November 1996).

This split between transnational and national unions could also be observed in the case of two other LO affiliates, the Industrial Workers' Union and the Union of Service and Communication Employees. Here, the unions did not give a recommendation, because they represented several sectors with different production structures and, thus, a unanimous position proved to be impossible. In the Industrial Workers' Union, the board and members were divided. Transnational sectors such as the textile and chemical industries were in favour, while the sugar sector, with no markets outside Sweden, was opposed (Interview no. 46; Stockholm, 13 November 1996). The Union of Service and Communication Employees also gave no recommendation at its 1993 congress. The transnational sectors such as telecommunications supported membership, but the postal workers were against, fearing that membership would imply further deregulation, the loss of the postal state monopoly and, thereby, the loss of jobs (Interview no. 58; Stockholm, 26 November 1996).

A similar division along the production structure was apparent in the TCO. The Swedish Association of Supervisors (Ledarna), which represented managers and supervisors working in production in both the private and the public sector, recommended a 'yes' on the ground of economic necessity. Moreover, the Swedish Union of Clerical and Technical Employees in Industry (SIF), and the Union of Financial Sector Employees, which organised white-collar workers in industry and finance respectively (that is, transnational social forces), exhibited a strong 'yes' tendency, though without official recommendation. On the other hand, the Swedish Teacher's Union, which represented teachers throughout the entire education system from pre-school to university level and, thus, public sector workers, had a tendency towards a 'no'. Its chairman even openly opposed membership. As in the case of the Municipal Workers' Union, EU membership was viewed as a threat to the Swedish welfare system and the equal treatment of women and men at the workplace (Interview no. 40; Stockholm, 11 November 1996).

The SACO considered the question of membership to be a matter of foreign policy and, therefore, beyond trade union competence. There was little internal discussion and no recommendation was made. The union only carried out a study about the pros and cons of membership with the result that no significant disadvantages for academic employees were identified. This did not, however, prevent affiliated unions from taking a position and a similar division between transnational and national social forces could be observed. The Swedish Association of Graduate Engineers recommended a 'yes' in 1994, a logical step considering its demand for application in May 1990. The Swedish Association of Graduates in Social Science, Personnel and Public Administration, Economics and Social Work, on the other hand, was rather reluctant. It did not recommend a 'no', but large numbers of its members, who were predominantly employed in the public sector, clearly opposed accession to the EU (Interview no. 41; Stockholm, 11 November 1996).

The position of the Swedish trade unions can be summed up as follows: the two major organisations, the TCO and LO, were positive towards membership, but they could not recommend a 'yes' for the referendum because of the different opinions of their affiliated unions. They argued that Sweden had to restructure its economy anyway due to transnational pressures, which implied the loss of government autonomy and trade union influence in economic matters. In this situation, co-operation at the European level offered the chance of partly regaining the control over capital lost at the national level and providing a more secure basis for the welfare system. The neo-liberal tendencies expressed in the convergence criteria were worrying, but there was some hope of joint action at the EU level to combat unemployment. The transnational sector unions, mainly unions in the industrial and financial sector, followed this position. They stressed in particular Sweden's export dependence on the EU and the fact that the big TNCs had already established themselves on the Internal Market. In contrast, the trade unions of the national sector, mainly the big public sector unions, opposed membership. They considered accession to the neo-liberal EU to be a threat to the Swedish Model and argued that the retaining of as many national policy tools as possible offered a better chance of preserving it.

The position of Swedish capital including the agricultural sector

The employers' associations immediately reacted positively towards the SAP's announcement of application to the EU. Their main arguments were of an economic nature. Participation in the Internal Market would lead to more competition and, thereby, more efficiency. This would result in higher economic growth and, eventually, more jobs. It was also pointed out that the higher degree of transnationalisation of production, with parts and finished products being increasingly traded to and fro across borders and the close links of Swedish companies to EU companies in this respect, had made membership necessary. Moreover, while the harmonisation of standards and regulations supported economic growth within the EU, companies from countries outside would face unequal terms of competition as a result (Interview no. 67; Stockholm, 29 November 1996).

The argument that membership would be a good way of getting rid of the Swedish Model played only a minor role. The Swedish Model was considered to have already been abandoned at the beginning of the 1990s (Interview no. 43; Stockholm, 12 November 1996; Interview no. 54; Stockholm, 19 November 1996). Some sections of industry, however, regarded membership as a safeguard against future Swedish experiments different from other countries' neo-liberal course. Membership would foreclose them for good (Interview no. 51; Stockholm, 15 November 1996).

There was no organised opposition from nationally-oriented companies. No branch as such opposed membership openly. This can partly be explained by the fact that many small and medium-sized companies were themselves export-oriented (about 15–23 per cent, estimated figure) and, thus, internationally-oriented forces. The removal of trade barriers was even more important for them than for TNCs, which could rely on production units within the EU (Interview no. 54; Stockholm, 19 November 1996). Hence, they were likely to support transnational capital's drive for liberalisation and deregulation. Another substantial group of small and medium-sized companies operated as subcontractors to TNCs and were, therefore, also internationally-oriented.

For several reasons, there was only moderate opposition within the food processing industry. First, 'Sweden's farmers, via their memberships of co-operative associations, are involved in the further processing and marketing of their agricultural products. These co-operatively owned processing industries are predominant in Sweden' (The Swedish Institute 1995: 1). Being in favour of membership as farmers, they were unlikely to vote differently in their capacity of owners in the food processing industry. Second, the LRF, which was in favour of membership from the beginning of the debate, represented most of the wholesale producers and could bring some pressure to bear on them (Interview no. 50; Stockholm, 14 November 1996). The structure in the food processing industry was, furthermore, extremely concentrated, including TNCs such as Nestlé. These companies viewed the EU as an opportunity of gaining access to a bigger market for their products (Interview no. 65; Stockholm, 28 November 1996).

The construction sector had always been protected in Sweden, but it collapsed when the bubble economic boom burst at the end of the 1980s. Consequently, it did not play a role in the debate on EU membership (Interview no. 65; Stockholm, 28 November 1997). Finally, despite the economic problems due to membership for the transport industry mentioned earlier, a vast majority of the companies came out in favour. One reason was that these changes had already been part of the EEA to a large extent. Second and more importantly, the argument prevailed that membership was essential for the Swedish economy as a whole, as it was dependent on equal access to the EU market. This would, eventually, also benefit the transport companies.[6]

At the same time, however, the opposition should not be underestimated. Företagarna, the Federation of Private Enterprises, which represented small and medium-sized companies, did not give a recommendation and only conducted an information campaign. There was uncertainty among its members and some were against accession to the EU, fearing more regulation from Brussels. A sectoral picture of resistance is not available, since the delegates at the association's general meeting represented either themselves or their district, but opposition came mainly from small companies in the North of Sweden, which were deeply integrated into the local community and produced exclusively for the local market. Firms in the South, on the other hand, often had export links to Germany, Denmark, and other EU countries and were, therefore, more positively inclined towards membership, which the Federation headquarters itself supported. It was accepted that the whole Swedish economy and, thereby, also the small and medium-sized companies depended on the TNCs. Their threat to leave Sweden in the case of non-membership loomed large and, although it was not openly acknowledged, decisively influenced the debate (Interview no. 69; Stockholm, 3 December 1996).

The LRF, which had been in favour of membership from 1990 onwards, gave a 'yes' recommendation for the referendum. There were some internal splits. Sections of the food processing industry were sceptical, as mentioned earlier, and some farmers, especially in the North, could never be convinced

(Interview no. 50; Stockholm, 14 November 1996). Farms in the North were generally small in contrast to the large farms in the southern part of Sweden (The Swedish Institute 1995: 1). The EU as a bigger market had hardly any significance for them. The LRF played an important role *vis-à-vis* the CP. It constantly put pressure on it, until the latter finally adopted a pro-EU position in spring 1994 (Interview no. 50; Stockholm, 14 November 1996).

To sum up, Swedish capital was overwhelmingly in favour of accession to the EU. Participation in the Internal Market was considered to be vital, first, in order to get equal access to it and second, in order to participate in its dynamic effects of stronger competition. Even small and medium-sized companies showed support for membership, partly because they were export oriented, and partly because they were sub-contractors of TNCs. The negotiation results were generally welcomed. For capital, it was important that Sweden became a member. The critical issues such as environmental standards did not affect these forces very much (Interview no. 43; Stockholm, 12 November 96; Interview no. 54; Stockholm, 19 November 1996; Interview no. 69; Stockholm, 3 December 1996). There was some hesitation, even rejection amongst nationally-oriented forces in the food processing industry and by small companies in the North, but they did not mount a 'no' campaign. The argument that the Swedish economy as a whole benefited from membership due to the gains of the TNCs, on which it depended, was too strong to be neglected. Splits parallel to the ones between transnational and national sector unions were not visible.

The employers' associations kept EMU off the referendum agenda. It was realised that this issue could tip the balance towards a 'no'. The later positive position on EMU – the SAF declared its support in spring 1995, the SI followed in February 1996 – however, demonstrated a different social purpose behind capital's interest in membership in contrast to the trade unions. It was argued that Sweden could not have an economic policy different from other countries in times of globalisation. Austerity and not further devaluations was, consequently, the way forward and the earlier there was a monetary union, the better (Interview no. 67; Stockholm, 29 November 1996). Small companies especially would benefit from EMU membership. While TNCs could hedge against fluctuating exchange rates, small companies had no opportunity to do so. Additionally, EMU membership was regarded as a necessary continuation of the changes in economic policy from the late 1980s towards a neo-liberal, market-oriented economy (Interview no. 54; Stockholm, 19 November 1996).

In view of the Swedish economic crisis, Per Magnus Wijkman, chief economist of the SI, argued that 'Sweden could indeed benefit from the peer pressure exercised in the framework of the Union's convergence and excessive deficit programmes' (Wijkman 1995: 7). By the same token, the employers' associations rejected a strong social dimension and Keynesian employment programmes at the European level. Instead, the neo-liberal drive should further continue in the EU so that European firms were competitive *vis-à-vis* the new industrialising countries of Asia (Interview no. 43; Stockholm, 12 November 1996). In short, rather than emphasising the need for co-operation at an international level to regain lost control over economic policy and to fight unemployment in a common effort, a continuation and stabilisation of neo-liberal restructuring was behind the employers' drive towards EU membership.

The political parties[7]

Two main positions characterised the pro-EU social forces which were chiefly organised in the MS, FP and the majority of the SAP and CP. First, in a compromise decision of June 1991, it had been decided that Sweden's policy of neutrality was compatible with EU membership. In May 1992 neutrality was redefined as military non-alignment to make it compatible with the CFSP (see chapter five). Second, while the convergence criteria of EMU were considered to be the basis for a sound economy, it was agreed that participation in the third stage of EMU would be decided later by the Swedish parliament and, thus, should not play a role in the referendum campaign.

The position of the MS and FP

Like the employers' associations, the MS and FP immediately supported the drive for membership, after the SAP's announcement in October 1990. The FP regarded the EU as a peace project. Further enlargement in Central and Eastern Europe could lead to a peaceful, prosperous and stable Europe from the Atlantic to the Urals. In addition, the FP emphasised economic issues. Membership would imply lower interest rates, attract inward FDI and be good for the economy in general (Interview no. 55; Stockholm, 19 November 1996). Membership would be necessary, because in times of a transnationalised economy, isolated national measures 'tend not to have effects that could previously be expected' (FP 1995: 16). The EU was further considered to be important for the fight against unemployment, though this was seen in terms of an emphasis on efficiency via competition in the Internal Market rather than EU common employment programmes.[8] The EU 'can play an important role to help increase the growth of the European economies through market oriented reforms. Europe shall be a continent of entrepreneurship, enterprise and competitiveness in order to fight unemployment and secure welfare systems' (FP 1995: 3). The social dimension was regarded as a system of unnecessarily detailed regulations on matters which should be dealt with at the national level (FP 1995: 7).

The MS similarly stressed economic arguments. Swedish industry would greatly suffer from non-membership. Additionally, membership would guarantee that Sweden remained on a neo-liberal course parallel to other countries. Finally, Sweden belonged to Europe and membership would be the only way to allow participation in the decision-making process of the EU (Interview no. 51; Stockholm, 15 November 1996).

Although EMU was kept off the agenda before the referendum, both parties considered EMU an improvement of the Internal Market and its positive competitive effects. They supported Swedish participation at the earliest possible date and argued that non-membership would cause doubts about Sweden's commitment to a hard currency on the global financial market. Higher interest rates would be the likely consequence (Interview no. 55; Stockholm, 19 November 1996). The negotiation results were welcomed by the MS and FP. In any case, membership as such, not particular issues, had been the main goal.

The position of the SAP

The SAP and CP, unlike the MS and FP, faced internal splits over membership, which both parties countered by allowing their members to form pro- and contra-EU campaign groups. The SAP 'yes' group argued in a similar way to the pro-EU sections of the trade union movement. The transnationalisation of capital and markets and the concomitant erosion of national sovereignty over economic policy were accepted as facts. Membership would allow European social democracy to recover some power *vis-à-vis* capital via co-operation at the international level. It was important, the 'yes' group argued, to create a political and trade-union counterbalance to capital, especially towards TNCs, in order to protect working conditions and rights, and to formulate a common strategy of employment and welfare (SAP 1993: 13). These common objectives at the European level needed to be defined as ambitiously as the convergence criteria for monetary co-operation. In short, 'in order to reinstall the chances for politics to control the capital markets it is necessary for politics to challenge the markets at an international level' (SAP 1996: 66).

Membership would, furthermore, improve the the prospects of combating transnational problems such as air and water pollution in a better way. Finally, the EU was considered to be a peace project. 'For Social Democrats our historical task as Europeans is to unite the countries in Eastern and Western Europe, thereby paving the way for increased prosperity and an all-embracing peace and security order on the European continent' (SAP 1996: 57). Only EU membership would allow Sweden to participate in the making of the future European order (Interview no. 47; Stockholm, 13 November 1996).

In contrast to some voices within the pro-EU trade union camp, however, a watering-down of the convergence criteria or an amendment with an employment criterion was not considered. EMU membership as such was to be discussed after the referendum at the SAP annual congress in September 1997, but the SAP committed itself to the policy of austerity as laid out in the criteria. Full employment was not dropped as a policy goal, but a different way to achieve it was put forward. Instead of budget deficit spending, the emphasis was now on a balanced economy and low levels of inflation (Interview no. 44; Stockholm, 12 November 1996). It was pointed out that in a global economy, where Swedish production had become increasingly transnationalised and the flow of capital had dramatically risen, new means were required to achieve old goals (Interview no. 48; Stockholm, 14 November 1997). Full employment was regarded as the result of the fulfilment of the convergence criteria and should not be confused with the criteria themselves (Interview no. 47; Stockholm, 13 November 1996).

The SAP 'no' group, on the other hand, criticised the loss of national sovereignty implied by membership. The removal of border controls would lead to a higher level of international crime, the CFSP was regarded as a danger for Sweden's policy of non-alignment and the Internal Market and EMU as a threat to the Swedish welfare system (Interview no. 44; Stockholm, 12 November 1996). The convergence criteria in particular would imply a risk for the solidaristic Swedish society, the tax system and, thereby, the Swedish Model itself (Interview no. 58; Stockholm, 26 November 1996). Margareta Winberg and Marita Ulvskog, both Ministers and leading SAP figures in the 'no' camp, published an article in the LO-owned newspaper *Aftonbladet* shortly before the referendum. They strongly warned against membership, which would result in a permanently high level of unemployment, and advocated an inflationary national economic policy to create new jobs (Svensson 1994: 3). In other words, the neo-liberal argument that higher competition would lead to more efficiency and economic growth and, eventually, to more jobs was rejected.

The two groups, established at the SAP annual congress in September 1993, prepared two motions for the extra-ordinary party congress in June 1994. The outcome of the vote was a moderate 'yes' recommendation for the referendum, but both groups were allowed to continue their campaigns until it was held. The SAP leader, Carlsson, made it clear that one could be a good social democrat whether one voted for or against membership (Interview no. 44; Stockholm, 12 November 1996). Clearly, the primary goal was to avoid splitting the party before the September 1994 general elections (Aylott 1997).

The position of the CP

After much hesitation, the CP annual congress of June 1991 decided to support closer co-operation with, and application to, the EU. The party's final decision on membership would be taken on the basis of the negotiation results. It was also demanded at the congress that the non-alignment policy and Sweden's higher environmental standards would be maintained and that there would be a development programme for Sweden's arctic regions. The more sceptical members of the party demanded the adoption of a new position after the Maastricht Treaty, but this was not deemed possible or necessary by the party leadership for two reasons. First, the party had signed a document, when it joined the new government in 1991, which stated its obligation towards a positive attitude on the question of EU membership; second, the Ministers of Agriculture, Labour and Environment were all from the CP. The party, consequently, felt it was in a strong position to make sure that the negotiations produced positive outcomes in the areas it was concerned about. Eventually, the party leadership was satisfied with the negotiation results. Non-alignment, which was not deemed threatened by the inter-governmental CFSP, was retained and the Swedish environmental standards did not need to be lowered. Of course, the four-year transition period was a set-back, but it was accepted that, overall, more could be done for the environment within the EU than outside it (Interview no. 42; Stockholm, 11 November 1996).

There were, however, two groups within the party. The 'yes' group argued that the EU was a pan-European peace project and membership would allow more to be done on a larger scale for the environment. The 'no' group, on the other hand, feared the negative impact on Sweden's higher environmental standards and the centralisation of decision-making in Brussels. In particular the CFSP and EMU – the loss of sovereignty, not the convergence criteria, which the party as a whole had supported as necessary to clean up the economy – gave rise to concern. Opposition within the party was represented in the youth organisation and roughly half of the party's women's group. On 2 and 3 May, 1994 a motion recommending a 'yes' in the referendum was passed by a two-thirds majority at the party's congress. Due to the many sceptical members, however, the party as such kept a low profile during the referendum campaign and only published a pamphlet with a short version of the congress recommendation (Interview no. 42; Stockholm, 11 November 1996).

In spite of this, many members still felt they had been overruled. The CP members and voters were predominantly small farmers from the North and the forestry areas, which hardly benefited from the potential access to a larger market. Many saw only tougher competition ahead as the result of membership and, therefore, disagreed with the CP on the EU question (Interview no. 42; Stockholm, 11 November 1996). The LRF's decision to support membership was crucial for the CP, since without its backing the party would hardly have decided in favour of membership (Interview no. 42; Stockholm, 11 November 1996). This was even more important with reference to the overall balance. If the CP had come out in opposition to the EU, the soft 'yes' recommendation would have been extremely difficult for the SAP, because it would no longer have been a leftist thing to be against membership (Interview no. 51; Stockholm, 15 November 1996). Of the four main parties, two strongly recommended a 'yes', while the other two came to a soft 'yes' conclusion.

The position of the VP and GP

The VP and GP were the only political parties, which opposed membership. They had rejected application and they continued on this course. The VP regarded the negotiation results as a failure. Transition periods, it was pointed out, were no guarantee of maintaining the higher environmental standards and keeping the alcohol monopolies. There was criticism that the EU had not explicitly acknowledged Sweden's status of neutrality (Interview no. 38; Stockholm, 8 November 1996). In general, the VP condemned the neo-liberal economic drive behind the EU. It opposed 'the EU rules about free movement of capital and economic standardisation' (VP 1995: 1) and the concentration on low inflation as embodied in the convergence criteria, because this would cement mass unemployment rather than create new jobs and exclude environmental and social conditions. 'For these reasons, the Left Party intends to oppose the monetary focus, working instead to ensure that full employment, good environment and equality between the sexes are given priority over demands of the marketplace' (VP undated: 4). This was to be supported by a global tax on currency transactions to control financial markets (VP undated: 16). The VP rejected the strengthening of supranational institutions. Their power should even be cut back, while national parliaments and their control of EU policy-making had to be enhanced.

This did not, however, mean that the VP sported a nationalist outlook. On the contrary, it envisaged pan-European co-operation via institutions such as the CSCE and the ECE of the UN, which encompassed most of the European states, and via more transnational links to parties and social movements in other countries. The goal was a just economic order through wide-ranging international co-operation in contrast to a 'Fortress Europe' of the rich against the developing countries (VP undated: 4–5). The EU, it was further argued, would compromise Sweden's policy of neutrality. The VP demanded that the connection between the EU and WEU be severed and that Sweden should be neither a member of, nor observer at, this organisation. 'Every similar connection diminishes the country's credibility when it comes to re-establishing Sweden's neutrality policy' (VP undated: 13). Overall, the VP rejected the idea that EU membership was a necessary response to global changes. A national strategy, combined with international intergovernmental co-operation, was still considered to be a better option to combat unemployment, to preserve the environment and to achieve equality between the sexes (Interview no. 38; Stockholm, 8 November 1996).

The GP argued along similar lines. The Maastricht Treaty significantly reinforced the party's opposition to the EU; the CFSP raised fears about the Swedish status of neutrality, and EMU was rejected because it would imply a loss of sovereignty, transferred to an undemocratic institution far away in Brussels (Interview no. 45; Stockholm, 12 November 1996). In order to maintain its non-aligned status, Sweden should neither be an observer at, nor become a member of, the WEU, and a common foreign policy department and joint financing of the CFSP were rejected (GP 1995: 2). With reference to the convergence criteria, the position was not entirely clear. While the third stage of EMU was rejected, the GP accepted the criteria at one stage as necessary to obtain a stable economy. It consequently supported the new SAP government and its convergence criteria plan in 1995. This view, however, was not shared by the whole party (Interview no. 70; Stockholm, 3 December 1996). In its programme for the 1995 elections to the EP, the GP even stated that 'Sweden shall . . . not accept the convergence criteria of the EMU as a goal for the economic policy and not join the third stage of the EMU' (GP 1995: 2). Apart from this, the line resembled again the VP's position.

This rejection of the EU did not imply a nationalist stance. Instead, pan-European co-operation should be conducted in a flexible way beyond the EU. For example, the GP suggested intergovernmental measures in order to control the financial markets, including fees on speculative currency transactions. In the area of security policy, the GP wanted to focus on the CSCE and included issues such as pollution in addition to military aspects. It was deemed to be timid to argue that Sweden would have to adapt to global changes in any case. The prospect of reforms at the EU level was discounted – four votes in the Council of Ministers would provide little influence – and many issues should anyway be dealt with at the national level. Environmental co-operation would also be possible outside the EU; in fact it would be necessary in many cases to solve such problems as the pollution of the Baltic sea, because the relevant countries were not EU members. There was, in short, not much hope for progress within the EU from the GP's point of view (Interview no. 70; Stockholm, 3 December 1996).

The referendum campaign

The 'yes' campaign

The first group formed to take part in the referendum was the group 'Yes to Europe' in 1991. It became the platform of the employers' associations and the MS and FP. As soon as it had become clear that the final decision on membership would be taken in a referendum, capital realised the importance of a well prepared and professionally run campaign (Interview no. 43; Stockholm, 12 November 1996). The two parties mainly provided the personnel, while industry funded a huge financial backup. The chairman of the group was a member of both the MS and industry and the work was predominantly carried out in local offices across the country (Interview no. 51; Stockholm, 15 November 1996). The MS and FP conducted their own pro-EU campaigns in addition to 'Yes to Europe' and the MS in particular wanted to make the EU an integrated issue of the party's appearance (Interview no. 51; Stockholm, 15 November 1996; Interview no. 55; Stockholm 19 November 1996).

The 'yes' group of the SAP set up its own campaign group after the party's 1993 annual congress and worked closely with the pro-membership forces of the LO. A common platform with 'Yes to Europe' was deemed impossible after their attacks on each other during the 1994 election campaign (Interview no. 44; Stockholm 12 November 1996), and too close a co-operation was regarded from both sides as dangerous. On some occasions, trade unions asked employers not to address the workers, because this could result in a negative opinion (Interview no. 66; Stockholm, 29 November 1996). Similarly, employers feared that a common platform could lead to a conspiracy theory amongst the population and thus be detrimental to the whole undertaking (Interview no. 43; Stockholm, 12 November 1996). There were, however, many informal contacts to exchange information about each other's strategy (Interview no. 47; Stockholm, 13 November 1996; Interview no. 58; Stockholm, 26 November 1996; Interview no. 61; Stockholm, 26 November 1996). Another reason for setting-up additional platforms was the fear that 'Yes to Europe' could not reach workers and the countryside. The SAP–LO group attracted workers, but pro-EU members of the CP, together with well known public figures and representatives of other small groups, formed the 'Network for Europe' with the financial help of the LRF in 1993 to cater for their particular constituency (Interview no. 50; Stockholm, 14 November 1996).[9] In general, the three different groups on the 'yes' side all addressed a different clientele and were thus regarded as complementing each other effectively (Interview no. 44; Stockholm, 12 November 1996).

There were, however, also programmatic reasons for the different campaign groups. All three groups regarded the EU as a peace project, capable of overcoming the separation between Eastern and Western Europe. Only membership would guarantee Sweden's participation in this project. It was also agreed that membership was an economic necessity and allowed such problems as the protection of the environment to be tackled at the international level.

The particular emphasis of the economic argument, however, differed significantly, in particular between the 'Yes to Europe' and the SAP–LO group. The former stressed the neo-liberal logic. Tougher competition, more inward FDI and lower interest rates as a result of membership would lead to higher economic growth and more jobs (Interview no. 54; Stockholm, 19 November 1996; Interview no. 55; Stockholm, 19 November 1996). Non-membership, on the other hand, would endanger the position of Swedish TNCs and, thereby, the whole Swedish economy (Interview no. 51; Stockholm, 15 November 1996; Interview no. 67; Stockholm, 29 November 1996). The EU was the best option along a neo-liberal economic policy course, which should not be undermined through the introduction of Swedish Model solutions such as an active manpower policy or the development of a strong social dimension at the European level (Interview no. 43; Stockholm, 12 November 1996). The SAP–LO group, in contrast, emphasised the need to combat unemployment at the European level and stated that they wanted a chapter on employment to be included in the revised Maastricht Treaty (Interview no. 58; Stockholm, 26 November 1996; Interview no. 66; Stockholm, 29 November 1996).

The 'no' campaign

The 'no' side, unlike the 'yes' groups, was united in the 'No to the EU' platform, which also had local organisations throughout the country. Membership was on an individual basis, but the various groups and associations had representatives on the board. These were mainly the SAP and CP sections against membership, the trade unions against membership, some interest groups such as 'People against Drugs', youth organisations and environmental groups, and the VP and GP. The latter two were extremely active, but did not want to, or were not allowed to, develop too high a profile. Both were electorally weak at the time and had a radical reputation, which threatened to endanger the 'no' side's non-partisan people's movement appeal. It was agreed that the most important task was to convince the SAP and CP voters. To the public, then, the platform was represented by the SAP–LO and CP networks (Interview no. 38; Stockholm, 8 November 1996; Interview no. 45; Stockholm, 12 November 1996).

'No to the EU' rejected the idea that Sweden could contribute to changes by being a member of the EU. A country as small as Sweden would have no say. Rather than Sweden influencing the EU, the EU would influence Sweden, causing lower environmental standards and undermining the welfare state via the harmonisation of systems. Instead of regarding the EU as an area of prosperity for everybody, 'No to the EU' viewed it as a fortress of the rich against the poor in the developing countries (Interview no. 47; Stockholm, 13 November 1996). Increased drug trafficking and lower food standards were presented as further possible dangers of membership (Interview no. 44; Stockholm, 12 November 1996). The EU was also rejected because of its democratic deficit, first, because of the diminution of national sovereignty and, second, due to undemocratic supranational institutions. The CFSP was regarded as a threat to Swedish neutrality. The VP's argument that the EU was a project of 'big capital' and that the convergence criteria would cement mass unemployment was not part of the platform's position. It has to be remembered that many CP politicians, who had supported the criteria as a good basis for a sound economy, were part of the platform and the VP did not want to break up the unity (Interview no. 38; Stockholm, 8 November 1996). The whole 'no' group also considered it difficult to put forward a strong economic case against membership, since this area was widely used and dominated by their opponents (Interview no. 70; Stockholm, 3 December 1996).

The outcome: a narrow 'yes' for membership

In contrast to Austria, the opposition had been in a much better position in Sweden in several respects. First, it was not divided into a nationalist and a progressive opposition and could therefore form a common platform. Second, the social forces of nationally-oriented labour were not constrained by organisational discipline and participated openly in the debate. Despite this, the 'yes' side still won, although by a very narrow margin. On 13 November 1994, 52.7 per cent voted 'yes' versus 47.3 per cent 'no', after the 'no' side had led from spring 1992 to shortly before the referendum (Luif 1996: 214).

The financial power behind the 'yes' group had been significantly larger, stemming mainly from industrial sources. An academic investigation found out that the ratio was about twenty to one in favour of the 'yes' side. Although there were separate campaign groups, this did not inhibit the SAP-LO group from accepting money from business (Interview no. 71; Stockholm, 4 December 1996). A second factor was that the 'no' side did not have a well-developed alternative to EU membership. What held them together was their rejection of accession to the EU. The fragility of the alliance was demonstrated immediately after the referendum by an inter-party competition between the GP and the VP for the support of those who had voted 'no' (Interview no. 70; Stockholm, 3 December 1997).

Although many reasons for opposing the EU were shared by all groups of the 'No to the EU' alliance, the differences could not have been clearer in the area of economic policy. While the VP and large sections of the GP and the SAP-LO 'no' group rejected the convergence criteria and their focus on low inflation at the expense of employment, the CP politicians, along with some SAP and LO members, still considered them to be a necessary basis for a sound Swedish economy, with or without EU membership. In this situation, it proved impossible to formulate an economic programme, which could rival the neo-liberal project. Considering the overall emphasis put on economic issues by the various 'yes' groups, such a programme would, however, have been a crucial prerequisite for success. This also demonstrates that the 'no' side had at no point managed to form a historical bloc. It had neither a common basis in the sphere of production nor a common ideological project. It was only a short-term alliance with a single goal, the prevention of Swedish EU membership. Some political commentators argued that this was responsible for the 'no' side's loss of supporters during the crucial final phase of the campaign (Svensson 1994: 1).

A further factor might have been the 'no' side's tactic of relying on comparatively little-known representatives to present its case to the public. Kenth Petterson, the President of the Commercial Workers' Union, Eva-Britt Svensson, a member of the SAP, and Eva Hellstrand, close to the CP, had a difficult time opposing well established, high profile politicians such as Prime Minister Carlsson and Bildt, the former Prime Minister and now leader of the main opposition party MS. The VP and GP as such, but especially the party leader of the VP and Per Gahrton of the GP, both well known politicians with a lot of experience in debates, might have been able to convince the public in a better way. In short, some sections within the VP and especially the GP criticised the 'no' side for having sidelined the VP and GP during the campaign, thereby failing to use two potentially strong factors (Interview no. 45; Stockholm, 12 November 1996). This point might have been of some relevance, taking into account the Swedish elections to the EP in September 1995, when the VP and the GP, with 12.9 per cent and 17.2 per cent respectively, scored a massive success mainly at the SAP's expense (The Swedish Institute 1996b: 2).

A few days before the referendum, nineteen out of the twenty-two Presidents of LO affiliated unions wrote an article, in which they declared their support for membership. This gave the 'yes' side a general boost, since many workers favoured a 'no' or still hesitated in their decision (Interview no. 56; Stockholm, 21 November 1997). Perhaps even more significantly, amongst the writers was Lillemor Arvidsson, the President of the Municipal Workers' Union. She also spoke out in favour of membership, despite the fact that her union had not given an official recommendation and that it was known that a majority of its members opposed the EU. Her decision came as a total shock to the 'No to the EU' group and damaged its campaign (Interview no. 45; Stockholm, 12 November 1996).

The SAP's move towards economic arguments during the last week of the campaign seemed to have been important. Prime Minister Carlsson and other high-profile SAP politicians, now free to campaign after the general elections had been won in September, threw their weight behind the 'yes' campaign. Membership, they argued, would lead to lower interest rates and more jobs, and was the only way to save the Swedish welfare state (Interview no. 44; Stockholm, 12 November 1996). Capital used its structural power to underline this argument. In open letters and advertisements in major Swedish newspapers in September 1994, 'the four largest companies explicitly threatened to move within the boundaries of the EU if Sweden did not join the Union' (Fioretos 1997: 315). The financial markets also lent their structural support. 'When the publication of a poll on 6 November 1994 showed the "no" side again gaining ground, interest rates went up in Sweden' (Luif 1996: 321). As a result, home owners feared that they would have to pay higher interest rates outside the EU. Everything boiled down to the question of who could be trusted with the economy. Eventually, it was the Prime Minister's credibility, which decided the point, something which was acknowledged by members of both the 'no' and the 'yes' sides (Interview no. 45; Stockholm, 12 November 1996; Interview no. 50; Stockholm, 14 November 1996). Again, the 'no' side's lack of an alternative economic programme and more high-profile representatives might have been crucial in this respect.

Conclusion

There was little new movement among the Austrian social forces in favour of membership after 1989. The pro-EU historical bloc had already been solidly formed in the process leading to application. During the referendum campaign, it was merely confirmed and reinforced. The main focus was on how to structure the campaign in order to achieve a 'yes' result in the referendum. The social forces opposed to the EU, on the other hand, attempted to mobilise their support and to form a stronger and broader alliance. Quantitatively, the FPÖ's shift towards a 'no' position strengthened the opposition, but in practice it undermined the cause of the anti-EU forces. The ideological rift was too wide to form an alliance and the social forces that opposed the EU but favoured international co-operation had constantly to distance themselves from nationalist, if not racist groups.

In Sweden, the debate started in earnest. To some extent, the formation of social forces showed interesting parallels to the Austrian situation. It was the transnational forces of capital and labour, not internationally-oriented forces based on the different production structure, which were in favour of application. Unlike in Austria, however, the social forces of the transnational sector of production formed a strong alliance only with reference to membership. They did not form a historical bloc. While they agreed on membership as a necessary response to globalisation and the Internal Market initiative, the social purpose for it differed significantly. Capital regarded the EU as a good means of continuing the neo-liberal restructuring of the Swedish state–society relations and rejected a strong social dimension and joint employment programmes at the European level. In contrast, transnational labour demanded additional joint employment programmes and sometimes even a relaxation of the convergence criteria and the acceptance of a slightly higher rate of inflation in order to create more jobs. In other words, transnational labour's support for EU membership did not signify that it had become part of a transnational historic bloc pursuing a neo-liberal hegemonic project. The conflict between capital and labour over the future form of the Swedish state was not resolved, but postponed and transferred to the European level.

As with Austria, the national forces opposed accession. It was the public sector in Sweden which was sheltered, and it was consequently the workers of this sector who played a leading role in opposing membership. An interesting difference was, however, the position of nationally-oriented capital, which can be explained by referring to the different economic structure of the two countries. In Sweden, the economic structure and the economic well-being of the whole country was dominated by TNCs. Many nationally-oriented companies either depended directly on the TNCs or argued that their good performance benefited the Swedish economy in general and, thereby, the nationally-oriented companies. There was, consequently, little incentive to oppose membership or campaign on the 'no' side. In contrast, small and medium-sized companies were predominant in the Austrian economic structure. They had always had a strong say in economic policy-making and faced little if no opposition by TNCs. At the same time, many would be negatively affected by membership and the concomitant deregulation of the sheltered sectors. It was natural for them to support the 'no' side during the campaign and to form alliances with nationally-oriented labour and, although to a lesser extent, the GA and FPÖ. In neither country, however, did the 'no' side manage to form a strong alliance, let alone a historical bloc. They failed to formulate a hegemonic project as an alternative to EU membership and, more critically, to present a coherent concept which could rival neo-liberalism. They were united only in their common rejection of membership. In Austria, even this proved to be impossible due to the ideological rift between the social forces around the GA and the FPÖ.

So far, the emphasis of the discussion has been on arguments over the political economy. It has been stated that mainly transnational forces in Sweden and internationally-oriented ones in Austria pursued membership, because it offered the best way to continue the accumulation of capital after the Keynesian arrangements at the national level of the post-war era had run out of steam. There are, however, serious claims, that it had actually been the changes in the international security structure which caused Austria and Sweden to join the EU. The next chapter explores this question.

5 Austria's and Sweden's accession to the EU and the changing security structure

Neo-realism, neutral states and the end of the Cold War

Neo-realists regard the bipolar Cold War period between 1947 and 1989, based on nuclear weapons and a balance of military capabilities between the USA and Soviet Union and their respective allies, as an extremely stable one that ensured a long-lasting peace in Europe (e.g. Mearsheimer 1990: 10–21). The end of the Cold War implied the destabilisation of this structure and, consequently, more instability, more insecurity and a greater likelihood of conflict in Europe. Neutral countries had benefited from the bipolar, peaceful structure as had those which were a member of one of the two military alliances. The end of the Cold War removed this cosy arrangement. New conflicts, real or potential, have emerged at the borders and endangered these countries' security. The conflicts in former Yugoslavia bordering Austria, and the potential conflicts between the three Baltic states and Russia in the vicinity of Sweden, underline this point. In this situation, it is argued along neo-realist lines, Austria and Sweden might have joined the EU in order to become part of a strong alliance of states. The close relationship between the EU and WEU and, therefore, NATO, as well as the emerging CFSP would provide security guarantees for Sweden and Austria without becoming a member of the WEU or NATO itself (Huldt: 1995: 149; Neuhold 1994: 110–11; Pedersen 1994: 83; Schneider 1994: 17–18).

This neo-realist argument directly contradicts the conclusions of chapters three and four that it was alliances of internationally-oriented capital and labour in Austria and transnational capital and labour in Sweden, which brought about EU membership in response to domestic economic recession, revived regional integration in Europe and global structural change.

In this chapter, the neo-realist argument is analysed from a neo-Gramscian perspective. At first sight, such a perspective and its focus on production seems unable to account for changes in the security structure and their impact on political processes. The globalisation concept of transnational production and finance appears to be contradicted by the territorial concept of security provision. These two concepts are, however, interrelated, because 'ultimately the security of globalisation depends upon military force with a territorial basis' (Cox with Sinclair 1996: 287). For example, during the war against Iraq, the USA, a state, responded as the principal guarantor and enforcer of the global economic order (Cox with Sinclair 1996: 287–92). Holman makes it clear that the emphasis on transnational social forces 'does not mean that [neo-Gramscians] argue for a simple replacement of a state-centric for a "TNC-centric" approach. In order to become effective, concepts of control . . . must also be translated into state policy' (Holman 1992: 19). In other words, hegemonic projects such as those behind Austria's and Sweden's accession to the EU must include a security component in order to have a chance of success. It is important to investigate how state interests in the security area were constructed at the Austrian and Swedish level against the background of the changes in the international structure. To ascertain whether the neo-realist hypothesis is correct or not, the focus has to be on the social forces' perception of the changes in the security structure, and the way they incorporated this perception in their attempt at forming a successful hegemonic project which made the combination of neutrality with membership feasible.

Austria: the silent redefinition of neutrality

The history of Austrian neutrality

Austrian neutrality is mainly a product of the Second World War and the Cold War. The Soviet Union could only accept Austrian independence if it was assured that Austria would not strengthen the rival bloc. Austria's status of neutrality was not part of the State Treaty of 15 May 1955, which gave Austria back independence and full sovereignty. Austria did not want to tie its neutrality to other countries' permission and it is often pointed out that only Austria decides on the formulation and contents of its neutral status (Jankowitsch and Porius 1994: 52). In the 'Moscow Memorandum' of 15 April 1955, however, Austria promised to commit itself constitutionally and via international law to permanent neutrality. On 26 October 1955, one day after the last foreign soldier had left Austrian territory, a constitutional law was, consequently, passed declaring a permanent neutral status. This was then notified to the states with which Austria had diplomatic relations at the time, which led to a quasi-treaty relationship with other states in respect of Austria's neutrality. Overall, although not part of the State Treaty, neutrality must be regarded as the Soviet Union's precondition for Austrian sovereignty (Neuhold 1987: 7–10; Ucakar 1991: 89).

It is generally accepted that permanent neutrals such as Austria are not only committed to neutrality in all wars, but that they also have to 'avoid such peacetime ties and policies as would make its neutrality in war impossible or unlikely' (Hakovirta 1988: 9). Neuhold presents a list of peacetime obligations from an Austrian perspective (Neuhold 1992: 88–9):

- no support for parties/states engaged in warfare;
- no permit for parties/states engaged in warfare to use Austrian territory and airspace;
- the restrictions related to private arms sales to war parties to be equal with reference to all war parties;
- prohibition of participation not only in military alliances, but also in systems of collective security because of possible military measures against aggressors from outside and inside the system;
- no participation in supranational economic organisations because of, for example, a possible one-sided embargo of weapon exports;
- maintenance of a strong national defence;
- intensive international activities to improve the respectability of neutrality.

Compared to Sweden, Austria's defence efforts were less determined (Kramer 1996: 162), but, like Sweden and Finland, Austria pursued an active internationalist policy. The link between foreign policy and active neutrality had already been made at the end of the 1950s, but the real upturn in internationalist policies occurred between 1970 and 1983 and was associated with the person of Chancellor Bruno Kreisky (SPÖ). Austria actively participated in the CSCE process and the United Nations (UN), handed a large centre in Vienna over to the UN and launched independent initiatives in respect of the North–South and Middle East conflicts (Kramer 1996: 156–69).

Application against the background of bipolarity

In 1989, a majority of Austrian social forces accepted that membership was compatible with neutrality. In contrast to Sweden, preparations for this had been made since 1987 and, thus, against the background of the Cold War (Lantis and Queen 1998: 155). In the government's report to parliament of April 1989, European Political Co-operation (EPC) – the predecessor of the CFSP– was considered to be of no risk to Austrian neutrality, because it excluded co-operation in military aspects. At the same time, it was declared that Austria would not participate in future developments towards a defence community or a binding foreign policy with majority decision-making (Luif 1996: 238). Nevertheless, application at this time implied that the definition of neutrality, which stated that neutrality was incompatible with membership in supranational economic organisations, was reinterpreted in an entirely opposite sense without a prior explicit change in the Austrian doctrine of neutrality (Hummer 1996: 13).

Chapter three demonstrated that the VÖI was the driving force behind application for economic reasons. It had, however, also realised that the question of neutrality needed to be addressed. It was the report by Waldemar Hummer and Michael Schweitzer (1987), commissioned by the VÖI, which provided the rationale for the reinterpretation of neutrality. The two experts in international law referred to the Luxembourg Compromise of 1966; Austria could declare neutrality a matter of important national interest in order to prevent majority decisions. They further noted that Articles 223 and 224 of the 1957 Treaty of Rome allowed exceptions for the protection of essential national security interests. Admittedly, Article 225 gives the ECJ the final say in these matters, but this problem could be overcome in that the EU agreed not to use the control powers of the ECJ when Austria sought exceptions because of its neutrality. On 1 March 1994, the Commission accepted this and supported an amendment to the Austrian accession treaty in this respect (Lantis and Queen 1998: 170).

It soon became clear that the Soviet Union had reservations about Austrian membership. They did not overtly oppose it, but they declined to give any positive signal either when Chancellor Vranitzky and Foreign Minister Mock visited Moscow in September 1988, or during the visit of the Soviet Foreign Minister Shevardnadze to Vienna in the same year (Interview no. 2; Vienna, 9 May 1995; Interview no. 14; Vienna, 17 May 1995). During Mock's discussions with Shevardnadze in Moscow, the latter said that he objected to Austrian participation in military alliances. Mock pointed out that the EU was not an alliance of this type, and the matter was not mentioned again (Interview no. 36; Vienna, 15 May 1996). The section within the Soviet Foreign Ministry responsible for policy formulation with reference to Germany and Austria consisted of old-style hard-liners who tried to influence Soviet foreign policy in a way that opposed Austria's EU membership. Overall, while they did not succeed in their task, it became clear that the Soviet Union would have preferred Austria to stay outside the EU (Interview no. 11; Vienna, 12 May 95). Not surprisingly, after Austria's official application to the EU on 17 July 1989, the Soviet Union issued an *aide-memoire*, in which the Austrian application was 'regretted'. It pointed out that the EU not only had an economic character, but also pursued the aim of establishing a political union with a common foreign and security policy. Membership of a permanently neutral country in such an organisation would lead to the loss of the real possibilities inherent in the neutral status. At the same time, the Soviet Union positively recognised Austria's insistence on maintaining its neutral status and it expected that Austria would honour the obligations, which stemmed from the State Treaty (Soviet Union 1989: 562).

Austria dealt with this pressure in a diplomatic way. On the one hand, it had tried to appease the Soviet Union from the beginning by writing its policy of neutrality into the application. Moreover, in an article clearly addressed to Soviet ears, Foreign Minister Mock emphasised both Austria's need to join the EU for economic reasons and its insistence on neutrality. The latter was a part of the Austrian national identity and would be used to further the dialogue between all European countries. Mock called the pursuit of both policies a 'double challenge'; they would not contradict each other, since the EU was not a military alliance, the EPC did not conflict with Austria's duties related to neutrality and the development of the EU into a political alliance was unlikely (Mock 1989). On the other hand, Austrian decision-makers ultimately ignored the Soviet reservations and applied to the EU despite them. The decline of the Soviet Union had already become noticeable and it was deemed possible to disregard Soviet opinion (Interview no. 9; Vienna, 11 May 1995). Furthermore, since Gorbachev had come to power in 1985, it had become clear that the Soviet Union had de-ideologised international relations and pursued a more liberal foreign policy. It would not launch a military attack on Austria to prevent it from joining the EU. In an official visit to Finland in 1991, Gorbachev stated that every country should be allowed to decide its own foreign policy. This new policy had already been apparent in the late 1980s (Interview no. 11; Vienna, 12 May 1995; Hafner 1992: 167–78).

To sum up, the changes in the international security structure, at this stage only expressed in the decline of the Soviet Union and in Gorbachev's liberal foreign policy, played a role as a background condition by making the re-interpretation of neutrality and the EU membership strategy by the VÖI a feasible option (Interview no. 2; Vienna, 9 May 95; Interview no. 33; Vienna, 9 May 1996). Since the drastic changes leading to the end of the Cold War and the break-up of the Eastern bloc did not occur until later, the decision on application cannot have been due to a higher degree of insecurity in the international system. Interviews with officials of the Foreign Ministry and the Chancellor's Office confirm that no higher level of international insecurity was perceived from 1985 onwards (Interview no. 2; Vienna, 9 May 1995; Interview no. 9; Vienna, 11 May 1995). Rather, the decision on membership was first taken for economic reasons, under pressure from the social forces of internationally-oriented capital and labour. The problem of how to combine this with neutrality was tackled later (Interview no. 33; Vienna, 9 May 1996).

Austria's new foreign and security policy after Maastricht

When the CFSP was added to the EU as an additional pillar in the Maastricht Treaty, Austria immediately stated its intention to be an active participant. Neutrality was neither renounced nor restated and the 1989 application to the EU was pragmatically, not officially, changed into application to the new, post-Maastricht EU. This implied that permanent neutrality was also considered to be compatible with the Maastricht Treaty and the CFSP (Hummer 1996: 26). The latter, it was pointed out, was not a military organisation, and its nature was purely intergovernmental, as decisions were taken according to the principle of unanimity. If there were changes towards a more supranational structure in this pillar, the Austrian government would ask for opt-out clauses (Interview no. 2; Vienna, 9 May 95; Interview no. 6; Vienna, 10 May 1995; Interview no. 9; Vienna, 11 May 95).

From a neo-realist perspective, one could argue that the real new international instability occurred after 1989 and that Austria was happy to continue its commitment to the EU application in 1991, as the EU included the new CFSP pillar, offering more security via membership. Various statements by Chancellor Vranitzky and Foreign Minister Mock indicate such a change in foreign and security policy:

> Considering the international conditions of security policy, the potential of the [EU] for peace and stability was also one of the central arguments of the Austrian government in favour of [EU] membership [author's translation].
>
> (Vranitzky 1995: 13)

> From a geopolitical point of view, we also have to take into account that Austria is situated in the new Europe along a dangerous area in East and South-East Europe [author's translation].
>
> (Mock 1994: 6)

Interviewees in Vienna, however, made it clear that Austria did not feel threatened militarily (Interview no. 2; Vienna, 9 May 1995; Interview no. 9; Vienna, 11 May 1995). The war in former Yugoslavia may have had an effect on the population and their decision in the referendum, but not on the political elite (Interview no. 6; Vienna, 10 May 1995; Interview no. 33; Vienna, 9 May 1996). Even this should not be overrated, since it did not change 'the fact that a majority of Austrians still preferred neutrality to [EU] . . . membership' (Luif 1996: 244).

Active participation in the CFSP was officially related to the establishment of a new European security system as the primary goal. Importantly, the definition of security was not limited to the military sphere, but included other areas as well. Chancellor Vranitzky stated that

> In this context, it appears to me to be important that European security policy will be defined in an encompassing way, beyond the framework of a merely military perspective and instruments and that it also consists of questions of social, ecological, democratic and of all policy areas described nowadays as 'internal security' – I only mention terms such as immigration, organised crime, terrorism [author's translation].
>
> (Vranitzky 1995: 13)

To conclude, EU membership even after the end of the Cold War was not seen as a method of gaining higher security, but rather as an opportunity to attain influence on the shaping of a new European security system that addressed issues beyond military concerns. In this sense, there was no contradiction between neutrality and active co-operation in the CFSP perceived (Interview no. 14, 17 May 1995).

Despite this rhetoric, however, traditional Austrian peacetime policies of neutrality were abandoned. In 1994, a new article was added to the Constitution to make the CFSP compatible with neutrality. It allowed Austria to participate in measures that restricted, suspended or cut economic relations with one or more states, thereby safeguarding its co-operation in possible economic sanctions of other countries by the EU (Hummer 1996: 27; Luif 1996: 334–5). EU membership, as already mentioned, contradicted the requirement of non-participation in supranational economic organisations, and the constitutional change related to the CFSP made Austrian support for a party or state engaged in warfare possible. Some observers correctly pointed out that Austria's neutrality had been reduced to its military core: non-participation in military alliances and combat (Hummer 1996: 44; Kunnert 1993: 321–3).[1]

Social forces and the construction of Austria's official position

This official Austrian position on neutrality was largely a compromise among the pro-EU social forces represented by the two governing parties, the SPÖ and ÖVP. A strong group within the SPÖ had mobilised against application, because it perceived neutrality as incompatible with membership. To minimise opposition to the EU, the SPÖ declared before the decision on application that neutrality was not negotiable. This demand was supported by the AK and ÖGB. The fact that a majority eventually decided in favour of compatibility was due, first, to a change in the frameworks of thought, partly brought about by the study of Hummer and Schweitzer (1987), and second, to the evaluation by the international law office in the Foreign Ministry, which sanctioned compatibility (see chapter three). After Maastricht, it was especially the SPÖ, which supported the wider definition of security with the goal of avoiding situations such as the crisis in former Yugoslavia from the beginning. It never regarded EU membership as a way of entering the WEU and/or NATO through the back door, since both were considered unsuitable as the basis for a future pan-European security system. Moreover, neutrality was deemed to be an untouchable issue, at least until the day the new all-encompassing security order had been established. But even in this event, membership in military alliances such as the WEU and NATO would not be on the social democratic agenda (Interview no. 4; Vienna, 9 May 1995). While the internal party opposition to EU membership supported this position, there was criticism of the lack of any clear concept of what this new order would look like or how it could be brought about (Interview no. 23; Vienna, 24 April 1996).

In contrast, the social forces, represented by the ÖVP were critical about making neutrality a non-issue of the debate. They were reluctant to include the neutrality clause in the application letter and large sections would have preferred neutrality to be renounced and Austria to become a member of WEU and NATO (though there was less support for the latter) (Kunnert 1993: 327; Interview no. 36; Vienna, 15 May 1996). Neutrality was deemed to be an obstacle to Austria's foreign and security policy, hindering it from taking up full responsibility in a new European security system. Should the CFSP move towards further integration in defence, the ÖVP would have preferred Austria not to demand opt-out clauses. Overall, however, the ÖVP had to pay attention to its coalition partner SPÖ and the Austrian population, for which neutrality was a 'sacred cow' (Interview no. 12; Vienna, 12 May 1995). Even former Foreign Minister Mock, who was in favour of membership of the WEU and NATO, identified merely traditional peace-keeping functions such as search and rescue as well as humanitarian operations, when it came to the question of Austria's active contributions to European security policy (Mock 1995: 9).

The opposition parties rejected this government compromise. The Liberal Forum argued that neutrality was obsolete after the end of the Cold War and should be replaced with WEU membership. The CSCE, with its fifty-three members, would be too inflexible and could not provide the basis for a new European security order. Instead, this order should be grounded in the transatlantic alliance between the EU and the USA via the WEU and NATO, the structures of which needed to be redefined (Hummer 1996: 43–4). The FPÖ also claimed that neutrality had been obsolete since the end of the 1980s because of the changes in the international security system. In the current situation, Austria's long borders with Eastern Europe and former Yugoslavia would require the country to look for whatever security it could get. As the WEU was considered to exist only on paper, NATO membership was the preferred option. Overall, a pan–European security order would be welcomed, but this was only regarded as a possibility in the long run (Interview no. 26; Vienna, 25 April 1996).

For its part, the GA rejected the government compromise because of its alleged negative implications for Austria's neutrality. In contrast to the SPÖ and ÖVP, the GA did not think that EU membership was compatible with neutrality and accused the government of deceiving the Austrian population in this respect. It would still use the word 'neutrality' to protect itself against the 'emotional shock' of losing it, while knowing perfectly well that neutrality was incompatible with the CFSP (GA 1993: 69–70). The EU was considered to have developed into a military bloc, which made the overcoming of aggressive structures towards a European peace order impossible. A higher degree of international instability, exemplified in the wars in former Yugoslavia and the former Soviet Union, and the danger of the proliferation of nuclear weapons, was acknowledged. This should not, however, be countered by an offensive Western European military strategy with military units designed for flexible intervention (GA 1993: 64–5). Instead, the WEU and NATO should be dissolved and make way for an integrated, co-operative security system, which also included Russia. Participation in the development of new transnational practices of peace-movements was one way of working towards such an alternative security policy. The extension and strengthening of all-European organisations, such as the CSCE, at the international level was another (GA 1993: 67–8). Finally, neutrality should not be undermined but reinstated in its full original meaning, as expressed in the internationalist policies of the former Chancellor Kreisky in the 1970s and early 1980s, to become one of the constitutive elements of the new European security system (GA 1996: 4–5).

During the referendum campaign, neutrality and questions of foreign and security policy did not play a dominant role, for supporters or for opponents of membership. They were respectively only the sixth and the fourth most important issues for voters (Luif 1996: 328). As outlined in chapter four, economic arguments and especially the irrational debate that turned the referendum into an anti-Haider campaign dominated the final stages of the struggle in Austria. The pro-EU social forces seem to have succeeded in convincing the population that membership was compatible with neutrality and that this, consequently, was not an issue of the campaign.

Sweden: neutrality redefined as non-alignment

The historical background of Swedish neutrality

Swedish neutrality dates from 1814–15 and the Europe of the Vienna Congress. Since then, Sweden has never been involved in a war (Logue 1989). During the Second World War, Swedish neutrality was stretched to its limits, though. In contrast to its neighbours Denmark and Norway, Sweden managed to stay out of war. Nevertheless, it supplied Germany with war material and even allowed a whole German division to cross its territory from Norway to Finland. According to Carlsnaes, this experience was decisive for the re-definition of Swedish neutrality after 1945 (Carlsnaes 1993: 72–3).

The official Swedish definition of its post-war neutrality was 'freedom from alliances in peace aiming for neutrality in war' (Sundelius 1989: 4). Although Sweden is considered to be a 'conventional neutral' without restrictions under international law (Hakovirta 1988: 10) and, thus, to be less limited in its foreign policy than Austria (Neuhold 1987: 3; Pedersen 1994: 17), there was no real difference in Sweden's foreign policy. 'Both types of neutral countries aim at maintaining their status during wartime. Therefore, they have to adjust their peacetime behavior accordingly' (Luif

1996: 132). Goldmann argues that the credibility of Sweden's neutral status rested primarily on a firm and consistent defence policy, demonstrating to others Sweden's ability to defend itself. Moreover, a strong public support for neutrality and the determination to remain unfettered in its foreign policy orientation further sustained Sweden's credibility. As in Austria, this was supported by an internationalist policy for peace and security with the focus on strengthening international law, especially via the UN, and on foreign aid to developing countries. Throughout the postwar era, neutrality was backed by a broad alliance of social forces from all the different parties and interest associations (Goldmann 1991: 123–30). It was the revival of European integration and the end of the Cold War that put neutrality on the agenda.

Neutrality and the application to the EU

As stated in chapter four, the FP and MS declared immediately after the fall of the Berlin Wall that Sweden should apply to the EU for membership while retaining its policy of neutrality. From their point of view, the changes in the European and international security structure had removed the last hindrances to the compatibility of membership and neutrality. The social democratic government, however, which had the last say in this matter, did not follow this line. In fact, Prime Minister Carlsson, assessing the changes in a speech to the Labour Movement Peace Forum in December 1989, maintained that 'a lower political temperature and the democratic process in several East European countries have not reduced the value of the Swedish policy of neutrality' (Carlsson 1989: 140). NATO and the Warsaw Pact still maintained large military arsenals and there might be possible setbacks and increasing international tension due to the severe economic problems in the Soviet Union. Closer co-operation with the EU would be attempted in various fields, but not those of foreign and defence policy. 'Swedish membership is not an objective in the discussions with the [EU] which are about to take place' (Carlsson 1989: 138). This position was confirmed in a publication by the Swedish Ministry of Foreign Affairs, which also acknowledged the changes in the European security structure, but repeated the party compromise of spring 1988 that membership was not an objective in the forthcoming EEA negotiations with the EU (Jacobsson 1990: 14).

As late as 27 May 1990, Carlsson stated in his article in the daily newspaper *Dagens Nyheter* that 'concern for the credibility of our policy of neutrality is the reason why we are not applying for [EU] membership' (quoted in Sundelius 1994: 179). He pointed to the EU's supranational character and its security and defence policy aspirations. In short, changes in the security structure did not cause a change in the SAP's neutrality policy. 'Although the Cold War came to an end . . . this need not have led to a change in [EU] policy, particularly not at this point in time'

(Gustavsson 1998: 192). As argued in chapter three, the economic crisis in general, and the flight of capital and the problems on the financial markets in particular, convinced SAP leaders that EU membership was the only way forward. The Ministry of Finance and the Prime Ministers' Office were at the centre of the decision in favour of application. The Ministry of Foreign Affairs was not in the forefront (Interview no. 60; Stockholm, 21 November 1996) and the announcement of application was not cleared in advance with its senior civil servants (Sundelius 1994: 191).

When the decision on application had been taken, its implications for neutrality needed to be clarified. The new situation led to the first official change in Swedish neutrality policy. Neutrality was not redefined or abandoned but simply declared compatible with membership due to the changes in the international security structure. Sten Andersson, the Minister for Foreign Affairs, stated that 'Sweden's attitude, I would say, is characterized more by continuity than by change. What has changed is not Sweden's position. It is Europe' (Andersson 1991: 48). According to Pierre Schori, the influential Under-Secretary of State for Foreign Affairs, membership had been impossible during the Cold War because of the division of Europe into two alliances. The EU had been perceived as a part of the Western bloc. Nevertheless, 'when the external environment changes, the prerequisites for the Swedish policy of neutrality also change' (Schori 1991: 62). With the Cold War over, Sweden could become a member of the EU, while retaining neutrality at the same time.

An overall assessment of foreign and security policy aspects by the Ministry for Foreign Affairs in consultation with the Advisory Council on Foreign Affairs in spring 1991 took fully into account the EU intergovernmental conference (IGC) on European Political Union, initiated in December 1990 (Swedish Ministry for Foreign Affairs 1991: 37–43). The discussions within the EU on a possible future common defence policy and common defence, but also some form of link between the EU and WEU were, consequently, known in Sweden before the eventual application on 1 July 1991. Prime Minister Carlsson's address to the Swedish parliament, on 14 June 1991, concerning Sweden's application to the EU, was based on this assessment. He acknowledged these EU-internal discussions but concluded that it was extremely unlikely that the EU would introduce qualified majority voting (QMV) for security and foreign policy questions (Carlsson 1991: 11). Sweden, he continued, could not participate in a common defence policy or a mutual defence commitment within the EU framework because of its neutrality. None the less, 'there is no reason to believe that the EU is now in the process of turning into a military alliance, or of creating other forms of binding common defence arrangements' (Carlsson 1991: 12).

It can be concluded that Sweden's application for membership was a response to severe economic problems, not an attempt to gain more security in a less stable world (Interview no. 53; Stockholm, 18 November

1996). If anything, Sweden was characterised by a general euphoria about the developments in Europe. In 1991, the Warsaw Pact was dissolved and Soviet troops withdrew all over Eastern Europe. The military threat lost much of its importance in the Swedish debate on European security (Lindahl 1995: 174; see also Interviews).[2] Two assessments by the Swedish Ministry of Defence in 1995 and 1996 further support this conclusion. They stated that there were no current military threats directed against Sweden (Swedish Ministry of Defence 1995: 4; 1996: 7). In the time between the decision in parliament on 12 December 1990 and the application on 1 July 1991, the implications for the neutrality policy were assessed and membership was declared compatible with it. While the changes in the international system did not cause Sweden's application, they formed an important background condition in that they allowed the SAP government to justify the change in its policy on membership and neutrality.

The redefinition of neutrality

The coming to power of the coalition government under Prime Minister Carl Bildt (MS) in October 1991 marked the start of a new phase in Sweden's neutrality policy. Margaretha af Ugglas, the new Minister for Foreign Affairs, indicated a first shift in parliament on 17 October 1991. She described the EU as the engine of international co-operation and argued that Sweden's foreign policy should have a clear European identity in contrast to the SAP's internationalist focus on 'exotic' places. Nevertheless, she reaffirmed the traditional neutrality policy for a last time: 'the strategic realities in our immediate vicinity mean that the main theme of our security policy – summarized as "non-participation in alliances in time of peace, aiming at neutrality in time of war" – retains its significance' (Ugglas 1991: 86). This was to change soon afterwards. Roughly a month later, Bildt spoke about the necessity of adjusting Sweden's foreign and security policy in the light of the new European realities and the development within the EU towards a CFSP. 'It is obvious', he argued, 'that the term "policy of neutrality" can no longer adequately be applied as an overall description of the foreign and security policies we wish to pursue within the European framework' (Bildt 1991a: 100). Neutrality and EU membership were no longer considered to be compatible. The SAP accepted this argument with surprisingly little opposition (Carlsnaes 1993: 84).

The result was a new compromise on foreign and security policy by all parties in parliament except for the VP (the GP was not in parliament between 1991 and 1994). In May 1992, two reports were passed. The first initiated the phasing out of the word 'neutrality'; 'military non-alignment' became the new official terminology. This had practical implications. 'The old formula "nonalignment in peacetime aiming at neutrality in wartime" was qualified so as to say that Swedish nonalignment aimed at "making it possible to be neutral" in case of a war in the neighboring area' (Huldt 1995: 158–9).

Lars-Åke Nilsson, Permanent Under-Secretary of State for Foreign Affairs, made clear that this change implied that neutrality 'is an option, not an absolute goal in every conceivable situation' (Nilsson 1993: 225). What remained of the old neutrality policy was the commitment to non-membership in military alliances and a strong national defence (Ugglas 1993: 300–1). The second report of the party compromise of May 1992 spelled out that 'the Maastricht Treaty was compatible with Sweden's aim of becoming a member of the [EU]' (Luif 1996: 247). Significantly, motions tabled by the VP and individual social democrats demanding a re-affirmation of the December 1990 party compromise, in which the intention of seeking membership while retaining neutrality was stated, were not endorsed by parliament. In sum, neutrality

> is now defined as the 'hard core' of Swedish defence policy, as distin-guished from a foreign and security policy outlook which will become much more adaptively orientated towards Europe and its emerging security arrangements than has been the case hitherto
>
> (Carlsnaes 1993: 84).

Membership in general, and the CFSP in particular, appeared to be the best way of participating in the establishment of a new, pan-European system of security, peace and prosperity. 'As we see it,' Ugglas stated, 'only the European [Union] is sufficiently powerful and comprehensive to serve as an engine for the reunification of Western and Eastern Europe' (Ugglas 1992: 120). Unlike neutrality, military non-alignment was deemed to be compatible with participation in the CFSP, provided unanimity in CFSP decision-making was retained. Consequently, Sweden's position for the 1996–7 IGC stated that 'there is no question of abolishing the right of veto for foreign and security policy decisions' (Swedish Government 1995: 27).

Bildt and the bourgeois government attempted to follow up the new definition in all its consequences. On 17 November 1993, in a speech to the Swedish Institute for International Affairs, Bildt referred to Russian threats against the Baltic States and stated that he 'finds it difficult to see neutrality as a probable choice in the predictable cases of conflict in our vicinity' (quoted in Bierfeld 1995: 186). This led to an intense conflict with the social democratic opposition (Huldt 1995: 156–7). While there was a consensus among all social forces on the need of supporting the three newly-independent Baltic States, the SAP did not want to give any quasi-guarantee of military assistance. Nevertheless, it was not only the SAP, but also the coalition partner CP, which criticised Bildt and demanded the maintenance of the 'limited' version of neutrality (Miles 1995: 14).

When the SAP returned to power in September 1994, it moved back to a stricter interpretation of non-alignment. During a parliamentary debate in February 1995, it stated that 'we must not lead other states to expect a Swedish military involvement in the event of an armed conflict. Sweden neither needs or wishes to impose restrictions on itself' (quoted in Miles 1995: 35). The 1996 security evaluation by the Swedish Ministry of Defence spelled this out even more clearly: 'it must . . . be perfectly clear that Sweden is not in a position to give security guarantees to the Baltic countries' (Swedish Ministry of Defence 1996: 6).

There were some indications that the MS and the FP would have preferred Swedish membership in the WEU and/or NATO to the defence policy of military non-alignment. Before the party compromise of May 1992, Bildt had not excluded Swedish membership in the WEU (Luif 1996: 246). Moreover, 'in 1995, the Liberal and Conservative members of the Parliamentary Defence Committee walked out in protest against Social Democratic refusal to discuss Swedish membership in a military alliance such as NATO' (Cordier 1995: 17). The FP affirmed that Sweden's current non-alignment policy did not mean that Swedish NATO membership might not be reconsidered in the future. It also demanded that the WEU was incorporated in the EU and that Sweden became a member of it (FP 1995: 13–14). Such a position, however, proved to be impossible with the SAP, the support of which was needed in the question of EU membership.

Both the VP and GP, however, argued that the EU and the CFSP compromised Sweden's status of neutrality, as outlined in chapter four. They demanded an end to the link between the EU and the WEU, and that Sweden be neither an observer at, nor a member of, the latter. Thus, these two parties represented those social forces, which still adhered to the traditional policy of neutrality and rejected the 1992 party compromise on redefinition.

At the annual meeting of the CSCE Parliamentary Assembly, 5–9 July 1996 in Stockholm, the GP together with the Green Group of the CSCE Parliamentary Assembly published its concept of a future European security order. It advocated a broader concept of security, which went beyond military power balance and international conflict resolution via force. Instead, 'aspects of an economic, social, ecological, religious, psychological and cultural nature must be a part of the security concept' (GP 1996: 1). The CSCE should take the leading role in the peaceful resolution of conflicts and the establishment of a pan-European, collective security system, in place of NATO or the WEU, which were attached to the 'old-fashioned', military-oriented security model. The conversion of the defence industry to civil production and the emphasis on economic cooperation on equal trade terms with developing countries were further aspects of the green security concept. Finally, the potentially positive role of neutral countries for negotiations, information and active conflict prevention was identified. 'The Greens therefore regard it as being of utmost importance that Sweden, Ireland, Austria and Finland can and may remain outside both WEU and NATO' (GP 1996: 1–2). Overall, the GP not only insisted on the traditional definition of neutrality, it also attempted to place it within a European-wide concept of security and to form transnational links, which could support this concept across borders.[3]

In conclusion, neutrality was redefined as non-alignment and reduced to its military core in 1992. However, this was not a response to a perception of increased international insecurity, since the basic decision on application had already been taken at that time. Rather, it was due partly to the new government's different emphasis in foreign policy and partly to the understanding that traditional neutrality was incompatible with the CFSP.

Despite this change in the official Swedish foreign and security policy, the population continued to be in favour of neutrality. 'In August 1992, 71 percent of all Swedes wanted the government to continue with neutrality policy. Only 18 percent thought that in view of the changing world Sweden should abandon its traditional foreign policy stance' (Luif 1996: 248). This implied potential problems for the 'yes' side in the referendum. In particular, the fact that the Maastricht Treaty mentioned a 'common defence policy' and 'common defence' could have had a decisive impact on voters' decision (Lindahl 1995: 176). The 'yes' side, consequently, concentrated on the non-military aspects of foreign and security policy and emphasised that the EU 'should be seen as having at its disposal the most important means – economic and political – of ensuring peace and stability in Europe' (Lindahl 1995: 178–9). Eventually, Sweden's security and non-alignment policy played only a minor role in the referendum, to the disadvantage of the 'no' side. 'Sweden's severe recession between 1990–93 meant that ultimately the electorate placed economic recovery above all else' (Miles 1995: 26).

Conclusion

In both countries, neutrality was reduced to its military core of non-partic-ipation in military alliances and combat. This was openly acknowledged in Sweden and silently brought about via political manoeuvres in Austria. Social forces represented by conservative parties in both countries, the ÖVP and FPÖ in Austria and the MS and FP in Sweden, would have preferred to abandon neutrality altogether and to join the WEU and/or NATO, while the social democratic parties and also the CP in Sweden opposed such a step. This discussion, however, was not related to EU membership, but had to do with general foreign policy. Conversely, the Green Parties in both countries and the VP in Sweden favoured the retaining of the traditional neutrality policy, which they continued to consider incompatible with accession to the EU.

The analysis of the impact of changes in the security structure has clearly shown that they were not a primary force behind the two countries' drive towards EU membership. There was no perception of higher levels of international insecurity in Austria and Sweden that made them apply to the EU in order to gain security guarantees from the WEU and/or NATO through the back door. Membership in the WEU could have provided some indirect security guarantees from NATO, since so many WEU members are also NATO members (Smith 1999: 57–8). Nevertheless, as a result of the security policy compromise in both countries discussed earlier, Austria and Sweden opted only for observer status at the WEU. Hence, the decision on application was taken first for economic reasons, and then neutrality was re-defined in a way that made it compatible with membership. The changes in the international security structure – Gorbachev's liberal foreign policy and a general decline in Soviet power in the case of Austria, and, in the case of Sweden, the end of the Cold War – were, however, important background conditions, which facilitated the redefinition of neutrality and made pro-EU strategies feasible. It allowed pro-EU forces to add the required security component to the hegemonic project which sustained the new neo-liberal model of capital accumulation in general, and the drive towards EU membership as a part of it in particular. The forces opposed to membership were better able to formulate a security component of their position than they had been in the economic sphere. They proved, however, unable to challenge the notion that membership and neutrality were compatible. Neutrality did not become a core issue in the struggles prior to the referenda.

In Austria, neutrality had been discussed from the very beginning of the EU debate and formed a part of the letter of application, while it was on the agenda in Sweden only after the SAP's turn-around in October 1990 and was not mentioned in the application. This can be explained by referring to the different timing of the two applications. Austria applied to the EU before the fall of the Berlin Wall and German reunification. The Cold War was still in its place and neutrality was a much more sensitive issue. Two years later, the issue was of much less concern to the Swedish government.

6 The future enlargement of the EU towards Central and Eastern Europe

A neo-Gramscian perspective on future EU enlargements

As a critical theory, the neo-Gramscian perspective used in this study 'does not envisage any general or universally valid laws which can be explained by the development of appropriate generally applicable theories' (Cox with Sinclair 1996: 53). So far, it has been applied to the Austrian and Swedish accession to the EU, but this analysis was not supposed to lead to general findings transferable to other instances of enlargement. Only the method of investigating such cases of accession and the concepts used in the analysis can be transferred. This is the approach with which this chapter looks at the possible EU enlargement to Central and Eastern Europe (CEE). While a full analysis of this process is not feasible in the limited space available, a possible application of a neo-Gramscian perspective is indicated.

When the communist regimes fell across CEE from 1989 onwards, dramatic processes of transformation were set in motion in the affected countries, including moves towards closer relationships with the EU. From 1991 onwards, Europe Agreements (EAs) were signed bilaterally between the EU and several CEE countries including Poland, the Czech Republic and Hungary (Grabbe and Hughes 1998: 31). Most importantly, they had the goal of creating a free trade area over a ten-year period. Although the EU regarded them as agreements in their own right, the applicant countries saw them from the very beginning not as an end in themselves, but as a stepping-stone towards full membership (Interview no. 73; London, 16 June 1999; Gower 1999: 5–7).[1]

At the 1993 European Council summit in Copenhagen, the EU accepted the prospect of enlargement and for the first time explicitly spelled out the criteria new members had to fulfil. They were asked to achieve a stable democracy, a functioning market economy, the ability to withstand competition within the EU, and to be prepared to take on the full *acquis communautaire* including the aims of political, and economic and monetary union (Gower 1999: 7).

In July 1997, the Commission published 'Agenda 2000', which set out its opinions on the applications and an analysis of EU development in view of enlargement, covering the potential for policy reforms in the areas of the CAP, regional policy, the institutional set-up and the future financing of the Union (Avery and Cameron 1998: 101–39). In December that year, the Luxembourg European Council summit decided to open negotiations with Hungary, the Czech Republic, Poland, Slovenia and Estonia (CEE-5). Bulgaria, Romania, Slovakia, Latvia and Lithuania were also given a pre-accession strategy, including an annual review by the Commission to determine whether negotiations may be opened. Negotiations were eventually launched on 30 March 1998 with the five Central and Eastern European states (the CEE-5) and Cyprus. Overall, however, despite these moves there were still severe doubts about the feasibility of enlargement.

The most important difference from the 1995 enlargement is the relatively poor situation of the ten aspirant states (the CEE-10). 'In absorbing all ten countries, the EU would add 28 per cent to its population but only 4 per cent to its GDP, and average per capita GDP in the CEE-10 is only one-third of the average EU level' (Grabbe and Hughes 1998: 90). In contrast to the 1995 enlargement, when all EU members were generally in favour (even if that support was primarily because the new members were going to be net contributors to the budget) their willingness to welcome the CEE-10 has been anything but assured. The EU has been faced with several severe problems, which had all been indicated by the Commission in its Agenda 2000. Some of them – the reform of the CAP and the new budget for the period of 2000–6 – had already been evident earlier, but were compounded by the prospect of enlargement. Others came on the agenda mainly because of enlargement: regional policy and the distribution of structural fund money, the free movement of labour and institutional reform (Ardy 1999; Grabbe and Hughes 1998: 90–108). The Treaty of Amsterdam in 1997 failed in particular to solve the institutional impasse. There was an agreement on a limit of seats in the EP and a modest extension of QMV, but the system of weighting countries' votes in the Council and the number of Commissioners remained unchanged (Grabbe and Hughes 1998: 103–4).

Since Amsterdam, however, significant progress has been made in all these areas. In March 1999 the European Council summit in Berlin finally agreed on the core issues of Agenda 2000. Compromises were agreed in the areas of CAP reform, the UK rebate, and the allocation of finances within the regional policy. This finally allowed the setting of the EU's budget for the seven years from 2000 to 2006. Although this compromise was regarded by many as rather messy and unsatisfactory, the completion of Agenda 2000 at least established a clear financial framework for enlargement. The EU set aside 4.14bn Euros for new members in 2002, which will be increased to 14.21bn Euros in 2006. This is modest in overall terms, but the fact that these funds are ring-fenced and cannot be used for other purposes shows the Union's clear commitment to enlargement (*Financial Times*, 27 March 1999: 2). At the European Council summit in Cologne in June 1999, the EU decided on an IGC to start and end in 2000 with the task of dealing with the institutional issues left over at Amsterdam in 1997 (*Guardian*, 4 June 1999: 15). Eventually, the Helsinki European Council summit in December 1999 decided in a dramatic step to open accession negotiations with the rest of the CEE-10 (Bulgaria, Romania, Slovakia, Latvia and Lithuania), as well as Malta and Turkey (*Guardian*, 11 December 1999: 5)

The potential enlargement to CEE has generated a host of academic studies (e.g. Avery and Cameron 1998; Curzon Price *et al.* 1999; Grabbe and Hughes 1998; Henderson 1999; Maresceau 1997; Mayhew 1998; Preston 1997). They are, however, predominantly state-centric and empiricist. They assume that enlargement is in general beneficial to all possible new members, and concentrate on the problems between the applicants and the EU and among EU members themselves. Little research has been carried out in relation to the potential conflicts between the losers and winners of EU membership among the applicants. Consequently, the potential opponents and their alternative approaches have been neglected. Similarly, the question of membership has not been linked to globalisation and the related restructuring processes which applicant countries have undergone since the end of the Cold War. It is especially in these two respects that a neo-Gramscian analysis can contribute to the debate.

The next part of this chapter investigates the impact of globalisation on the former communist states in CEE, focusing on the two upsurges of liberalism in this area: the economic restructuring according to neo-liberal criteria and the establishment of liberal democracies (Holman 1992: 13–14). The latter is crucial in providing legitimacy and mobilising support for the former. The analysis concentrates on Hungary, Poland and the Czech Republic which, since 1989–90, have been generally perceived as the front-runners in the transformation into market economies and liberal democracies, and in the bid for EU membership. Estonia and Slovenia joined them only later, after achieving the status of sovereign states in 1991. The final section attempts a first examination of the potential internal divisions over EU membership within these countries.

Globalisation and the transformation of Poland, the Czech Republic and Hungary

During the 1970s and especially the 1980s, the accumulation regime of the state socialist mode of production in CEE had become exhausted and unsustainable (Bryant and Mokrzycki 1994: 2). At the ideological level, Gorbachev's concepts of *perestroika* and *glasnost* further undermined the established order. The related promotion of domestic democratisation and revision of Cold War Soviet foreign policy was crucial in the decision to put an end to the Soviet bloc (Köves 1992: 10). In the ensuing political and economic transformation, these countries were fully exposed to the neo-liberal pressures of globalisation.

The transnationalisation of finance

Hungary and Poland had already been integrated into the global financial market through the international debt they accumulated in the attempt to stop economic decline in the 1970s and 1980s, amounting in 1990 to $21.3bn and $49.4bn respectively (Business Central Europe, http://www.bcemag.com/, 3 June 1999). 'The huge foreign debts with which the new rulers were confronted immediately after coming to power clearly constrained their capacity to act in the economic sphere' (Holman 1998: 18). It left little alternative to austerity programmes and submitted both countries to the harsh neo-liberal restructuring measures of the IMF.

The financial markets in all three countries were deregulated and liberalised incrementally throughout the 1990s. In Poland, convertibility for current transactions was introduced in 1995 (Curzon Price 1999: 28). Since February 1999, foreign banks and insurance companies have been allowed to open branches in Poland under the same conditions as Polish banks. Foreign banks had, in fact, already acquired stakes in the financial sector via participation in the privatisation process. As of 1999, about 50 per cent of the banking sector is in foreign hands. Moreover, with the exception of some regulations in the area of short-term financial investment, Poland lifted all restrictions on currency convertibility in 1999. By the beginning of 2000, Poland was due to abolish the remaining restrictions and exchange controls, which are not compatible with OECD guidelines (Interview no. 72; London, 15 June 1999). Finally, Warsaw has emerged as the most transparent stock market in the region and is becoming a regional financial centre (*Financial Times*, 11 April 1997, Survey: 2).

The Czech Republic, at that time still part of the Czech and Slovak Federation, had already introduced currency convertibility for all current and most capital transactions in 1992 (Curzon Price 1999: 28). In comparison with Hungary and Poland, it is most advanced in the liberalisation of capital transactions. According to the capital account liberalisation index of the European Bank for Reconstruction and Development (EBRD), the Czech Republic had a ranking of 73.7 out of a possible maximum of 100 in December 1997, while Hungary rated 59.5 and Poland 55.3 (EBRD 1998: 89).[2]

In Hungary, convertibility for current transactions was established in January 1996 (Curzon Price 1999: 28). Since 1 January 1998, foreign banks and insurance companies have been able to open branches in Hungary freely. In practice, there are no exchange controls for Hungarian companies that want to invest abroad. Permission is granted automatically. Foreign investment can come in freely and profits can be repatriated. Hungary complies fully with its OECD commitments in this respect. Regulations still apply only as far as short-term financial flows are concerned and the recently established pension funds are not allowed to invest abroad. The latter two measures are, however, only temporary. The high level of financial transnationalisation is most explicit in the fact that about 60 per cent of the banking sector is in foreign hands (Interview no. 73; London, 16 June 1999). In short, all three countries have been to a large extent integrated in the global financial market.

The transnationalisation of production

The transformation from a command to a market economy in all three countries started in 1989–90 and has been dominated by foreign capital ever since (Holman 1998: 18–19). 'Among the CEE-10, Hungary, Poland and the Czech Republic have received the bulk of the [FDI] inflows, with over two-thirds of the total' (Grabbe and Hughes 1998: 20). Table 6.1 shows that there was a dramatic increase in Poland from US$ 89 million in 1990 to US$ 7500 million in 1998. In the Czech Republic, there was a development from US$ 100 million in 1992 to US$ 2540 million in 1998, having already peaked at of US$ 2500 million in 1995. Hungary too experienced dramatic increases over the same time period peaking in 1995 with US$ 4500 million.

In an international comparison, these flows are significant. Within four to five years of transformation, the three countries were matching or coming close to the level of inward FDI into the largest FDI recipients among developing countries. Compared with EU members, 'in 1994, both Hungarian and Polish inflows were greater than those into Greece, Ireland and Portugal. Czech inflows were substantially higher than Irish inflows and comparable to Greek and Portuguese inflows' (Estrin *et al.* 1997: 39). In short, the production structure of all three countries has been increasingly transnationalised in recent years. Estimates assume that TNCs are, for example, responsible for 25 per cent of Hungarian GDP (Interview no. 73; London, 16 June 1999).

Some economic sectors have been more attractive to transnational capital than others. In the early years, manufacturing proved to be most attractive, while FDI in services has become more prominent recently. 'Within manufacturing, food processing and consumer goods were most important, with

Table 6.1 Inward FDI in Poland, the Czech Republic and Hungary (in million US $), 1990–98

	1990	1991	1992	1993	1994	1995	1996	1997	1998
Poland	89	100	300	600	500	1100	2800	3000	7500
Czech Rep.	—	—	100	600	700	2500	1400	1300	2540
Hungary	300	1500	1500	2300	1100	4500	2000	2100	1150

Source: Business Central Europe, http://www.bcemag.com/ (3 June 1999)

vehicles also very significant' (Estrin *et al.* 1997: 48–9). In the Czech Republic, transport and communications are of primary importance, while property and financial services are significant in Hungary and Poland respectively.

Economic transformation also included a redirection of trade, which was particularly necessary due to the break-up of the old Communist Council for Mutual Economic Assistance in 1991. Exports to the EU from six countries of the CEE-10 (Bulgaria, the Czech Republic, Hungary, Poland, Romania and Slovakia) rose from 35 per cent in 1989 to 63 per cent in 1995. The EU had become the most important market for CEE countries (Grabbe and Hughes 1998: 13; see also Avery and Cameron 1998: 19–20). Overall, there are significant transnational and internationally-oriented social forces in Poland, the Czech Republic and Hungary. They are likely to be in conflict with nationally-oriented social forces, mainly engendered by the agricultural sector and the steel and mining industries, but also the public sector.

The restructuring of the state

After the collapse of the communist regimes in CEE, neo-liberalism played a predominant role in the restructuring of these states. 'Neo-liberal economists spoke with great assurance, filled the vacuum, and advised the new regimes in Poland, Czechoslovakia and Hungary that a rapid [transformation] to capitalism was feasible' (Bryant 1994: 59). The most rapid transformation, the Balcerowicz Plan, named after the then Polish Finance Minister and heavily influenced by the IMF and the neo-liberal Harvard economist Jeffrey Sachs, was implemented in Poland in 1990. Its goal was to stabilise the economy, get hyperinflation under control, and, most importantly, bring about the radical transformation of the whole system into a market economy. As part of the package, most prices were freed, subsidies to companies were reduced and the Polish *zloty* was made internally convertible. Moreover, the package included deep cuts in public expenditure, a tight monetary policy and the imposition of a restrictive incomes policy.

The privatisation programme, passed by the Polish parliament in July 1990 was a crucial part of the neo-liberal transformation strategy. This programme, however, took longer to be implemented. It was very successful in the retailing sector of small sized enterprises, and with respect to medium-sized enterprises, which were privatised either by auction or through liquidation. Nevertheless, 'large-scale privatization in Poland has proceeded very slowly' (Duke and Grime 1994: 160). In 1997, the 'crown jewels' such as LOT, the state airline, Polska Miedz, the copper miner and refiner, and Polska Telecom were still awaiting privatisation (*Financial Times*, 11 April 1997, Survey: 2).

In the Czech Republic, the shock therapy was delayed by about a year after the political revolution. Nevertheless, some important preconditions for a market economy had been established in April 1990, including the abolition of the Planning Commission, the Prices Board and the state monopoly of foreign trade. On 1 January 1991, 'some 85 percent of retail and wholesale prices were freed from state control . . . and the *koruna* became convertible for current account purposes' (Dangerfield 1997: 442). Further neo-liberal policies over the years included an emphasis on the control of inflation, cutbacks in unemployment benefits, social security and education expenditures, and the lowering of the basic corporate tax rate from 41 to 39 per cent in 1996. Finally, as in Poland, an extensive privatisation programme was enacted. Small-scale privatisation proceeded very quickly, covering small shops, pubs and restaurants (Duke and Grime 1994: 162). The privatisation act for large-scale enterprises was passed in February 1991. The first wave of large-scale privatisation was completed in May 1993, the second in autumn 1994 (Dangerfield 1997: 445). While there had been some social market policies at the beginning of transition, the Czech Republic took a clearly neo-liberal course under the Klaus government between 1992 and 1996, the crucial years in this process (Dangerfield 1997: 446).

Economic transition in Hungary is frequently considered to have been more gradual than in Poland and the Czech Republic. Yet Halpern and Wyplosz point out that 'in fact, restructuring has been a shock therapy: the very tough bankruptcy law adopted in 1991 has been vigorously implemented, resulting in the closing down of thousands of firms' (Halpern and Wyplosz 1998: 2). Against the background of high levels of foreign debt, the initial reforms did not improve the economic situation, resulting in a situation of relatively small economic growth combined with growing budget deficits. The stabilisation package, passed in March 1995 to rescue the situation, consisted of three key measures: first, budget spending was cut by more than 15 per cent in real terms; second, the currency was devalued and its regime was changed from a fixed to a crawling peg; and third, a commitment to the containment of nominal wage increases was adopted (Halpern and Wyplosz 1998: 5). In addition, the link between the government and central bank was cut and, after the end of 1996, the latter was no longer permitted to finance budget deficits of the state. Large-scale privatisation, relying heavily on FDI, moved rapidly, but 'Hungary's small privatization programme was delayed by uncertainties over the question of reprivatization of property' (Duke and Grime 1994: 166).

Thus, all three countries pursued a strategy of neo-liberal restructuring in their transformation towards a market economy. Most importantly, they relied on austerity budgets to combat high inflation. These were achieved through cut-backs in public spending, vast privatisation programmes and the abolition of planning. Measured in terms of the private sector share of GDP, the transformation can be regarded as a success. In 1997, the private sector was responsible for 75 per cent of GDP in the Czech Republic and Hungary, and 65 per cent in Poland (EBRD 1998: 163, 171, 183). Considering that the communist regimes were discredited and neo-liberalism had gained predominance throughout the Western World, it proved impossible to put forward an alternative. Glasman points to the Solidarity programme of 1981, 'based on the idea of self-organised democratic power and the Catholic social doctrine with its stress on solidarity and co-operation' (Glasman 1994: 195–6), and argues that it provided the basis for a possible social market model along German lines. However, pressure by the West in the form of IMF conditions against the background of high Polish external debt, an increasingly important role of foreign capital in industry and banking, and the inability of the Solidarity movement to contest the prevailing orthodox paradigm meant that neo-liberal restructuring prevailed. At the very outset of transformation, the particular social structure of accumulation of the command economy, Cox argues, included the potential for democratisation combined with socialist reform. This could have taken 'the form either of producer self-management, or of a democratization of the central planning process, or conceivably of some combination of the two' (Cox 1991: 187). In the event, privatisation and the turn to the market economy made this outcome impossible.

Initially, the transformation led to dramatic economic downturns in all three countries. GDP declined especially drastically in Poland, the Czech Republic and Hungary in 1991, by 7, 11.5 and 11.9 per cent respectively (see Table 6.2). Inflation also reached dramatic levels, rising to 585.8 per cent in Poland in 1990 (see Table 6.3). Unemployment rose to more than 10 per cent, a level unprecedented in any of the three countries (see Table 6.4). The only country in the region to escape this trend was the Czech Republic, where unemployment was kept relatively low until 1996 largely due to state intervention through active labour market policies (Pollert 1997: 208–9; see also Bell and Mickiewicz 1999: 142–5). Following wage deregulation and the unravelling of social peace from 1995 onwards, the picture started to resemble that in Poland and Hungary. Unemployment reached levels of 5.2 per cent in 1997 and 7.5 per cent in 1998, and seemed likely to rise further.

In recent years, a general tendency of economic improvement can be identified as far as economic growth rates are concerned, though the Czech Republic in 1997 and 1998 was the exception to this rule (see Table 6.2). Hyper-inflation has clearly been brought under control, but inflation remained above 10 per cent in all three countries in 1998 (see Table 6.3) and was, thus, markedly higher than in the EU (OECD 1998: 206). Most importantly, however, unemployment levels remained high (see Table 6.4). A policy of full employment had been one of the economic priorities of the

Table 6.2 Economic growth in Poland, the Czech Republic and Hungary 1990–98 (% change in GDP from previous period)

	1990	1991	1992	1993	1994	1995	1996	1997	1998
Poland	-11.6	-7.0	2.6	3.8	5.2	7.0	6.1	6.8	4.8
Czech Rep.	-1.2	-11.5	-3.3	0.6	3.2	6.4	3.9	1.0	-2.7
Hungary	-3.5	-11.9	-3.1	-0.6	2.9	1.5	1.3	4.6	5.1

Source: Business Central Europe, http://www.bcemag.com/ (3 June 1999)

Table 6.3 Inflation/Consumer Price Index in Poland, the Czech Republic and Hungary 1990–98 (% change from previous period)

	1990	1991	1992	1993	1994	1995	1996	1997	1998
Poland	585.8	70.3	43.0	35.3	32.2	27.8	19.9	14.9	11.8
Czech Rep.	9.7	56.6	11.1	20.8	10.0	9.1	8.8	8.5	10.7
Hungary	28.9	35.0	23.0	22.5	18.8	28.2	23.6	18.3	14.3

Source: Business Central Europe, http://www.bcemag.com/ (3 June 1999)

Table 6.4 Unemployment rates in Poland, the Czech Republic and Hungary 1990–98 (%)

	1990	1991	1992	1993	1994	1995	1996	1997	1998
Czech Rep.	0.8	4.1	2.6	3.5	3.2	2.9	3.5	5.2	7.5
Hungary	1.9	7.4	12.3	12.1	10.4	10.4	10.5	10.4	9.1
Poland	6.3	11.8	13.6	16.4	16.0	14.9	13.2	10.3	10.4

Source: Business Central Europe, http://www.bcemag.com/ (3 June 1999)

communist regimes in CEE (Standing 1997: 133–4). As in Austria and Sweden, which had pursued a policy of full employment within a capitalist economy along Keynesian lines (see chapter two), neo-liberal restructuring against the background of globalisation has led to persistent high levels of unemployment in all three countries, converging around the EU average of 10 to 11 per cent (OECD 1998: 211). These high levels of unemployment indicate that large sections of the population are excluded from the gains of transformation. They may become the source of resistance to further neo-liberal restructuring, and also to EU membership.

The establishment of liberal democracies

Arguably, some of the most important features of liberal democracies are the open competition between several political parties in free elections, and the formation of trade unions and employers' associations independent from the state. This section concentrates on these issues.

The first two free elections in Poland were contested by a vast array of different parties, and it was not until the 1997 elections that a clearer picture emerged (Król 1999; Vinton 1999). The elections were won by the Solidarity Electoral Action (AWS), which was still a very fragmented assemblage of about thirty centre-right groups. It gained 33.8 per cent of the popular vote and formed a governing coalition with the neo-liberal Democratic Union (UW) which, led by Balcerowicz, won 13.4 per cent of the vote. Attracting 27.1 per cent of the vote, the Democratic Left Alliance (SLD) – an alliance formed around the Social Democracy of the Polish Republic, the successor party of the Polish Communist Party – changed role from governing to main opposition party. The Polish Peasant Party (PSL) continues to play a minor role with 7.3 per cent, and the Movement to Rebuild Poland (ROP) also gained seats in parliament with 5.6 per cent of the vote (Vinton 1999: 73).

The two big trade unions, the OPZZ with 4 million and Solidarity with 2.3 million members have both supported neo-liberal restructuring, the former as an ally of the SLD–PSL government between 1993 and 1997, the latter in the period 1989–93 being closely aligned with the various 'Solidarity' governments. Instead of defending workers' rights together, the two unions are divided between 'post-Communists' (OPZZ) and 'Polish patriots' (Solidarity) (Bartosz 1996: 44). Finally, there is the small Solidarity-80 union, which gained support in its opposition to the Balcerowicz Plan. It is radically anticapitalist in its orientation, but can muster only a few hundred members at its demonstrations. As in other CEE countries, the Polish employers' association, established in 1991, has not been very effective (Standing 1997: 147).

The party system of the Czech Republic was characterised until the 1996 elections by a strong and united centre-right grouping around the neo-liberal Civic Democratic Party (ODS) of prime minister Václav Klaus (Kavan and Palouš 1999: 82). While the unreformed Communist Party (KSCM) retained about 10 per cent of the vote throughout the 1990s, the Czech Social Democratic Party (CSSD), reconstituted shortly after the Velvet Revolution of 1989, emerged as the strongest force on the centre-left in 1996 with 26.4 per cent of the vote, up from 6.5 per cent in 1992. In the elections of 1998, it gained the biggest share of the vote with about 32 per cent and formed a minority government. The extreme right Republican Party (SPR-RSC), which is xenophobic, racist and populist, is another important political force, having gained 8 per cent in the 1996 elections (Pehe 1999: 45).

In contrast to other CEE countries, in the Czech Republic the communist unions were replaced by new ones in 1989–90. The most important union became the Czech and Moravian Confederation of Trade Unions (CMKOS). Initially, the unions supported the neo-liberal economic policies of the government, partly due to their involvement in corporatist institutions and partly due to low unemployment. By 1995, however, it was clear that the government wanted to dismantle corporatism and give up the policy of full employment. As a consequence, mass demonstrations took place and the trade unions took a more adversarial line with government (Pollert 1997: 209–15). There are several independent employers' associations in the Czech Republic, the actions of which are co-ordinated in the Co-ordination Board of Unions and Associations of Employers (Standing 1997: 147).

In Hungary, the first years of transformation were governed by christian-conservative parties, with the Hungarian Democratic Forum (MDF) as the most important. (Bozóki 1999: 109). In 1994, however, the Hungarian Socialist Party (MSZP), the re-formed former Communist Party, won a clear election victory with 54.1 per cent of the vote. This was reversed in 1998 when public dissatisfaction with the MSZP's economic austerity policies led to its electoral defeat. This time, the neo-liberal Alliance of Young Democrats (FIDESZ) won the election with 38 per cent of the vote. On the extreme right of the party system is the anti-liberal and radical rightist Party of Hungarian Truth and Life (MIEP), which gained parliamentary representation in 1998 for the first time with 3.6 per cent of the vote (Fricz 1999: 84, 86 and 88). Finally, some unreformed communists set up the Workers' Party (MP). It has failed to enter parliament, 'although it is still probably the strongest extra-parliamentary party, with roughly 3 per cent of the vote' (Bozóki 1999: 112).

In 1990, the National Trade Union Council of the communist period dissolved itself into four successor organisations. Despite their past, they remained stronger than two newly formed unions (Girndt 1996). As elsewhere in the region, employers' associations are extremely fragmented; in the tripartite council, nine different organisations represent the employers' side (Girndt 1996: 50–1). In all three countries, corporatist institutions have been established, but they clearly lack the degree of representativeness and effectiveness in wage setting, which their counterparts in Austria and Sweden (until 1990–91) have enjoyed (Bell and Mickiewicz 1999: 131–4).

In sum, liberal democratic party systems and independent trade unions and employers' associations have been established in all three countries and form important parts of the institutional framework within which social forces have struggled over EU membership. All the main parties, be they from the centre-right or reformed former communist parties, have accepted neo-liberal transformation and, by extension, EU membership (as discussed in the next section). In all three countries, however, there are also extreme right-wing parties and, with the exception of Poland, unreformed small communist parties. They attract the losers in the transformation process and may be well placed to lead the resistance to accession to the EU, which is correctly perceived as a continuation of neo-liberal restructuring.

Poland, the Czech Republic, Hungary and the question of EU membership

Hungary applied to the EU for membership on 31 March 1994, and Poland a few days later on 5 April; the Czech Republic followed on 17 January 1996. In the case of all three countries, application to the EU had been part of a twofold strategy to integrate with the West. On the one hand, 'joining NATO has come to be seen by the CEE countries as the only credible guarantee of long-term defence' (Grabbe and Hughes 1998: 110; see also Avery and Cameron 1998: 158–74). Poland, the Czech Republic and Hungary were invited to become NATO members in July 1997. In the economic sphere, they looked to the prosperous EU. Hence, as in Austria and Sweden, EU membership was not regarded as a way of gaining security guarantees. This may be a motive for those countries, which have been refused NATO membership, but even this is doubtful (Smith 1999: 61–2).

In contrast to neutral Austria and Sweden, the CFSP is less likely to cause domestic problems for the three NATO members.

Against the background of global pressures and neo-liberal restructuring in all three countries, applying to join the EU can clearly be regarded as a logical step. The EU itself had been undergoing neo-liberal restructuring in its Internal Market programme and the Treaty of Maastricht and, due to geographical proximity and its promises of wealth, had been the obvious regional organisation to join. Nevertheless, while application was a logical extension of neo-liberal restructuring at home, it also implied a reinforcement of this process. The most important elements of the EU's enlargement strategy clearly demanded adaptation to EU rules, and thus measures of liberalisation and deregulation. The EAs mainly focused on the free movement of goods and had the task of achieving alignment of the applicants' laws with EU norms, in particular in the areas of competition and state aid rules. Importantly, 'they can tie the CEE countries into trade liberalization and counter domestic pressure for protection' (Grabbe and Hughes 1998: 33).

In June 1995, the Cannes European Council passed the Internal Market White Paper, which extended the alignment process to the free movement of services and capital. It identified the key areas of legislation and the necessary administrative and technical structures for its implementation (Preston 1997: 202–3). Applicant countries were left with the task of drawing up programmes and timetables for implementation of legislation. In short, again, the CEE-10 were locked into a process of neo-liberal restructuring on their way towards membership.

The move towards membership was strongly impelled by foreign TNCs and international finance companies which had invested in the three countries, and by the domestic business communities in export-oriented sectors, which have re-oriented their trade towards the EU since 1989. Trade unions have been less involved so far, since they are weakened due to their fragmentation and the need to restructure themselves (Grabbe and Hughes 1998: 76; Interview no. 73; London, 16 June 1999). Thus, transnational social forces and internationally-oriented forces of capital are clearly behind the drive for membership. In all three countries, they captured the major parliamentary parties, which have subscribed to neo-liberal restructuring and EU membership. This is most clearly visible in the fact that both issues remained at the top of the agenda despite changes in government. Coalition governments led by reformed former communist parties continued the drive towards membership between 1994 and 1998 in Hungary, and between 1993 and 1997 in Poland, a movement which had been started in both countries by centre-right coalition governments. Similarly, the change in power from the ODS-led, centre-right government to the CSSD government in the Czech Republic in 1998 did not derail the membership course.

Although popular support for membership is high in all three countries

(Grabbe and Hughes 1998: 82), this does not signify that referenda on eventual accession treaties will inevitably be an easy win for the 'yes' sides. It is frequently pointed out that there is a general lack of detailed knowledge of the EU and debate about the implications of membership (Bozóki 1999: 120; Król 1999: 71; Millard 1999: 203). When the costs and losers of membership become apparent during the negotiation of difficult issues, stronger anti-EU movements may by formed. 'In all the countries there remain many sectors which have low productivity and survive behind protective barriers of one sort or another' (Mayhew 1998: 353). It is these sectors of nationally-oriented social forces, which are most likely to generate opposition to membership. Additionally, as stated earlier, transformation has meant the social exclusion of significant portions of the population, and they are also potential opponents of the EU.

In Poland, it is the mining industry and the steel sector in particular which may cause problems. They would lose state aid in the form of, for example, tax exemptions, and some coal mines may even have to be closed down as a consequence of EU membership. While it is argued that restructuring and especially privatisation of these sectors is necessary anyway, it may be linked to the question of membership, especially as some within the government use the preparation for entry as an argument to make these developments appear inevitable. In 1996, coal mining and the steel industry were responsible for 7.6 per cent and 4.2 per cent of the country's global export production respectively. This may appear small, but restructuring implies drastic job losses. It is estimated that restructuring of the steel industry will lead to 40,000 unemployed workers. In the coal mining industry, employment sank from 312,000 in 1993 to 243,000 in 1997 and is expected to fall to approximately 204,000 in 2002 (Interview no. 72; London, 15 June 1999). In September 1997, angry miners organised by the Solidarity-80 trade union attacked Balcerowicz, the architect of Polish neo-liberal transformation, for bankrupting the coal mines (*Financial Times*, 16 September 1997: 3). Solidarity-80 may well be able to organise nationally-oriented labour against membership more generally.

The second problematic Polish sector is agriculture. Prices are much lower than under the CAP regime and some efficient Polish farmers would gain from accession. Agriculture in general, however, is an extremely inefficient, if not backward sector. It employs 27 per cent of the working population, but produces only 6 per cent of GDP. The majority of the two million small farms, which do not produce for export, are unlikely to survive membership, and this raises the prospect of rising unemployment in rural areas (*Financial Times*, 25 March 1998, Survey: 4).[3] These worries are compounded by the EU's intention not to extend farm subsidies available to current members to farmers in the new member states from the beginning of accession. There is a general fear of the inflow of highly subsidised EU products, with which Polish farmers could not compete. Finally, there are worries about the possibility of West Europeans buying up the significantly cheaper Polish land (Interview no. 72; London, 15 June 1999).

In short, there is a large reservoir of possible discontent by nationally-oriented forces in the agricultural sector. This potential opposition may be organised by Solidarity RI, the trade union's rural arm. Although it supports the current coalition government of AWS and UW, it has already organised a demonstration by farmers in Warsaw demanding that farmers must benefit from the CAP regime from day one of membership (*Financial Times*, 25 March 1998, Survey: 4). The PSL, whose support comes predominantly from small farmers, may be another institution rallying these forces. Although it is generally supportive of membership, it makes its support dependent on a negotiation outcome that is acceptable for agriculture (Interview no. 72; London, 15 June 1999; see also Millard 1999: 206–7).

The AWS itself is not necessarily united in favour of full neo-liberal restructuring and EU membership. The broad electoral alliance includes significant forces of anti-European clerical nationalists, and strong sections of labour in mining and shipbuilding, exactly those areas, which require restructuring prior to accession (Millard 1999: 211–14). Finally, the ROP, although not openly against membership, had spoken out against restructuring and privatisation, trying to defend small and medium-sized Polish companies against competition by foreign capital. This stance could easily lead to an anti-EU position and indeed, the ROP is frequently described as 'comparable to the anti-establishment and anti-European parties of the extreme right in western Europe such as Haider's Freedom Party of Austria or Le Pen's National Front in France' (Millard 1999: 212–13).

In the Czech Republic, agriculture and the issue of land purchase by foreigners, especially of privatised state farm land, is a potential problem for the negotiations with the EU and may, if not satisfactorily solved, create resistance to EU membership (*Financial Times*, 10 November 1998: 3). Overall, however, agriculture is of little importance for the national economy and employs only 5 per cent of the workforce (*Financial Times*, 8 July 1998: 2). Economic restructuring had been accepted by workers and trade unions until 1994–5, mainly due to the continuing low rate of unemployment. The unravelling of industrial peace from 1995 onwards resulted, however, in open conflict. Between 1995 and 1997, strikes against low wages and restructuring in the public sector involved rail workers, teachers, doctors and nurses (Pollert 1997: 213). Further restructuring is required prior to accession and it is acknowledged that this may lead to open resistance to EU membership.[4] Restructuring of the steel and mining sectors to prepare the Czech Republic for membership may also cause public friction. Trade unions enjoy strong support in both sectors (Pollert 1997: 212) and could provide leadership for the resistance to the EU, if membership is linked to further restructuring. The extreme right-wing SPR-RSC and the communist KSCM, which both enjoyed considerable electoral success in the 1990s, also have a strong potential to rally opposition. The former follows a clearly nationalist and xenophobic strategy and opposes EU membership. The latter not only rejected the Czech privatisation programme, but has also objected to the country's integration with the western institutions of NATO and the EU (Pehe 1999: 40).

As in Poland and the Czech Republic, the purchase of agricultural land may be a problem for Hungary during the negotiations and, in the event of an unfavourable outcome, cause domestic hostility to membership. The country's negotiators are likely to ask for a transition period in this respect. Similarly, the EU's refusal to extend CAP payments to new members from the beginning may cause unrest in this sector. Overall, however, agriculture is much smaller and more efficient than in Poland – 6.6 per cent of the workforce are employed full-time contributing 8 per cent of GDP – and should not be a serious obstacle to membership. Further resistance may come from some small domestic transport companies and some professions such as lawyers and economists, which may lose out to higher competition within the EU (Interview no. 73; London, 16 June 1999). This resistance may be taken up by the right-wing MIEP and/or the communist MP. Both have rejected integration into Western institutions, whether NATO or the EU (Bozóki 1999: 119).

To conclude, in all three countries neo-liberal hegemonic projects were formulated in response to the fall of the communist regimes after 1989. In order to become effective, these projects needed to be translated into domestic and foreign policy at the state level (Holman 1998: 26). This was achieved via neo-liberal restructuring of the economic and political systems at the domestic level, and integration into NATO and (most likely) the EU at the international level, the latter strategy reinforcing the former. Thus, the three countries have been fully integrated into the global economy and transnational class formation, the drive towards EU membership being part and parcel of this process. The possible resistance to membership clearly needs more analysis, but it is already visible to some extent at this stage.

7 Conclusions

Globalisation, EU enlargement and the limits of neo-liberalism

A neo-Gramscian perspective as an alternative approach to European integration

Throughout the post-war era, Austria and Sweden remained outside the EU, because both countries considered membership to be incompatible with their neutral status and a threat to their social democratic achievements of full employment, a generous welfare state and increasing equality in society. Against the background of globalisation, however, Austria and Sweden, like other Western countries, although slightly later, experienced the end of the Fordist accumulation regime and endured dramatic economic recessions at the beginning of the 1980s. Belief in the superiority of the two countries' economic and political systems was eroded, and they were eventually abandoned, in Austria in 1985–6 and in Sweden approximately five years later, when the 'third way' strategy had also failed. In this situation, rather than appearing a threat, the EU, revived around the Internal Market initiative, offered some hope for a fast recovery and help with the necessary restructuring of the apparently backward Austrian and Swedish state–society relations. In addition, the international security system was changing. While this did not push Austria and Sweden towards membership, it ensured that neutrality was a much less severe obstacle to EU membership than during the previous four decades. Gorbachev's liberal foreign policy and the decline of the Soviet Union in the case of Austria, and the end of the Cold War in the case of Sweden made a redefinition of neutrality and, thus, the formulation of a pro-membership project feasible. While the rough outlines of the story can be told quickly, this does not throw much light upon the actual processes leading first to application and then to membership after a referendum. It does not reveal anything about the main actors involved, the opposition put forward against the EU and the reasons why the pro-membership forces won. To do this, a theoretical lens is required for the analysis.

In chapter one, it was demonstrated that established theories of integration have to date been unable to provide an adequate lens in this respect. Neo-functionalism, although it experienced a revival in the wake of the new dynamics of European integration from 1985 onwards, was a partial explanation at best. It was employed to highlight the role of transnational actors and central EU institutions, but the original notion of automatic spill-over excluded a full-scale neo-functionalist analysis of Austria's and Sweden's accession to the EU. Intergovernmentalist approaches also had their limits. They failed to take into account the impact of neo-liberalism as a set of economic ideas and the role of transnational actors such as Swedish TNCs. Their concentration on the negotiations between states overlooked the crucial importance of the processes leading to application and the conflicts around the referenda on membership. In sum, because neo-functionalist and intergovernmentalist approaches took existing power structures as given, they, first, could not take into account the structural change of globalisation since the early 1970s. Furthermore, their determinism incorrectly made enlargement appear to have been a historically inevitable development.

The neo-Gramscian perspective developed in this study focused on social forces, engendered by the production process, as the most important collective actors. Thus, globalisation became accessible, since the emergence of new social forces resulting from the transnationalisation of finance and production could be incorporated. This led to an intra-class conflict in both countries. In Austria, nationally-oriented social forces of capital and labour opposed internationally-oriented forces. Both were engendered by a domestic production structure, but had a different geographical orientation as expressed in their trading patterns. By contrast in Sweden, labour mainly from the national, public sector opposed transnational social forces represented in the Swedish TNCs.

In addition, the focus on class struggle as the heuristic model for understanding structural change showed that there are no inevitable developments in history. Swedish and Austrian accession to the EU was neither an automatic process of spill-over, nor a response to structural necessity in the wake of a new international distribution of economic and military capabilities. Rather, it was one of several possible outcomes of an open-ended struggle between different social forces against the background of global structural change.

The focus on social forces did not imply that the state was excluded from the analysis. In contrast to state-centric approaches, however, it was not assumed to be a unitary actor, but split into the various state institutions, which were treated according to their place in the global economy. A distinction was made between institutions linked to the global economy and those which merely dealt with national issues. Moreover, parties and interest associations were deemed important in the domestic policy-making process. Nevertheless, they were not regarded as unitary actors, but as institutions, within which various social forces attempted to establish their particular interest as the one generally accepted.

Finally, in contrast to established integration theories, the neo-Gramscian perspective was able to account adequately for the role of ideas. The importance of neo-liberalism as a part of the structure in the form of intersubjective meanings could thus be highlighted. This made it extremely difficult for forces opposed to the EU to formulate a convincing alternative to membership. At the same time, pro-EU social forces gained credibility for their course of action by justifying accession to the EU in neo-liberal terms. Membership simply appeared to be the natural solution to Austria's and Sweden's economic problems.

Although this study showed that a neo-Gramscian perspective is a viable alternative approach to EU enlargement, some qualifications need to be made. In chapters one and two, it was argued that globalisation is likely to result in cross-class alliances between transnational/internationally-oriented capital and labour on the one hand and national capital and labour on the other. This proved to be correct in the Austrian and Swedish cases. Nevertheless, the firmness of such inter-class alliances should not be exaggerated. It was previously pointed out that the alliance of transnational capital and labour in favour of EU membership in Sweden was formed to achieve an identical goal for totally different purposes. In Austria, the alliance was strong enough to form a historical bloc. This did not, however, imply that there were no conflicts between internationally-oriented capital and labour. As the Association of the Austrian Textile Industry made clear, while labour and capital of this sector pursued membership for the same reasons, no combined strategy was devised. The employers did not want to give labour any kind of bargaining chip for future wage-negotiations (Interview no. 24; Vienna, 24 April 1996). In short, inter-class alliances are likely against the background of globalisation, but the main conflict in capitalism is still between capital and labour as such.

A second qualification is that the neo-Gramscian emphasis on organic intellectuals and hegemonic projects tended to give the impression that events such as the application and accession to the EU could only occur via a well-developed project. The Swedish case contradicted this. Considering transnational capital's pressure on the SAP through the transfer of production units to the EU, it can be concluded that structural power might make long-term political strategies unnecessary. A hegemonic project in Sweden can only be identified by looking at a longer period between the mid-1970s and the early 1990s, when transnational Swedish capital led by the SAF was engaged in the successful launch of a neo-liberal project against the Swedish Model. EU membership was only the logical last step in this undertaking.

Finally, as stated earlier, the results of this analysis cannot be generalised and transferred to other cases of EU enlargement. It is not the goal of critical theories such as this neo-Gramscian perspective to generate general findings. Chapter six on the possible enlargement of the EU towards CEE demonstrated, however, that the method itself can successfully be transferred.

There are several further studies, which attempt to analyse aspects of European integration from a neo-Gramscian perspective. Holman investigates the general integration of Spain into the Western European capitalist system (Holman: 1996). Other studies employ neo-Gramscian concepts for the explanation of the role of the European Round Table of Industrialists in the process leading to the Internal Market (van Apeldoorn and Holman 1994; Holman and van der Pijl 1996). Gill analyses EMU as a case of 'new institutionalism', defined as a disciplinary framework of governance, which seeks to separate economic policies from political accountability (Gill 1998). A more comprehensive attempt at explaining an instance of European integration is van Apeldoorn's analysis of the possible developments of a future European model of capitalism (van Apeldoorn 1996). Further case studies are also contained in Holman *et al.* (1998). In short, it is clear from these studies that neo-Gramscian perspectives may be useful as an approach to the study of European integration more generally beyond the narrow empirical focus of EU enlargement.

Social forces behind the Austrian and Swedish accession to the EU

During the process leading to application between May 1987 and June 1989, a historical bloc was formed in Austria which consisted of an alliance of internationally-oriented social forces of capital and labour. It was rooted in the economic structure through its location in the internationally-oriented sector of production; it extended into the superstructure by defining the dominant ideas of a neo-liberal economic policy and a re-interpretation of neutrality deemed compatible with EU membership. It formed a solid structure of political society and civil society by encompassing both institutions of the state apparatus (such as the ANB and the Finance and Economic Ministries) and organisations of civil society including the two main parties SPÖ and ÖVP and the four social partners, the BWK, the LK, the AK and the ÖGB. The driving force behind the establishment of this historical bloc was provided by the organic intellectuals of the VÖI. They developed the hegemonic project based on the re-interpretation of neutrality and on neo-liberalism, arguing that EU membership and participation in the Internal Market would lead to more efficiency via higher competition and eventually to the creation of wealth and more jobs. The historical bloc was reconfirmed after the success of the negotiations. The protected industrial sectors and the agricultural sector were guaranteed help for financial restructuring and the setting-up of work foundations. While an ideological consensus was an important element of the historical bloc, material pay-outs were also crucial in attracting other social forces.

In Sweden, there was an alliance of transnational social forces of capital and labour and forces emanating from the agricultural sector in favour of membership. They were supported by the institutions linked to the global economy, notably the Prime Minister's Office and the Ministry of Finance. In contrast to Austria, however, this alliance did not develop into a historical bloc. While its members agreed on the need for EU membership, their social purposes differed significantly. On the one hand, transnational capital regarded membership as a way of continuing the neo-liberal drive which had dismantled the Swedish Model in the early 1990s. They were not interested in a strong social dimension or joint employment programmes at the EU level. The convergence criteria, regarded as a guarantee for the continuation of neo-liberalism, should not be watered down or amended. Transnational social forces of labour, on the other hand, viewed the EU as a broader context in which to regain some control over capital. Globalisation, it was argued, made autonomous national economic policy-making impossible. The EU, therefore, provided a platform to counter the increased power of the global financial market and TNCs and to modify, if not to halt, neo-liberalism.

A second apparent difference in Sweden was the lack of a hegemonic project related to EU membership. There was no institution similar to the VÖI, which provided the platform for organic intellectuals to launch a project of this type. Two clear reasons for this can be identified. First, in contrast to the SPÖ, the SAP had been hegemonic in the Swedish party system and, therefore, it had to take the decision on application. Until the economic recession of 1989–90, the SAP had always considered an EEA-type strategy *vis-à-vis* the EU to be sufficient. Only when it had lost confidence in its own ability to run the economy differently from the rest of Europe after the 'third way' strategy had failed, did the SAP start to change its economic policy. In the course of 1990, it first accepted that full employment could no longer be the primary policy objective and then announced its decision in parliament to apply to the EU. Second, Swedish capital did not face the same absolute necessity of formulating a political strategy as in Austria. The transnational production structure and the deregulation of the Swedish financial markets gave it the structural power to transfer production units to the EU. Thereby, it became a part of the Internal Market and applied pressure on the SAP government towards application at the same time. In the end, the ongoing capital flight was a major reason why the SAP saw no other option than to seek EU membership. In Austria, on the other hand, internationally-oriented capital, with its national production structure, had to achieve membership in order to gain access to the Internal Market. The transfer of production units was not a viable option.

In both countries, significant opposition had formed against EU membership. Chapter six identified the potential for similar resistance in Poland, the Czech Republic and Hungary. The final section analyses the extent to which these forces may become the basis for a counter neo-liberal hegemonic project at the national and European level.

The possibilities for a counter neo-liberal project

As indicated in chapter one, this neo-Gramscian perspective as a critical theory is also interested in social and political transformation. An analysis of empirical events is not an end in itself. Rather, it is a 'useful way of understanding the social and political world in order to change it' (Cox 1987: 393). The analysis of Austria's and Sweden's accession to the EU provides a clear picture of the configuration of social forces at the Austrian and Swedish form of state level. In this way, it helps to identify those social forces and ideas, which could be the basis of a future alliance or even historical bloc against neo-liberalism.

As Cox outlines, Gramsci distinguished between 'war of movement' and 'war of position'. In Russia, Gramsci argued, the administrative and coercive apparatus of the state had been well developed, but civil society was rather weak. Therefore, a 'war of movement' by Lenin and the Bolsheviks, which immediately occupied state power, was able to succeed. In Western Europe, by contrast, the rule of the bourgeois state was closely linked to a much more developed civil society. Hence, a 'war of position' was required, 'which slowly builds up the strength of the social foundations of a new state' (Cox 1983: 165). The high development of civil society and its close links to the political state apparatus in Western European countries make Gramsci's analysis about the impossibility of 'war of movements' even more valid in today's context. A counter neo-liberal historical bloc must be prepared and established within civil society before an assault on the state can be successful. Importantly, this has to occur from the bottom up since, if it happens from the top down, the hegemonic forces 'influence the development of [the] current version of civil society towards making it an agency for stabilizing the social and political status quo' (Cox 1999: 11).

The levels of such a bottom-up strategy, however, are not exactly clear. Murphy, for example, speaks about an international civil society, which he identifies as public and private institutions such as governmental and non-governmental international organisations (Murphy 1994: 14). This would indicate that a counter neo-liberal 'war of position' at the international level was feasible. Germain and Kenny, however, point out that Gramsci's concept of society was closely linked to the state and, since there is no international state, there can be no international society (Germain and Kenny 1998: 14–17). It is consequently correct to agree with Cox that 'the task of changing world order begins with the long laborious effort to build new historical blocs within national boundaries' (Cox 1983: 174).

Nevertheless, the EU can be perceived as a macro-region within the capitalist world economy with specific, historically-determined socio-economic and political structures, where supranational institutions such as the EP and the Commission adopt similar roles to their counterparts within states and complex policy-making processes link a host of interest groups to decision-making (van Apeldoorn 1996: 19). Caporaso, defining 'state' as an enduring structure of governance, concludes that 'the EU . . . is already an international state' (Caporaso 1996: 33). It may, thus, be possible to think about a European civil society in addition to national civil societies. A counter neo-liberal movement could, therefore, also be developed at the EU level from within European civil society.

The possibility of counter neo-liberal projects at the Austrian and Swedish level

The Austrian historical bloc achieved its aim of accession to the EU, but only obtained a position of supremacy, not hegemony. As indicated in chapter one, resistance to capitalist exploitation of the reproduction sphere can be of a progressive or a nationalist type. In Austria, the FPÖ's xenophobic anti-EU campaign, concentrating on issues such as anti-immigration with 'Austria first' slogans and stressing the importance of national sovereignty including the maintenance of the AS, clearly represented the latter type. The same is valid with regard to the anti-EU *Bürgerinitiative gegen den Verkauf Österreichs an die EU*, which warned against the flooding of Austria by foreigners and the sell-out of Austria's wealth. These forces can hardly be considered a potential part of an emancipatory project against and beyond capitalist exploitation.

The GA, in contrast, put up progressive opposition to EU membership. The *Initiative Österreich und Europe* before the application and the *Kritische Europainformationen* during the campaign exhibited a similar tendency. Instead of retreating inside a nationalist outlook, the GA favoured active co-operation in Europe between sovereign states in tandem with reforms at the national level. Rather than concentrating on efficiency via neo-liberal convergence criteria, it gave economic priority to environmental and social standards and an environmentally-friendly agriculture. An expansive fiscal policy to create employment was also demanded. At the security level, an integrated, co-operative security system based on all-European organisations such as the CSCE was favoured over the EU, which was alleged to have developed into a military bloc. Austria's neutral status in its original meaning could provide a useful role in building bridges between Eastern and Western Europe and, thus, become one of the constitutive elements of a future European security system.

By contrast, there was no nationalist, reactionary challenge to the neo-liberal EU membership project in Sweden. All opposition forces were part of the same anti-EU campaign group. The VP and GP had been sceptical about closer ties with the EU throughout the 1980s and rejected the party compromise of spring 1988. After the Swedish application to the EU, these forces were joined by large parts of the SAP and CP, but also national sector trade unions mainly from the public sector. Membership was opposed as a threat to the Swedish Model with its policies of full employment, a generous welfare system and gender equality. In the same way as the Austrian GA, the VP and GP argued that the EU and CFSP compromised Sweden's neutrality and, thus, undermined its potential role as a bridge-builder between East and West in the new European security order.

While the social forces opposing the EU were quite strong in Austria, they proved unable to form a joint platform based on a common project which offered a credible alternative to the EU. Co-operation with the FPÖ seemed to be neither possible nor desirable for the GA. Nevertheless, the links between the GA and nationally-oriented labour and, where possible, nationally-oriented capital and dissatisfied forces in the agricultural sector could be improved. Only this would undermine the support for the FPÖ, which is supported by many dissatisfied workers and small farmers. More importantly, this would provide a clear economic basis for a counter neo-liberal project, which must be rooted in the structure in order to have any chance to challenge the Austrian neo-liberal pro-EU bloc successfully.

Furthermore, within the superstructure, a hegemonic project should be developed around issues of a collective security system via the CSCE and an economic strategy which considers good environmental and social standards and full employment to be more important than efficiency, competition and high levels of economic growth. In this respect, it is important to challenge the neo-liberal wisdom, which has acquired a status of natural truth during the processes of globalisation. Economic co-operation is not to be excluded, but should move away from the EMU convergence criteria. This will not be easy and requires a long 'war of position'. Institutions should be set up, which could provide the platform for organic intellectuals and for the development and promotion of an alternative to neo-liberalism.

The situation was similar in Sweden. Although there was no right-wing competitor in the rejection of the EU, apart from opposing membership, the 'no' side did not develop a coherent alternative to membership. The potentially strong platform that national labour and the GP and VP might have shared was undermined by the refusal of the former to give the two parties a stronger role within the 'no' camp. Provided this can be remedied, an economic basis exists from which to mount the challenge to neo-liberalism. At the ideological level, a strong hegemonic project could be formed around the traditional values of the Swedish Model. The economic area was where the 'no' side failed most notably during the referendum campaign, and this weakness needs to be corrected, even if it means the loss of some forces of the CP, which have supported a neo-liberal economic policy. As in Austria, the continuing importance of neutrality and the emphasis on the CSCE for the formation of a collective security system in Europe could be put forward as security policy.

The struggle against EU membership was lost at the national level in Austria and Sweden. European integration, however, is not static and may offer new areas for resistance in the future. In Sweden, for example, which unlike Austria did not join the final stage of EMU in January 1999, EMU will be one of the most important issues in the near future and it is here that the forces opposed to neo-liberalism can open up a new site of struggle. EMU may even provide an issue around which transnational and national labour, split over EU membership, could form an alliance.

The European level

In Sweden, labour in the transnational sector favoured EU membership, hoping that some countervailing measures against pure neo-liberalism could be devised at the European level in co-operation with forces from other member states. There has been no similar fraction of social forces in Austria. Both internationally-oriented capital and labour regarded EU membership and the convergence criteria as an economic necessity. Nevertheless, Austrian social forces of labour were disappointed about the lack of a social dimension or employment target in the convergence criteria. Although they did not express it as clearly as Swedish trade unions, they also hoped that the social dimension of the EU offered some compensation for lost influence at the national level and opportunities to control TNCs in a better way. Additionally, Austrian internationally-oriented capital had never been in favour of pure neo-liberalism. The VÖI did not regard the end of consultations with organised labour within the corporatist institutions of the ESP as desirable (Interview no. 18; Vienna, 22 May 1995). The employers' association of the textile industry even demanded the regulation of social standards and wage costs at the European level to create a level playing field for the companies from all countries in this sector (Interview no. 24; Vienna, 24 April 1996). In the end, it was also Austrian capital's more co-operative outlook, which helped to form the historical bloc in favour of membership. Thus, the forces of Austrian internationally-oriented capital and labour might both become part of an alliance which attempts to achieve some social regulation of the market economy.

While neo-liberalism is firmly entrenched in the EU via the Internal Market and the EMU convergence criteria, a full neo-liberal course is not the only possible future development for the Union. Van Apeldoorn identifies four ideal-typical ideological and strategic orientations currently put forward by different alliances of social forces: neo-liberalism (globalism), neo-mercantilism (Europeanism), embedded neo-liberalism and European social democracy (van Apeldoorn 1996: 17–27). The further development of the social dimension and a common policy against unemployment are currently the most important issues in the struggle against neo-liberalism at the European level.

The chances for success of a counter neo-liberal strategy at the European level are, however, unclear. In 1989, the Commission put forward an action programme of forty-seven proposed measures, the so-called 'Social Charter', focusing primarily on the establishment of common minimum standards and employee information and consultation procedures. The European Works Councils directive in June 1994 was the most far-reaching result of the Social Charter in that it laid the basis for transnational industrial relations procedures within TNCs operating across the EU (Hall 1994: 299). The Social Chapter/Social Policy Protocol of the Treaty of Maastricht extended the more informal arrangements of the Social Charter and incorporated it into the EU Treaty. It gave the Community direct and extensive legal competence in the social policy field, and provided for direct participation of trade unions and employers' associations (Hall 1994: 301). Nevertheless, how far a common social policy will go remains to be seen (for a recent evaluation, see Falkner 1998).

Even less has been achieved in the area of common policies against unemployment. It was the Commission's White Paper on 'Growth, Competitiveness, Employment', which brought the issue of unemployment on to the agenda of the EU in 1993. Although it still expressed some traditional social democratic values, the paper as such accepted the neo-liberal explanation of unemployment by transnational European capital. Hence, lower unemployment was linked to the notion of higher competitiveness and labour market flexibility (van Apeldoorn 1998: 25–30). In June 1997, the new French Prime Minister, Lionel Jospin, demanded a chapter on employment in the Amsterdam Treaty. This was in exchange for France's acceptance of the Stability Pact, which aimed to ensure countries' compliance with the convergence criteria after the final stage of EMU had started. A compromise was found in the 'Resolution on Growth and Employment', which provided Union employment guidelines while employment policy as such remained a national competence (Devuyst 1998: 624).

In contrast to the hopes of transnational labour, the EU has shown little inclination so far to provide the platform for a successful regulation of neo-liberalism and transnational capital. In the post-war era, it has been at the national level that unions have exercised influence. As Falkner (1998) demonstrates, a corporatist policy community has emerged in EU social policy since the Treaty of Maastricht in 1991. Capital and labour can negotiate collective agreements and then request the Council of Ministers to implement these agreements without discussing their contents. She also points out, however, that while the institutional framework for labour's influence on social policy-making has at least partly been established at the EU level, this does not imply that the outcome is automatically a regulation of neo-liberalism. This is only one possible result of an open-ended struggle.

Counter neo-liberal forces in Poland, the Czech Republic and Hungary

Nationally-oriented capital is unlikely to mount a challenge to membership. It is simply overpowered by foreign TNCs and finance companies. Additionally, many of the companies in the nationally-oriented sectors of mining and steel are still state-owned and the government may use the EU as an excuse for pushing through restructuring and privatisation. Trade unions in these sectors may oppose membership, but in general they are too fragmented to pose a serious challenge. They have also steadily lost members in recent years. For example, in the Czech Republic, 'CMKOS's membership had declined from 3.5 million in 1993 to 2.7 million in 1994 and unions reported increasing difficulties in organizing members, both because of anti-union employers and the fragmentation of former large state companies into small units' (Pollert 1997: 220). Moreover, workers may actually benefit from membership, since 'EU standards promise better working conditions, equal opportunities, improvements in living standards and the introduction of means to enforce these rights' (Bell and Mickiewicz 1999: 145).

Cirtautas points out that nationalism is gaining in strength throughout CEE and may rival neo-liberal transformation (Cirtautas 1994; see also Mayhew 1998: 202). In Poland, a project of nationalist resistance, similar to the one of the Austrian FPÖ, could be led by the ROP, which wants to defend Polish interests against foreign exploitation. It may be supported by the PSL, especially if the negotiation settlement in agriculture is unsatisfactory, and important parts of the AWS which, as noted in chapter six, contains strong elements of clerical nationalism. The right-wing SPR–RSC may lead resistance in the Czech Republic around a nationalist anti-EU movement. Its overall chance of success, however, looks thin considering that it failed to re-enter parliament in the 1998 elections (*Economist*, 27 June 1998). Finally in Hungary, it is the right-wing MIEP, which could develop nationalist resistance. The positions of the KSCM in the Czech Republic and the MP in Hungary are still unclear and it is yet to be seen which type of rejection their programme will take, once the negotiations have been completed and the referenda come closer.

In sum, resistance to membership is likely to be small in all three countries. In contrast to Austria and Sweden, where the post-war Keynesian welfare state had not lost complete credibility, the communist systems in CEE are fully discredited and it has, therefore, been much easier for neo-liberalism to triumph. If resistance to the EU and neo-liberal restructuring is going to occur, then it is most likely to be of the nationalist, reactionary variant. With the possible exception of the small Solidarity-80 union in Poland, there is currently no party or interest association in the three countries that is likely to develop progressive resistance to capitalist exploitation.

To conclude, EU enlargement against the background of globalisation has clearly been a neo-liberal project and thus part and parcel of transnational restructuring. The success of enlargement indicates the strong global position of neo-liberalism. First it overcame the Keynesian welfare state in Austria and Sweden and now it is presented to the former communist systems in CEE as the only possibility of transformation.

Nevertheless, resistance to neo-liberalism has not completely been overcome. At the European level, there are attempts at regulation and while the chances of success currently look dim, this may not be the case in the future. Resistance at the national level is still strong in Austria and Sweden and, although to a much lesser extent, present in Poland, the Czech Republic and Hungary. With increasing exploitation of the production and reproduction spheres, these forces may become stronger. They could form an alliance with other national forces and with those forces which try to overcome neo-liberalism at the European level, and eventually be in a position to challenge neo-liberalism more successfully at both the national and European level. Importantly, a progressive and internationalist hegemonic project needs to be formed, around which these forces can rally, because the nationalist, reactionary response to exploitation cannot provide an emancipatory way forward.

Notes

1 Introduction

1   It is only since the Treaty of Maastricht in 1991 that one speaks of the European Union. Nevertheless, for the sake of consistency the term EU is used throughout the book.
2   The WEU was established in 1954 by those Western European countries, which were willing to co-operate in military matters. It was reactivated from October 1984 onwards because of the perceived need for a European view on security and has nine members, made up of all EU members at the time of the signing of the Treaty of Maastricht except for Ireland, Denmark and Greece.
3   For a detailed outline of a neo-Gramscian perspective on the agency–structure problem in IR, see Bieler and Morton (1999).
4   Other neo-Gramscians also make the distinction between the two concepts. Rupert considers the historical bloc to be a precondition for hegemony (Rupert 1995: 29). This implies that there is no hegemony without a historical bloc, but not the other way round. Augelli and Murphy speak about a period during which the USA under Reagan in the 1980s was hegemonic within the Western World and exerted coercive domination over various Third World countries. In other words, they conceive a situation in which a historical bloc combines hegemonic rule in some areas with coercive rule in others (Augelli and Murphy 1993: 134–6).
5   The concept of 'hegemonic project' is sometimes also referred to as a 'comprehensive concept of control'. Both terms are defined in the same way and often used interchangeably (e.g. Holman 1996; Overbeek and van der Pijl 1993).

2 Austria and Sweden in an era of global structural change

1   For an overview of the literature on globalisation, see Clark (1998) and Higgott and Reich (1998).
2   'Transnationalisation' is used here to indicate structural change beyond the state system such as the organisation of production on a transnational scale, while changes in levels of cross-border flows such as trade are referred to as instances of 'internationalisation'.
3   For a collection of analyses of states' and non-state actors' role and authority in the global system, see Higgott et al. (2000).
4   For the inherent conflict potential between these two different capitalist class fractions, see van der Pijl's discussion of the ideal-types of money-capital and productive-capital concepts of control (van der Pijl 1984: 8–20).

5   Importantly, corporatism is here not understood as a system of policy-making. Instead, it is regarded as a particular set-up of political institutions, within and through which social forces operate.

6   Parris *et al.* give lower figures: in 1982, the public enterprise sector accounted for 14.3 per cent of employment of the whole Austrian economy, for 17.8 per cent of the production in terms of value added and for 21.1 per cent of capital investment (Parris *et al.* 1987: 29). This was, however, still the largest public sector in Western Europe (Parris *et al.* 1987: 27).

7   'Hard' is understood here as the absence of depreciations or devaluations of the currency, measured via the nominal exchange rate as the relative price between two national currencies, and the pursuit of price stability, often achieved through the pegging of the national currency to a foreign currency with a stable real value (Hörngren and Lindberg 1994: 133).

8   The recent elections of 3 October 1999 may, however, indicate a more general shift away from the two-thirds majority of the SPÖ–ÖVP. The SPÖ dropped to 33.2 per cent of the vote, while it was the FPÖ that came second with the same result as the ÖVP, both obtaining 26.9 per cent (http://www.agora.stm.it/elections/election/austria.htm; 18 December 1999).

9   The Christian Democratic Party had a dramatic success in the 1998 elections, when it obtained 11.8 per cent of the votes cast (information provided by the Swedish Embassy in London). In the future, it is likely to play a more significant role on the centre-right of the Swedish party system.

10   'Union membership peaked at about 86 per cent of all employees in 1986, went down to about 81 per cent in 1991, but is on its way up again amidst growing unemployment' (The Swedish Institute 1994: 2).

11   For 1994, the Swedish Institute presented the following membership figures: LO 2.2 million; TCO 1.3 million; SACO 370,000 (Swedish Institute 1994: 2).

12   For an account of the wage earner fund debate, see Heclo and Madsen 1987: 253–85.

13   It is theoretically possible for a conflict to occur between transnational and internationally-oriented social forces, if the latter depend on state support for their exports. In the case of Austria and Sweden, however, the move in both countries towards neo-liberalism and the concomitant abolition of export support schemes makes this unlikely. For example, Austria's nationalised industry was formerly subsidised and, therefore, supported in its export efforts. This ended with its privatisation and the turn towards efficiency and competitiveness in the market place. In Sweden, the government used to boost exports via devaluations. Since the adoption of a hard currency policy in the 1980s, this support has also ceased to exist.

3 Social forces and the struggle for application in Austria and Sweden

1   An open letter to the Chancellor and Foreign Minister together with a list of signatures, demanding that they should not send a letter of application because the debate about the advantages and disadvantages of such a move had not developed far enough, was printed in *Profil* 26 (1989): 53.

2   Gösta Dahlström worked as an economist at the LO, Jan Olsson (Olsson 1988a) was a researcher previously employed by the Metal Workers' Union, Hans Olsson (Olsson 1988b) was the Head of the Research Department at the Metal Workers' Union, and Rune Molin was the Vice Chairman of LO.

3   It is often alleged in the literature that a change towards a pro-membership position within the trade unions contributed to the SAP's turn-around in 1990 (e.g. Jerneck 1993: 34; Miles 1996: 64). The empirical evidence presented here does not corroborate this position.

4   This position was reiterated in official government declarations and state-
    ments by Prime Minister Carlsson and ministries throughout 1987–9 (e.g.
    Carlsson 1988: 230; Carlsson 1989: 137–8; Gradin 1988: 246; Swedish
    Government 1988a: 223–4; Swedish Ministry for Foreign Affairs 1987: 16,
    26).
5   SAP sources deny the charge that there had been no debate. Apparently,
    Ingvar Carlsson attempted to start a debate on application at the annual party
    conference in September 1990, but party members had just not been inter-
    ested (Interview no. 48; Stockholm, 14/11/1996). Two articles by Carlsson in
    the daily newspaper Dagens Nyheter on 27 May and 5 July 1990, may also be
    cited. They were allegedly written with the intention of adjusting the party's
    position. Neither article, however, inspired a widespread response (Interview
    no. 52; Stockholm, 15/11/1996).
        In his introduction to a parliamentary debate on Europe on 10 October
    1996, Sten Andersson, the Minister for Foreign Affairs, stated that 'in a more
    long-term perspective, the question of membership may become relevant'
    (Andersson 1990: 95). Then, however, he added five reasons why this was still
    premature. 'They had to do with Swedish unity, the time process, the security
    situation, the negotiating situation and the [EU's] discussion of a political
    union' (Lindmarker 1991: 5).

4 The conflict over the EU referenda in Austria and Sweden

1   It is sometimes incorrectly argued that the step from the EEA to membership
    implied only small additional economic gains (e.g. Gstöhl 1994: 334).
2   One interviewee, however, pointed out that it would have been much more dif-
    ficult to achieve a majority in favour of application, if the CFSP had been in
    place two and a half years earlier (Interview no. 25; Vienna, 25 April 1996).
3   In October 1991, the EU and Austria had concluded a transit agreement with
    the general aim of reducing pollution caused by heavy goods vehicles
    (Schaller 1994a: 200–4).
4   The details in relation to Austrian neutrality were finalised on 1 March 1994
    (see chapter five).
5   This declaration was not only important to the applicants. It also satisfied
    those critical voices within the member states, which doubted the neutral
    countries' willingness to co-operate in matters of foreign and security policy
    (Interview no. 36; Vienna, 15 May 1996).
6   Telephone call with the EU expert of the Biltrafikens Arbetsgivareförbund
    (Road Transport Employers' Association); Stockholm, 26 November 1996.
7   With reference to the positions of the political parties, some material is used
    which was published by the parties after the referendum, whether as their posi-
    tion for the elections to the EP in September 1995 or a general position on
    Europe. This is justified, because the parties' positions on the EU have not
    changed since the referendum.
8   The FP regarded co-ordinated actions concerning the infrastructure as an
    exception in this respect (FP 1995: 16–17).
9   Some people argued that the SAP–LO platform and the 'Network for
    Europe' actually formed one group (Interview no. 50; Stockholm, 14
    November 1996), but this was denied by SAP–LO group activists (Interview
    no. 44; Stockholm, 12 November 1996; Interview no. 47; Stockholm, 13
    November 1996). While there were two different groups, the unclear
    boundaries may indicate strong co-operation and overlapping interests in
    contrast to the 'Yes to Europe' group.

5 Austria's and Sweden's accession to the EU and the changing security structure

1   Austria's decision to allow the use of its air and ground space for the transit of weapons and military personnel during the Gulf War in 1991, and legal changes which declared that measures taken by the UN against aggressors did not constitute an instance of war within the meaning of the term in international law (Jankowitsch and Porius 1994: 54; Luif 1996: 144–5), further underlined this restriction of neutrality.

2   A contrary evaluation is presented by Wæver. He argues that the Swedish discussion about EU membership, neutrality and non-alignment 'points to an intense feeling of insecurity, of loss of ground' (Wæver 1992: 90). He offers, however, little empirical evidence for his conclusion.

3   The fact that the Austrian GA was a part of the Green Group of the CSCE Parliamentary Assembly and, thus, co-author of this concept for a future European security order indicated the first forms of such transnational links.

6 The future enlargement of the EU towards Central and Eastern Europe

1   So far, ten CEE countries (CEE-10) have officially applied for membership: Hungary (March 1994), Poland (April 1994), Romania (June 1995), Slovakia (June 1995), Latvia (October 1995), Estonia (November 1995), Lithuania (December 1995), Bulgaria (December 1995), Czech Republic (January 1996) and Slovenia (June 1996).

2   The index gives values between 0 and 100, with 100 representing the maximum degree of liberalisation of capital flows.

3   Polish estimates differ here. While agriculture is an important sector, it is argued that only 10 per cent of the working population are employed full-time in agriculture (Interview no. 72; London, 15 June 1999).

4   Telephone call with the EU expert of the Czech Embassy in London, 20 August 1999.

Bibliography

For the sake of clarity, the bibliography is divided into primary and secondary sources, with the former further divided into subsections of Austria, Sweden and Interviews. Official documents of states, state institutions, political parties and interest organisations, as well as statements by leading officials of these institutions are considered primary sources. All other references are included in secondary sources.

Primary sources

Austria

AK (1989) *Europa Stellungnahme des Österreichischen Arbeiterkammertages*, Vienna: AK.

Arbeitsübereinkommen (1987) 'Arbeitsübereinkommen zwischen der Sozialistischen Partei Österreichs und der Österreichischen Volkspartei über die Bildung einer gemeinsamen Bundesregierung für die Dauer der XVII. Gesetzgebungsperiode des Nationalrates vom 16.01.1987', in A. Khol, G. Ofner and A. Stirnemann (eds) *Österreichisches Jahrbuch für Politik 1986*, Vienna/Munich: Verlag für Geschichte und Politik/R. Oldenbourg Verlag: 641–95.

Aussenministerium (1992) 'Erklärung des Bundesministers für Auswärtige Angelegenheiten, Dr. Alois Mock, anlässlich der Unterzeichnung des Vertrags über die Europäische Union am 07.02.1992', in G. Kunnert (1992) *Spurensicherung auf dem österreichischen Weg nach Brüssel*, Vienna: Verlag der Österreichischen Staatsdruckerei: 113–15.

Bielka, E. (1989) 'Neutralitätspolitik und europäische Integration', *Österreichische Zeitschrift für Politikwissenshaft* 18, 3: 258–60.

Blau-Meissner, F. (1987) 'Erklärung von Klubobfrau Abg. z. NR. Freda Blau-Meissner im NR. am 25.03.1987 zur österreichischen Integrationspolitik (Auszug)', in G. Kunnert (1992) *Spurensicherung auf dem österreichischen Weg nach Brüssel*, Vienna: Verlag der Österreichischen Staatsdruckerei: 345–6.

Bundeskanzleramt/Aussenministerium (1993) 'Betreff: Europäische Gemeinschaft; Aufnahme der Beitrittsverhandlungen; grundsätzliche österreichische Verhandlungsposition; Verhandlungsvollmacht; 21.01.1993', in H. Neisser (1993) *Das Politische System der EG*, Vienna: Holzhausen: 330–40.

Bundessektion Industrie (1989) *Österreichs Industrie und der EG-Binnenmarkt: Branchenstudien über die wirtschaftlichen Auswirkungen*, Vienna: Bundessektion Industrie.

BWK (1987) 'Stellungnahme der Bundeswirtschaftskammer zur Europäischen

Integration; 09.12.1987 (Auszug)',.in G. Kunnert (1992) *Spurensicherung auf dem österreichischen Weg nach Brüssel*, Vienna: Verlag der Österreichischen Staatsdruckerei: 457–9.

—— (1992) 'PBK 204/92 (WM), Pressedienst der Bundeswirtschaftskammer (13.04.1992)', in G. Kunnert (1992) *Spurensicherung auf dem österreichischen Weg nach Brüssel*, Vienna: Verlag der Österreichischen Staatsdruckerei: 468–9.

Dillersberger, S. (1994) 'FPÖ und Europa', in A. Khol, G. Ofner and A. Stirnemann (eds) *Österreichisches Jahrbuch für Politik 1993*, Vienna/Munich: Verlag für Geschichte und Politik/R. Oldenbourg Verlag: 707–14.

Food Processing Trade Union (1988a) 'Hintergrund: Die österreichische Nahrungsmittelindustrie und die europäische Gemeinschaft', *Der Lebensmittelarbeiter* 4.

—— (1988b) 'Wortprotokoll, Diskussion, Schlussworte und Kurzfassung der Referate', in *EG-Podiumsdisskussion anlässlich der LUGA-Gesamtvorstandssitzung (8 März)*, Vienna: Food Processing Trade Union.

FPÖ (1985) 'Parteiprogramm der FPÖ, beschlossen am 02.06.1985', in G. Kunnert (1992) *Spurensicherung auf dem österreichischen Weg nach Brüssel*, Vienna: Verlag der Österreichischen Staatsdruckerei: 320–2.

—— (1987) 'Entschliessungsantrag der FPÖ im NR vom 27.11.1987 betreffend die Aufnahme von Beitrittsverhandlungen mit der EG', in G. Kunnert (1992) *Spurensicherung auf dem österreichischen Weg nach Brüssel*, Vienna: Verlag der Österreichischen Staatsdruckerei: 328.

—— (1993) *Österreich Zuerst – Unser Weg nach Europa: Für ein Europa der Bürger und Völker, für ein Europa als Freiheits-, Friedens- und Wohlstandsordnung (08.05.1993)*, Vienna: FPÖ.

GA (1989) 'Europamanifest der Grünen Alternative, beschlossen auf dem Europa-Kongress in Innsbruck vom 17.–19.02.1989', in G. Kunnert (1992) *Spurensicherung auf dem österreichischen Weg nach Brüssel*, Vienna: Verlag der Österreichischen Staatsdruckerei: 348–52.

—— (1993) *Ja Zu Europa – Nein Zur EG*, Vienna: Grüne Bildungswerkstatt.

—— (1996) Europa Verwandeln: Europapolitisches Manifest der Grünen, Vienna: GA.

Lanc, E. (1989) 'Politische und ökonomische Aspekte der Beziehungen Österreichs zur Europäischen Gemeinschaft', *Österreichische Zeitschrift für Politikwissenshaft* 18, 3: 253–7.

Landeshauptmännerkonferenz (1987) 'Beschluss der Landeshauptmännerkonferenz vom 13. November 1987 betreffend die europäische Integration', in G. Kunnert (1992) *Spurensicherung auf dem österreichischen Weg nach Brüssel*, Vienna: Verlag der Österreichischen Staatsdruckerei: 514.

LK (1989) *Memorandum zur Europäischen Integration: Zukunftchance ökosozialer Weg; Februar*, Vienna: Präsidentenkonferenz der Landwirtschaftskammern.

Mock, A. (1987) 'Bericht des BMA im Einvernehmen mit dem BMW an die BReg vom 30.11.1987 über das Konzept der österreichischen Integrationspolitik und bisherige Ergebnisse bei seiner Verwirklichung (präsentiert am 01.12.1987)', in G. Kunnert (1992) *Spurensicherung auf dem österreichischen Weg nach Brüssel*, Vienna: Verlag der Österreichischen Staatsdruckerei: 23–8.

—— (1989) 'A View From Vienna', *International Affairs (Moscow)* 2: 15–19.

—— (1994) *Erklärung des Bundesministers vor dem Nationalrat aus Anlass der parlamentarischen Genehmigung des EU-Beitrittsvertrages (11 November)*, Vienna.

—— (1995) *The Present Challenges of the European Union. Opening Statement to the Participants of the Austro-Belgian Symposium on the European Union (3 April)*, Brussels.

ÖGB (1988) *Europa Memorandum (Dezember)*, Vienna: ÖGB.

—— (1991) 'ÖGB-Präsident Fritz Verzetnitsch: 'Enttäuscht vom EG-Gipfel', ÖGB-Pressedienst (12.12.1991)', in G. Kunnert (1992) *Spurensicherung auf dem österreichischen Weg nach Brüssel*, Vienna: Verlag der Österreichischen Staatsdruckerei: 447–8.

ÖGB-Rednerdienst (1988) '*EG – EFTA: Österreichs Rolle in Europa*', No.3 (August).

Österreichischer Bauernbund (1988) 'Entschliessung des Bundesbauernrates des Österreichischen Bauernbundes an die BReg vom 22.10.1988', in G. Kunnert (1992) *Spurensicherung auf dem österreichischen Weg nach Brüssel*, Vienna: Verlag der Österreichischen Staatsdruckerei: 273–5.

ÖVP (1988) 'Maria Plainer Beschluss des erweiterten ÖVP-Bundesparteivorstandes vom 08.01.1988 zur österreichischen Europapolitik', in G. Kunnert (1992) *Spurensicherung auf dem österreichischen Weg nach Brüssel*, Vienna: Verlag der Österreichischen Staatsdruckerei: 245.

Parteienvereinbarung (1994) *Europa-Abkommen zwischen SPÖ und ÖVP vom 22. April 1994*, Vienna.

Sallmutter, H. (1993) 'Diskussionsstand in der GPA zur europäischen Integration', in GPA (ed.) *Der Countdown läuft: Österreichs Arbeitnehmer auf dem Weg nach Europa*, Vienna: Gewerkschaft der Privatangestellten: 161–7.

Soviet Union (1989) 'Aide-mémoire der Sowjetunion zu den österreichischen EG-Beitrittsansuchen vom 10.08.1989', in G. Kunnert (1992) *Spurensicherung auf dem österreichischen Weg nach Brüssel*, Vienna: Verlag der Österreichischen Staatsdruckerei: 562.

Sozialpartnerstellungnahme (1989) *Österreich und die Europäische Integration (01.03.1989)*, Vienna.

Thalberg, H. (1989) 'Die immerwährende Neutralität: Eckpfeiler der österreichischen Sicherheitspolitik', *Österreichische Zeitschrift für Politikwissenshaft* 18, 3: 261–4.

Voggenhuber, J. (1995) 'Die EU reformieren! Die europäische Integration und die Politik der GRÜNEN vor und nach der österreichischen Volksabstimmung', in A. Khol, G. Ofner and A. Stirnemann (eds) *Österreichisches Jahrbuch für Politik 1994*. Vienna/Munich: Verlag für Geschichte und Politik/R. Oldenbourg Verlag: 379–412.

Vogler, H. (1991) 'Zukunft der Sozialpartnerschaft im Binnenmarkt aus der Sicht der Arbeitnehmer', in H. Kienzl (ed.) *Österreichs Wirtschafts- und Währungspolitik auf dem Weg nach Europa. Festschrift für Maria Schaumayer*, Vienna: Österreichische Nationalbank: 179–82.

VÖI (1987a) *Europa – Unsere Zukunft. Eine Stellungnahme der Vereinigung Österreichischer Industrieller zur Europäischen Integration*, Vienna: Schreiftenreihe der Vereinigung Österreichischer Industrieller.

—— (1987b) '"Österreich muss sich zum Westen bekennen", Pressedienst der Industrie (15.05.1987)', in G. Kunnert (1992) *Spurensicherung auf dem österreichischen Weg nach Brüssel*, Vienna: Verlag der Österreichischen Staatsdruckerei: 495.

—— (1989) *Euro–Info, Nr.6/ 24 (Juli 1989)*, Vienna: Vereinigung Österreichischer Industrieller.

—— (1991) '"Kessler: EWR ist nur Zwischenschritt", Pressedienst der Industrie (23.04.1991)', in G. Kunnert (1992) *Spurensicherung auf dem österreichischen Weg nach Brüssel*, Vienna: Verlag der Österreichischen Staatsdruckerei: 508.

—— (1992) '"Das Ziel bleibt Vollmitgliedschaft", Pressedienst der Industrie (04.05.1992)', in G. Kunnert (1992) *Spurensicherung auf dem österreichischen Weg nach Brüssel*, Vienna: Verlag der Österreichischen Staatsdruckerei: 510.

—— (1994) 'EWR von A – Z', *Europainformation Nr. 28/94*.

Völkerrechtsbüro (1988) 'Mitgliedschaft Österreichs in den Europäischen Gemeinschaften und immerwährende Neutralität (22.11.1988)', in G. Kunnert (1992) *Spurensicherung auf dem österreichischen Weg nach Brüssel*, Vienna: Verlag der Österreichischen Staatsdruckerei: 34–40.

Vranitzky, F. (1988) 'Die Rolle Österreichs im neuen Europa. Referat des SPÖ-Vorsitzenden Dr. Franz Vranitzky am 15.10.1988 auf dem Europa-Kongress der SPÖ in Bregenz', in G. Kunnert (1992) *Spurensicherung auf dem österreichischen Weg nach Brüssel*, Vienna: Verlag der Österreichischen Staatsdruckerei: 172–83.

—— (1989) 'Österreich in Europa. Bericht des Parteivorsitzenden an das Parteipräsidium und den Bundesparteivorstand am 03.04.1989', in G. Kunnert (1992) *Spurensicherung auf dem österreichischen Weg nach Brüssel*. Vienna: Verlag der Österreichischen Staatsdruckerei: 188–200.

—— (1995) 'Europäische Herausforderungen – Europäische Lösungen', *Lecture by the Austrian Chancellor to the 'Schweizerische Institut für Auslandsforschung' (17 January)*, University of Zurich.

Zourek, H. (1989) 'Der EG-Beitritt aus der Sicht der Arbeitnehmervertretungen', in H. Glatz and H. Moser (eds) *Herausforderung Binnenmarkt: Kopfüber in die EG?*, Vienna: Service: 185–94.

Sweden

Andersson, S. (1990) 'Introductory statement by the Minister for Foreign Affairs, Mr. Sten Andersson, in the parliamentary debate on Europe (10 October)', in Swedish Ministry for Foreign Affairs (1991) *Documents on Swedish Foreign Policy 1990*, Stockholm: 92–6.

—— (1991) '"Sweden in a new Europe" – Speech by the Minister for Foreign Affairs, Mr. Sten Andersson, in Oslo at the annual dinner of the European Movement in Norway (12 February)', in Swedish Ministry for Foreign Affairs (1992) *Documents on Swedish Foreign Policy 1991*, Stockholm: 47–53.

Bildt, C. (1991a) '"Sweden – from a reluctant to an enthusiastic European" – Remarks by the Prime Minister, Mr. Carl Bildt, at the Office of the Commission of the European Communities in Bonn (13 November)', in Swedish Ministry for Foreign Affairs (1992) *Documents on Swedish Foreign Policy 1991*, Stockholm: 94–101.

—— (1991b) 'Statement by the Prime Minister, Mr. Carl Bildt, after consultations with the Advisory Council on Foreign Affairs (11 December)', in Swedish Ministry for Foreign Affairs (1992) *Documents on Swedish Foreign Policy 1991*, Stockholm: 117–8.

Carlsson, I. (1988) 'Introductory remarks by the Prime Minister, Mr. Ingvar Carlsson, at a meeting with the Commission of the European Communities (16 May)', in Swedish Ministry for Foreign Affairs (1990) *Documents on Swedish Foreign Policy 1988*, Stockholm: 229–32.

—— (1989) 'Address by the Prime Minister, Mr. Ingvar Carlsson, to the AIC and the Labour Movement Peace Forum in Stockholm, concerning among other things developments in Eastern Europe and Sweden and the European Community (2 December)', in Swedish Ministry for Foreign Affairs (1990) *Documents on Swedish Foreign Policy 1989*, Stockholm: 128–43.

—— (1991) 'Statement to the Riksdag by Prime Minister Ingvar Carlsson on June 14

1991, on Sweden's Application for Membership of the European Community', in M. Ärnborg and S.-O. Allard (eds) (1991/2) *Sweden, the EC and Security Policy Developments in Europe*, Stockholm: Ministry for Foreign Affairs: 7–14.

Dahlström, G. (1987) 'EFTA–EC relations as seen by the Swedish trade unions', *EFTA-Bulletin* 28, 1: 4–7.

Dinkelspiel, U. (1991) 'Parliamentary briefing on the EEA agreement by the Minister for European Affairs and Foreign Trade, Mr. Ulf Dinkelspiel (24 October)', in Swedish Ministry for Foreign Affairs (1992) *Documents on Swedish Foreign Policy 1991*, Stockholm: 268–71.

—— (1993) 'Statement by the Minister for European Affairs and Foreign Trade, Mr. Ulf Dinkelspiel, at the opening of Sweden's negotiations on accession to the EC (1 February)', in Swedish Ministry for Foreign Affairs (1994) *Documents on Swedish Foreign Policy 1993*, Stockholm: 28–35.

FP (1995) *Seizing the Opportunities – A Liberal Programme for Europe. Election platform by the Swedish Liberal Party for the September 17, 1995 elections to the European Parliament*, Stockholm: FP.

GP (1995) *Main Points of the Green Party Election Programme for the Elections to the European Parliament, September 17*, Stockholm: GP.

—— (1996) *A Green View on Security Policy (OSCE – 5th Annual Session Parliamentary Assembly, 5–9 July 1996, Stockholm; Forum of Green and Alternative Forces)*, Stockholm: GP.

Gradin, A. (1987) 'Speech by the Minister for Foreign Trade, Ms. Anita Gradin, in the Riksdag debate on Europe (12 November)', in Swedish Ministry for Foreign Affairs (1990) *Documents on Swedish Foreign Policy 1987*, Stockholm: 300–4.

—— (1988) 'Excerpt from an address by the Minister for Foreign Trade, Ms. Anita Gradin, at a meeting of Swedish ambassadors to Western Europe in Lidingö (22 August)', in Swedish Ministry for Foreign Affairs (1990) *Documents on Swedish Foreign Policy 1988*, Stockholm: 246–251.

—— (1989) '"On the threshold of Europe: Industry and social policy". Excerpt from an address by the Minister for Foreign Trade, Ms. Anita Gradin, at a seminar arranged by the Swedish Social Work Federation in Malmö (14 August)', in Swedish Ministry for Foreign Affairs (1990) *Documents on Swedish Foreign Policy 1989*, Stockholm: 270–4.

—— (1990a) 'Parliamentary briefing by the Minister for Foreign Trade, Ms. Anita Gradin, concerning EFTA–EC relations (18 January)', in Swedish Ministry for Foreign Affairs (1991) *Documents on Swedish Foreign Policy 1990*, Stockholm: 219–22.

—— (1990b) 'Address by the Minister for Foreign Trade, Ms. Anita Gradin, at a youth seminar on Europe at Rosenbad (12 September)', in Swedish Ministry for Foreign Affairs (1991) *Documents on Swedish Foreign Policy 1990*, Stockholm: 263–71.

Jacobsson, R. (1990) *Sweden and West European Integration*, Stockholm: Swedish Ministry for Foreign Affairs.

LO (1994) *Trade Unions and the EC: The Trade Union Evaluation of the Membership Negotiations*, Stockholm: The Swedish Trade Union Confederation.

Molin, R. (1988) 'Bringing a social dimension into European economic integration', *Inside Sweden* 1: 10–11.

Nilsson, L.-Å. (1993) '"Sweden's foreign and security policy in a changing Europe" – Address by the Permanent Under-Secretary of State for Foreign Affairs, Mr. Lars-Åke Nilsson, to representatives of the Norwegian National Defence College during a visit to Stockholm (22 February)', in Swedish Ministry for Foreign Affairs (1994) *Documents on Swedish Foreign Policy 1993*, Stockholm: 221–7.

Ohlsson, L. (1988) *Consequences of the EC for Swedish Manufacturing Industry. Industry & EC 7*, Stockholm: Industriförbundets Förlag.

Olsson, J. (1988a) 'The Swedish labour movement needs a European vision', *Inside Sweden* 1: 5–6.

Olsson, H. (1988b) 'From Eurosclerosis to Eurocapitalism', *Inside Sweden* 1: 8–9.

SAP (1993) *Social Democracy on the Eve of the EC membership negotiations (final version, discussed by the Party Executive and adopted by the Parliamentary Group at 12.30 on 19 January 1993)*, Stockholm: SAP.

—— (1996) *Sweden into the 21st centruy: A social democratic policy for a new age – political guidelines adopted by the Congress of the Swedish Social Democratic Party 15–17 March 1996 in Stockholm*, Stockholm: SAP.

Schori, P. (1991) '"Sweden and new developments in Europe" – Address by the Under-Secretary of State for Foreign Affairs, Mr. Pierre Schori, at Chatham House, London (14 May)', in Swedish Ministry for Foreign Affairs (1992) *Documents on Swedish Foreign Policy 1991*, Stockholm: 60–70.

Swedish Government (1988a) 'Government statement on trade policy (4 May)', in Swedish Ministry for Foreign Affairs (1990) *Documents on Swedish Foreign Policy 1988*, Stockholm: 220–9.

—— (1988b) 'Memorandum on Government consideration of European issues (5 July)', in Swedish Ministry for Foreign Affairs (1990) *Documents on Swedish Foreign Policy 1988*, Stockholm: 242–5.

—— (1990) 'Excerpt from a Government Document addressed to Parliament concerning measures to stabilize the economy and limit growth in public expenditure (26 October)', in Swedish Ministry for Foreign Affairs (1991) *Documents on Swedish Foreign Policy 1990*, Stockholm: 305–6.

—— (1995) *The EU Intergovernmental Conference 1996. Government Report 1995/96:30*, Stockholm.

The Swedish Institute (1994) *Labour Relations in Sweden. Fact Sheets on Sweden (FS 3 t Oha)*, Stockholm: Swedish Institute.

—— (1995) *Agriculture in Sweden. Fact Sheets on Sweden (FS 22 u Qd)*, Stockholm: Swedish Institute.

—— (1996a) *The Swedish Political Parties. Fact Sheets on Sweden (FS 16 n Oc)*, Stockholm: Swedish Institute.

—— (1996b) *Sweden in the European Union. Fact Sheets on Sweden (FS 94 b Qadd)*, Stockholm: The Swedish Institute.

Swedish Ministry for Foreign Affairs (1987) *On Sweden and West European Integration: Extracts from the Swedish Government's bill 1987/88:66 (unofficial translation; chapters 1, 2 and 5)*, Stockholm.

—— (1991) 'Europe 1991: Security Policy and the Development of the EC (summary of parts of the Ministry for Foreign Affairs Report, spring 1991)', in M. Ärnborg and S.-O. Allard (eds) (1991/2) *Sweden, the EC and Security Policy Developments in Europe*, Stockholm: Ministry for Foreign Affairs Information: 15–44.

Swedish Ministry of Defence (1995) *Renewal of Swedish Defence. Press Release No.102 (5 October)*, Stockholm.

—— (1996) *Sweden's Defence and Security Policy in an International Perspective (23 September)*, Stockholm.

TCO (1993) *A Trade Union Policy for Europe*, Stockholm: TCO.

—— (1994) *TCO's Assessment of the EU Agreement*, Stockholm: TCO.

Ugglas, M. af (1991) '"Sweden's foreign policy in a changing international environment" – Speech in Parliament by the Minister for Foreign Affairs, Mrs. Magaretha af Ugglas (17 October)', in Swedish Ministry for Foreign Affairs (1992) *Documents on Swedish Foreign Policy 1991*, Stockholm: 85–9.

—— (1992) '"Sweden at the heart of Europe" – Address by the Minister for Foreign Affairs, Mrs. Margaretha af Ugglas, at Chatham House, London (26 November)', in Swedish Ministry for Foreign Affairs (1993) *Documents on Swedish Foreign Policy 1992*, Stockholm: 118–23.

—— (1993) '"Sweden's foreign and security policy in a changing Europe" – Address by the Minister for Foreign Affairs, Mrs. Margaretha af Ugglas, to the Commission on Foreign Affairs and Security of the European Parliament in Brussels (3 December)', in Swedish Ministry for Foreign Affairs (1994) *Documents on Swedish Foreign Policy 1993*, Stockholm: 298–304.

VP (1995) *Strengthen democracy – reduce the power of EU: The election platform of the Left Party for the EU election, September 17*, Stockholm: VP.

—— (undated) *More democracy – less union: The EU programme of the Left Party of Sweden (Vänsterpartiet)*, Stockholm: VP.

Wijkman, P.M. (1995) 'To Be or Not to Be a Member: The Swedish Referendum Debate', *Industriförbundet: Working Paper 8* (December).

Interviews

1 Political Advisor, Section for Foreign Trade and Integration, *Arbeiterkammer* (Chamber of Labour, AK); Vienna, 2 p.m., 8 May 1995.
2 Director of the Section for Fundamental Questions of European Integration responsible for the 1996 IGC, *Foreign Ministry*; Vienna, 10 a.m., 9 May 1995.
3 Political Advisor, *Verband Österreichischer Banken und Bankiers* (Federation of Austrian Banks and Bankers, VÖB); Vienna, 2 p.m., 9 May 1995.
4 Political Advisor, International Secretariat, *Sozialdemokratische Partei Österreichs* (Austrian Social Democratic Party, SPÖ); Vienna, 4 p.m., 9 May 1995.
5 Political Advisor, Section for Integration and Trade Policy, *Bundeswirtschaftskammer* (Chamber of Commerce, BWK); Vienna, 10 a.m., 10 May 1995.
6 Political Advisor, Section for European Integration, *Chancellor's Office*, Vienna, 1 p.m., 10 May 1995.
7 Political Advisor, Section for European Integration, International and Economic-Political Issues/Section for Budget Policy, *Finance Ministry*; Vienna, 9 a.m., 11 May 1995.
8 Director of *Austrian Industries* (1986–1993) and Member of the European Round Table of Industrialists (1989–1993); Vienna, 11 a.m., 11 May 1995.
9 Director of the Section for Coordination of Emergency Supply, State Crisis Management and Foundation of Security Policy/Director of the Section for Coordination of Emergency Supply and Foundation of Security Policy, *Chancellor's Office*, Vienna, 2 p.m., 11 May 1995.
10 Director of the Section for fundamental Issues of European Economic Integration, *Economic Ministry*; Vienna, 10 a.m., 12 May 1995.
11 Journalist, *Austria Presse Agentur*; Vienna, 1 p.m., 12 May 1995.
12 Director of the Political Section, *Österreichische Volkspartei* (Austrian People's Party, ÖVP); Vienna, 3 p.m., 12 May 1995.
13 Political Advisor, Section for National Economy, *Österreichischer Gewerkschaftsbund* (Austrian Federation of Trade Unions, ÖGB); Vienna, 4.30 p.m., 12 May 1995.

14 Director of the Section for Questions of Political Integration, *Chancellor's Office*, Vienna, 12 a.m., 17 May 1995.

15 Member of the Board of Directors, *Creditanstalt-Bankverein*, and Member of the Association for Monetary Union in Europe; Vienna, 3.30 p.m., 17 May 1995.

16 Director of the Section for Issues of Integration and International Financial Organisation, *Österreichische Nationalbank* (Austrian National Bank, ANB); Vienna, 10 a.m., 18 May 1995.

17 General-Secretary Deputy, Section for Trade Policy, EU and Integration, *Präsidentenkonferenz der Landwirtschaftskammern Österreichs* (Confederation of regional Chambers of Agriculture, LK); Vienna, 2 p.m., 18 May 1995.

18 Director of the Europe Information Service, *Vereinigung Österreichischer Industrieller* (Federation of Austrian Industrialists, VÖI); Vienna, 9 a.m., 22 May 1995.

19 Member of the Board of Directors, *AgrarMarkt Austria* (regulatory institution for the agricultural market, 1993–1995), Director of the Economic-Political Section of the *Arbeiterkammer* (Chamber of Labour, AK) (1985–1993); Vienna, 9 a.m., 23 May 1995.

20 Central Secretary, *Gewerkschaft Agrar, Nahrung, Genuß* (Trade Union of Food Processing Industry, ANG); Vienna, 10 a.m., 22 April 1996.

21 Managing Director, *Federal Association of Bakers, Millers, Confectioners, Butchers and Food Processing Industry* (affiliated to the BWK); Vienna, 8 a.m., 23 April 1996.

22 President of the *Trade Union for Textile, Clothes and Leather* and Head of the ÖGB Integration Committee since 1987, responsible in the SPÖ for the drawing up of the coalition agreement of 26 June 1989; Vienna, 10 a.m., 23 April 1996.

23 Foreign Secretary (1983–84) and co-founder of the '*Initiative Österreich und Europa*', Vienna, 11 a.m., 24 April 1996.

24 Political Advisor, Section International Trade and Environment, *Association of the Austrian Textile Industry*; Vienna, 3 p.m., 24 April 1996.

25 Second President of the *Nationalrat*, responsible in the ÖVP for the drawing up of the coalition agreement of 26 June 1989; Vienna, 10 a.m., 25 April 1996.

26 Member of European Parliament and Head of the Fraction in the EP (until April 1996), Party Deputy-Director, *Freiheitliche Partei Österreich* (Austrian Freedom Party, FPÖ); Vienna, 1 p.m., 25 April 1996.

27 Political Advisor on Europe in the *Grüne Alternative* fraction of the Nationalrat/ Europe – Co-ordinator of the *Grüne Alternative* (Green Alternative Party, GA); Vienna, 11.30 a.m., 2 May 1996.

28 Head of the Section for Goods and Processing, *Österreichischer Raiffeisenverband*; Vienna, 9 a.m., 3 May 1996.

29 General-Secretary, '*Österreichische Gesellschaft für Europapolitik*'; Vienna, 1 p.m., 3 May 1996.

30 Head of the Section for International Employment Policy, *Ministry for Labour and Social Affairs*, Vienna, 6 p.m., 6 May 1996.

31 Political Advisor, Office of the Minister, *Ministry for Public Industry and Transport* (1995–96), Office of the Minister, *Finance Ministry* (1996–); Vienna, 2 p.m., 7 May 1996.

32 State-Secretary for Integration and Development Co-operation in the *Chancellor's Office*, responsible together with Dr. Mock for the accession negotiations (1993–4), State-Secretary for European Affairs in the *Chancellor's Office* (1994–1995), Managing-Director of the *SPÖ* (since 1995); Vienna, 1 p.m., 8 May 1996.

33 General-Secretary, *International Institute for Peace*, Vienna, 3 p.m., 9 May 1996.

34 Political Scientist, *Institut für Konfliktforschung*, Vienna, 5 p.m., 10 May 1996.
35 Head of the President's Office, *Gewerkschaft der Privatangestellten* (White Collar Workers' Union, GPA); Vienna, 8 a.m., 14 May 1996.
36 Foreign Secretary (1987–94), Chairman of the *ÖVP* (until 1989), Austria's main negotiator in Brussels (1993–4); Vienna, 11 a.m., 15 May 1996.
37 Senior Advisor, International Secretariat, *Sveriges Riksbank* (Swedish Central Bank); Stockholm, 2 p.m., 7 November 1996.
38 Head of Swedish EU-Secretariat, *Vänsterpartiet* (Left Party, VP); Stockholm, 10 a.m., 8 November 1996.
39 Political Scientist, *Fackföreningsrörelsens Institut för Economisk Forskning* (Trade Union Institute for Economic Research); Stockholm, 1 p.m., 8 November 1996.
40 International Secretary, *Tjänstemännens Centralorganisation* (Swedish Confederation of Professional Employees, TCO); Stockholm, 11 a.m., 11 November 1996.
41 Senior Advisor, *Sveriges Akademikers Centralorganisation* (Swedish Confederation of Professional Associations, SACO); Stockholm, 2 p.m., 11 November 1996.
42 Director of Information, *Centerpartiet* (Centre Party, CP); Stockholm, 4 p.m., 11 November 1996.
43 Director of International Affairs, *Svenska Arbetsgivareföreningen* (Confederation of Swedish Employers, SAF), Stockholm, 9 a.m., 12 November 1996.
44 Europe-Co-ordinator, *Socialdemokratiska Arbetarepartiet* (Swedish Social Democratic Party, SAP); Stockholm, 11 a.m., 12 November 1996.
45 Party Secretary, *Miljöpartiet de Gröna* (Green Party, GP); Stockholm, 2 p.m., 12 November 1996.
46 International Officer, *Industri Facket* (Industrial Workers' Union, LO affiliate); member of the LO Committee on the EU; Stockholm, 10 a.m., 13 November 1996.
47 Political Advisor, *Ministry of Finance*, Leading activist in the SAP-internal 'yes' group; Stockholm, 2 p.m., 13 November 1996.
48 Political Advisor, *Ministry of Industry and Trade*, employed in various ministries between 1990 and 1995, SAP member; Stockholm, 9.30 a.m., 14 November 1996.
49 Deputy Auditor General, *The Swedish National Audit Office* (since 1995), *Ministry of Finance* (1980–95), Head of inter-ministerial co-ordination team on European integration, expert aid to Finance Minister on economic questions during accession negotiations; Stockholm, 1 p.m., 14 November 1996.
50 Director of Strategic Planning, *Lantbrukarnas Riksförbund* (Federation of Swedish Farmers, LRF); Stockholm, 3.30, 14 November 1996.
51 Political Co-ordinator European Affairs, *Moderata Samlingspartiet* (Moderate Party, MS), Political Advisor to Prime Minister Bildt responsible for co-ordination of coalition partners in the areas of foreign affairs, defence, labour and trade (1991–94); Stockholm, 10 a.m., 15 November 1996.
52 Political Advisor, *Prime Minister's Office* (since 1995), Journalist for Swedish National Broadcasting 1981–94, based in Brussels 1989–93, Political Advisor to Mats Hellström, Minister for Foreign Trade and European Affairs (1995–96); Stockholm, 1 p.m., 15 November 1996.
53 Research Associate, *Utrikespolitiska Institutet* (Swedish Institute of International Affairs); Stockholm, 9 a.m., 18 November 1996.
54 Senior Advisor, *Industriförbundet* (Federation of Swedish Industries, SI); Stockholm, 12 a.m., 19 November 1996.
55 Member of Parliament, *Folkpartiet liberalerna* (Liberal Party, FP), Minister for Health and Social Affairs (1991–94); Stockholm, 2 p.m., 19 November 1996.

56 Political Advisor, International Department, *Landsorganisationen i Sverige* (Swedish Trade Union Confederation, LO); Stockholm, 10 a.m., 21 November 1996.
57 Researcher, *Transportarbetareförbundet* (Transport Workers' Union, LO affiliate), member of the LO Committee on the EU; Stockholm, 12 noon, 21 November 1996.
58 Press Officer, *Facket för Service och Kommunikation* (The Union of Service and Communication Employees, SEKO, LO affiliate), member of the SAP 'yes' campaign; Stockholm, 9 a.m., 26 November 1996.
59 International Secretary, *Kommunalarbetare Förbundet* (Municipal Workers' Union, LO affiliate), member of the LO Committee on the EU; Stockholm, 1 p.m., 26 November 1996.
60 Special Advisor on European Security, *Ministry of Foreign Affairs*, Political Advisor in *Ministry of Defence* (until 1995); Stockholm, 4 p.m., 26 November 1996.
61 President of the *Swedish Trade Council*, senior civil servant under SAP government (1987–91), Chief Negotiator of EEA (1989–92), Chief Negotiator of EU accession treaty (1993–94), Minister for Trade and European Affairs (1991–94); Stockholm, 5 p.m., 26 November 1996.
62 Member of Steering Committee Secretariat, *Landsorganisationen i Sverige* (Swedish Trade Union Confederation, LO); Stockholm, 8.45 a.m., 27 November 1996.
63. Administrator, *Studieföbundet Näringsliv och Samhälle* (Centre for Business and Policy Studies, SNS); Stockholm, 10 a.m., 27 November 1996
64. Director, *Arbetsmarknadsstyrelsen* (Swedish National Labour Market Board, AMS); Stockholm, 9 a.m., 28 November 1996.
65 Deputy Director, *Industriens Utredningsinstitut* (The Industrial Institute for Economic and Social Research, IUI); Stockholm, 1.30 p.m., 28 November 1996.
66 EU-Co-ordinator, Research Department, *Metallindustriarbetareförbundet* (Metal Workers' Union, LO affiliate); Stockholm, 9 a.m., 29 November 1996.
67 Senior Vice President, Public Affairs, *Verkstadsindustrier* (Association of Swedish Engineering Industries, SAF and SI affiliate); Stockholm, 11 a.m., 29 November 1996.
68 State Secretary, *Ministry for Foreign Affairs*, Chief Negotiator in the 1996 IGC; Head of Foreign Affairs Department, *Ministry of Finance* (1982–8), State Secretary, *Ministry of Finance* (1988–91); Stockholm, 10.45 a.m., 2 December 1996.
69 Project Manager, *Företagarna* (Federation of Private Enterprises representing small and medium-sized companies); Stockholm, 9 a.m., 3 December 1996.
70 Secretary of the standing advisory committee on the EU, *Miljöpartiet de Gröna* (Green Party, GP); Stockholm, 10 a.m., 3 December 1996.
71 Political Scientist, *Department of Political Science*, University of Stockholm; Stockholm, 4 p.m., 4 December 1996.
72 Counsellor in the Political Section, *Embassy of the Republic of Poland*; London, 3 p.m., 15 June 1999.
73 Third Secretary, EU Affairs, *Hungarian Embassy*; London, 11 a.m., 16 June 1999.

Secondary sources

Agnew, J. and Corbridge, S. (1995) *Mastering Space: Hegemony, Territory and International Political Eonomy*, London/New York: Routledge.
Ahlén, K. (1989) 'Swedish Collective Bargaining Under Pressure: Inter-union Rivalry and Income Policies', *British Journal of Industrial Relations* 27, 3: 330–46.

Althaler, K. S. *et al.*(1988) *AUSWEG - EUROPA? Wirschaftspolitische Optionen für Öster-reich*, Vienna: Falter Verlag.

Amin, A. and Thrift, N. (1994) 'Living in the Global', in A. Amin and N. Thrift (eds) *Globalization, Institutions, and Regional Development in Europe*, Oxford: Oxford University Press: 1–22.

Andersson, T., Fredriksson, T. and Svensson, R. (1996) *Multinational Restructuring, Internationalization and Small Economies: The Swedish Case*, London/New York: Routledge.

Ardy, B. (1999) 'Agricultural, Structural Policy, the Budget and Eastern Enlargement of the European Union', in K. Henderson (ed.) *Back to Europe: Central and Eastern Europe and the European Union*, London: UCL Press: 107–28.

Augelli, E. and Murphy, C. N. (1993) 'Gramsci and International Relations: a General Perspective and Example from Recent US Policy toward the Third World', in S. Gill (ed.) (1993a) *Gramsci, Historical Materialism and International Relations*, Cambridge: Cambridge University Press: 127–47.

Avery, G. and Cameron, F. (1998) *The Enlargement of the European Union*, Sheffield: Sheffield Academic Press.

Aylott, N. (1997) 'Between Europe and Unity: The Case of the Swedish Social Democrats', *West European Politics* 20, 2: 119–36.

Bartosz, J. (1996) 'Polish Trade Unions: Caught up in the Political Battle', *Labour Focus on Eastern Europe* 55: 38–46.

Bell, J. and Mickiewicz, T. (1999) 'EU Accession and Labour Markets in the Visegrad Countries', in K. Henderson (ed.) *Back to Europe: Central and Eastern Europe and the European Union*, London: UCL Press: 129–50.

Bellak, C. (1992) 'Die wesentlichsten Entwicklungen österreichischer Direkt-investitionen anhand der Statistik', in W. Clement (ed.) *Neue Entwicklungen – neue Formen – neue Herausforderungen. Internationalisierung Band VI*, Vienna: Signum Verlag: 17–73.

Berg, J. O. (1994) 'Outcome of Sweden's EU Referendum is Hard to Predict', *Current Sweden* 405 (September).

Bergström, H. (1991) 'Sweden's Politics and Party System at the Crossroads', *West European Politics* 14, 3: 8–30.

Bieler, A. (1998) 'Austria's and Sweden's Accession to the European Community. A Comparative neo-Gramscian Case Study of European Integration', unpublished PhD. thesis, University of Warwick.

Bieler, A and Morton, A. D. (1999) 'The Gordian Knot of Agency–Structure in International Relations: a Neo-Gramscian Perspective', paper presented at the 24th annual conference of the British International Studies Association, Manchester, 20–22 December.

Bierfeld, U. (1995) 'Sweden's Foreign Policy After the End of the Cold War – from Neutrality to Freedom of Action', in R. Lindahl and G. Sjöstedt (eds) *New Thinking in International Relations: Swedish Perspectives. The Yearbook of the Swedish Institute of International Affairs:*, Stockholm: 183–94.

Biersteker, T. J. (1995) 'The "Triumph" of Liberal Economic Ideas in the Developing World', in B. Stallings (ed.) *Global Change, Regional Response: the New International Context of Development*, Cambridge: Cambridge University Press: 174–96.

Bjørklund, T. (1996) 'The Three Nordic 1994 Referenda Concerning Membership in the EU', *Cooperation and Conflict* 31, 1: 11–36.

Bonefeld, W. (1995) 'Monetarism and Crisis', in W. Bonefeld and J. Holloway (eds) *Global Capital, National State and the Politics of Money*, Houndmills: Macmillan: 35–68.

Bozóki, A. (1999) 'Democracy in Hungary, 1990–97', in M. Kaldor and I. Vejvoda (eds) *Democratization in Central and Eastern Europe*, London/New York: Pinter: 105–120.

Braunerhjelm, P. and Oxelheim, L. (1996) 'Structural Implications of the Investment Response by Swedish Multinational Firms to the EC 1992 Program', in S. Hirsch and T. Almor (eds) *Outsiders' Response to European Integration*, Copenhagen: Handelshøjskolens Forlag: 99–118.

—— Ekholm, K., Grundberg, L. and Karpaty, P. (1996) 'Swedish Multinational Corporations: Recent Trends in Foreign Activities', *The Industrial Institute for Economic and Social Research: Working Paper* 462.

Breit, J. and Rössl, D. (1992) 'Internationalisierung der Klein- und Mittelbetriebe', in W. Clement (ed.) *Neue Entwicklungen – neue Formen – neue Herausforderungen. Internationalisierung Band VI*, Vienna: Signum Verlag: 191–222.

Breuss, F. and Stankovsky, J. (1988) *Österreich und der EG-Binnenmarkt*, Vienna: Signum Verlag.

Bryant, C. G. A. (1994) 'Economic Utopianism and Sociological Realism: Strategies for Transformation in East-Central Europe', in C. G. A. Bryant and E. Mokrzycki (eds) *The New Great Transformation? Change and Continuity in East-Central Europe*, London/New York: Routledge: 58–77.

Bryant, C. G. A. and Mokrzycki, E. (1994) 'Introduction: Theorizing the Changes in East–Central Europe', C. G. A. Bryant and E. Mokrzycki (eds) *The New Great Transformation? Change and Continuity in East-Central Europe*, London/New York: Routledge: 1–13.

Bulmer, S. (1983) 'Domestic Politics and European Community Policy-Making', *Journal of Common Market Studies* 21, 4: 349–63.

—— (1998) 'New Institutionalism and the Governance of the Single European Market', *Journal of European Public Policy* 5, 3: 365–86.

Burley, A.-M. and Mattli, W. (1993) 'Europe before the Court: A Political Theory of Legal Integration', *International Organization* 47, 1: 41–76.

Burnham, P. (1991) 'Neo Gramscian Hegemony and the International Order', *Capital and Class* 45: 73–93.

—— (1994) 'Open Marxism and Vulgar International Political Economy', *Review of International Political Economy* 1, 2: 221–31.

Cameron, D. R. (1992) 'The 1992 Initiative: Causes and Consequences', in A. M. Sbragia (ed.) *Euro-Politics: Institutions and Policymaking in the 'New' European Community*, Washington, D.C.: The Brookings Institution: 23–74.

Caporaso, J. (1996) 'The European Union and Forms of State: Westphalian, Regulatory or Post-Modern?', *Journal of Common Market Studies* 34, 1: 29–52.

Carlsnaes, W. (1993) 'Sweden Facing the New Europe: Whither Neutrality?', *European Security* 2, 1: 71–89.

Castles, F. G. (1978) *The Social Democratic Image of Society: A Study of the Achievements and Origins of Scandinavian Social Democracy in Comparative Perspective*, London/Henley/Boston: Routledge and Kegan Paul.

Cirtautas, A. M. (1994) 'In Pursuit of the Democratic Interest: The Institutionalization of Parties and Interests in Eastern Europe', in C. G. A. Bryant and E. Mokrzycki (eds) *The New Great Transformation? Change and Continuity in East-Central Europe*, London/New York: Routledge: 36–57.

Clark, I. (1998) 'Beyond the Great Divide: Globalization and the Theory of International Relations', *Review of International Studies* 24, 4: 479–98.

Cordier, S. S. (1995) 'Scandinavian Security in a Global Framework', *School of Economics and International Studies/University of Humberside: Occasional Papers in*

Nordic Studies 5.
Cox, R. W. (1981) 'Social Forces, States and World Orders: Beyond International Relations Theory', *Millennium: Journal of International Studies* 10, 2: 126–55.
—— (1983) 'Gramsci, Hegemony and International Relations: An Essay on Method', *Millennium: Journal of International Studies* 12, 2: 162–75.
—— (1987) *Production, Power And World Order: Social Forces in the Making of History*, New York: Columbia University Press.
—— (1989) 'Production, the State, and Change in World Order', in E.-O. Czempiel and J. N. Rosenau (eds) *Global Changes and Theoretical Challenges: Approaches to World Politics for the 1990s*, Lexington, Mass./Toronto: Lexington: 37–50.
—— (1991) '"Real Socialism" in Historical Perspective', in R. Miliband and L. Panitch (eds) *Communist Regimes: The Aftermath. Socialist Register 1991*, London: The Merlin Press: 169–93.
—— (1992) 'Global Perestroika', in R. Miliband and L. Panitch (eds) *New World Order? Socialist Register 1992*, London: The Merlin Press: 26–43.
—— (1993) 'Structural Issues of Global Governance: Implications for Europe', in S. Gill (ed.) (1993a) *Gramsci, Historical Materialism and International Relations*, Cambridge: Cambridge University Press: 259–89.
—— (1994) 'The Crisis in World Order and the Challenge to International Organization', *Cooperation and Conflict* 29, 2: 99–113.
—— (1995) 'Critical Political Economy', B. Hettne (ed.) *International Political Economy: Understanding Global Disorder*, London/New Jersey: Zed Books: 31–45.
—— with Sinclair, T. (1996) *Approaches to World Order*, Cambridge: Cambridge University Press.
—— (1999) 'Civil Society at the Turn of the Millennium: Prospects for an Alternative World Order', *Review of International Studies* 25, 1: 3–28.
Curzon Price, V. (1999) 'Reintegrating Europe: Economic aspects', in V. Curzon Price, A. Landau and R. G. Whitman (eds) *The Enlargement of the European Union: Issues and Strategies*, London/New York: Routledge: 25–53.
Curzon Price, V. Landau, A. and Whitman R. G. (eds) (1999) *The Enlargement of the European Union: Issues and Strategies*, London/New York: Routledge.
Dachs, H. (1991) 'Grünalternative Parteien', in H. Dachs *et al.* (eds) *Handbuch des Politischen Systems Österreichs*, Vienna: Manz: 263–74.
Dangerfield, M. (1997) 'Ideology and the Czech Transformation: Neoliberal Rhetoric or Neoliberal Reality?', *East European Politics and Societies* 11, 3: 436–69.
Devetak, R. (1996) 'Critical Theory', in S. Burchill and A. Linklater (eds) *Theories of International Relations*, Houndmills: Macmillan: 145–78.
Devuyst, Y. (1998) 'Treaty Reform in the EU: the Amsterdam Process', *Journal of European Public Policy* 5, 4: 615–31.
Dörfel, A., Eggl, B. and Schubert, A. (1993) 'Insider Or Outsider? The Case Of Austria', in K. Gretschmann (ed.) *Economic and Monetary Union: Implications for National Policy-Makers*, Maastricht: European Institute of Public Administration: 115–46.
Duke, V. and Grime, K. (1994) 'Privatization in East-Central Europe: Similarities and Contrasts in its Application', in C. G. A. Bryant and E. Mokrzycki (eds) *The New Great Transformation? Change and Continuity in East-Central Europe*, London/New York: Routledge: 144–70.
EBRD (1998) *Transition Report 1998*, London: European Bank for Reconstruction and Development.
Eduards, M. L. (1991) 'The Swedish Gender Model: Productivity, Pragmatism and Paternalism', *West European Politics* 14, 3: 166–81.

EFTA (1991) *EFTA Trade 1990,* Geneva: European Free Trade Area.

Esping-Andersen, G. (1985) *Politics Against Markets: The Social Democratic Road to Power,* Princeton, N.J.: Princeton University Press.

Estrin, S., Hughes, K. and Todd, S. (1997) *Foreign Direct Investment in Central and Eastern Europe: Multinationals in Transition,* London/New York: Pinter.

Falkner, G. (1998) *EU Social Policy in the 1990s: Towards a Corporatist Policy Community,* London/New York: Routledge.

Fioretos, K.-O. (1997) 'The Anatomy of Autonomy: Interdependence, Domestic Balances of Power, and European Integration', *Review of International Studies* 23, 3: 293–320.

Fricz, T. (1999) 'Hungary', in J. Smith and E. Teague (eds) *Democracy in the New Europe: The Politics of Post-Communism,* London: The Greycoat Press: 77–96.

Gamble, A. and Payne, A. (eds) (1996) *Regionalism and World Order,* Houndmills: Macmillan.

George, S. (1996) *Politics and Policy in the European Community (third edition),* Oxford: Oxford University Press.

Germain, R. D. and Kenny, M. (1998) 'Engaging Gramsci: International Relations Theory and the New Gramscians', *Review of International Studies* 24, 1: 3–21.

Gill, S. (1990) *American Hegemony and the Trilateral Commission,* Cambridge: Cambridge University Press.

—— (1992) 'The Emerging World Order And European Change: The Political Economy Of European Union', in R. Miliband and L. Panitch (eds) *New World Order? Socialist Register 1992,* London: The Merlin Press: 157–96.

—— (ed.) (1993a) *Gramsci, Historical Materialism and International Relations,* Cambridge: Cambridge University Press.

—— (1993b) 'Epistemology, Ontology and the "Italian School"', in S. Gill (ed.) (1993a) *Gramsci, Historical Materialism and International Relations,* Cambridge: Cambridge University Press: 21–48.

—— (1995) 'Globalisation, Market Civilisation, and Disciplinary Neoliberalism', *Millennium: Journal of International Studies* 24, 3: 399–423.

—— (1998) 'European Governance and New Constitutionalism: Economic and Monetary Union and Alternatives to Disciplinary Neoliberalism in Europe', *New Political Economy* 3, 1: 5–26.

Gill, S. and Law, D. (1988) *The Global Political Economy: Perspectives, Problems and Policies,* London: Harvester-Wheatsheaf.

—— (1989) 'Global Hegemony and the Structural Power of Capital', *International Studies Quarterly* 33: 475–99.

Gilpin, R. (1981) *War and Change in World Politics,* Cambridge: Cambridge University Press.

Girndt, R. (1996) 'Hungary's Trade Unions: Division and Decline', *Labour Focus on Eastern Europe* 55: 47–58.

Glasman, M. (1994) 'The Great Deformation: Polanyi, Poland and the Terrors of Planned Spontaneity', in C. G. A. Bryant and E. Mokrzycki (eds) *The New Great Transformation? Change and Continuity in East-Central Europe,* London/New York: Routledge: 191–217.

Gmeiner, M. (1996) 'EU-Opposition in Österreich', in A. Rothacher *et al.* (eds) *Österreichs europäische Zukunft: Analysen und Perspektiven,* Vienna: Signum: 259–81.

Goldmann, K. (1991) 'The Swedish Model of Security Policy', *West European Politics* 14, 3: 122–43.

Gower, J. (1999) 'EU Policy to Central and Eastern Europe', in K. Henderson (ed.)

Back to Europe: Central and Eastern Europe and the European Union, London: UCL Press: 3–19

Grabbe, H. and Hughes, K. (1998) *Enlarging the EU Eastwards*, London: The Royal Institute of International Affairs.

Gramsci, A. (1971) *Selections from the Prison Notebooks* (ed. and trans. Q. Hoare and G. Nowell Smith), London: Lawrence and Wishart.

Granell, F. (1995) 'The European Union's Enlargement Negotiations with Austria, Finland, Norway and Sweden', *Journal of Common Market Studies* 33, 1: 117–41.

Gstöhl, S. (1994) 'EFTA and the European Economic Area or the Politics of Frustration', *Cooperation and Conflict* 29, 4: 333–66.

—— (1996) 'The Nordic countries and the European Economic Area (EEA)', in L. Miles (ed.) *The European Union and the Nordic Countries*, London/New York: Routledge: 47–62.

Gustafsson, A. (1986) 'Rise and Decline of Nations: Sweden', *Scandinavian Political Studies* 9, 1: 35–50.

Gustavsson, J. (1998) *The Politics of Foreign Policy Change. Explaining the Swedish Reorientation on EC membership*, Lund: Lund University Press.

Haas, E. B. (1958) *The Uniting of Europe: Political, Social and Economic Forces, 1950–1957*, London: Stevens.

Hafner, G. (1992) 'The Impact of Developments in the East European "Socialist" States on Austria's Neutrality', in H. Neuhold (ed.) *The European Neutrals in the 1990s: New Challenges and Opportunities*, Boulder/San Francisco/Oxford: Westview: 165–83.

Hakovirta, H. (1988) *East–West Conflict and European Neutrality*, Oxford: Clarendon.

Hall, M. (1994) 'Industrial Relations and the Social Dimension of European Integration: Before and After Maastricht', in R. Hyman and A. Ferner (eds) *New Frontiers in European Industrial Relations*, Oxford/Cambridge, Mass.: Blackwell: 281–311.

Halpern, L. amd Wyplosz, C. (1998) 'The Hidden Hungarian miracle', in L. Halpern and C. Wyplosz (eds) *Hungary: Towards a Market Economy*, Cambridge: Cambridge University Press: 1–19.

Hamilton, C. B. and Stålvant, C.-E. (1989) 'A Swedish View of 1992', *RIIA: Discussion Paper 13*.

Heclo, H. and Madsen, H. (1987) *Policy and Politics in Sweden: Principled Pragmatism*, Philadelphia: Temple University Press.

Helleiner, E. (1994) *States and the Reemergence of Global Finance: from Bretton Woods to the 1990s*, Ithaka/London: Cornell University Press.

—— (1996) 'Post-Globalization: Is the Financial Liberalization Trend Likely to be Reversed?', in R. Boyer and D. Drache (eds) *States Against Markets: the Limits of Globalization*, London/New York: Routledge: 193–210.

Henderson, K. (ed.) (1999) *Back to Europe: Central and Eastern Europe and the European Union*, London: UCL Press.

Higgott, R. (1997) 'Globalisation, Regionalisation and Localisation: Political Economy, the State and Levels of Governance', *paper presented at the 25th Joint Sessions, The European Consortium for Political Research*, Bern, Switzerland, 27 February–4 March.

Higgott, R. and S. Reich (1998) 'Globalisation and Sites of Conflict: Towards Definition and Taxonomy', *CSGR Working Paper* 01/98.

Higgott, R., Underhill, G. and Bieler, A. (eds) (2000) *Non-State Actors and Authority in the Global System*, London/New York: Routledge.

Hirst, P. and Thompson, G. (1996) *Globalization in Question: the International Economy and the Possibilities of Governance*, Cambridge: Polity Press.

Hix, S. (1994) 'The Study of the European Community: the Challenge to Comparative Politics', *West European Politics* 17, 1: 1–30.

—— (1999) *The Political System of the European Union*, Houndmills: Macmillan.

Hoffmann, S. (1966) 'Obstinate or Obsolete? The Fate of the Nation State and the Case of Western Europe', *Daedalus* 95, 3: 862–915.

Holloway, J. (1995) 'The Abyss Opens: The Rise and Fall of Keynesianism', in W. Bonefeld and J. Holloway (eds) *Global Capital, National State and the Politics of Money*, Houndmills: Macmillan: 7–34.

Holman, O. (1992) 'Transnational Class Strategy and the New Europe', *International Journal of Political Economy* 22, 1: 3–22.

—— (1996) *Integrating Southern Europe: EC Expansion and the Transnationalization of Spain*, London/New York: Routledge.

—— (1998) 'Integrating Eastern Europe: EU Expansion and the Double Transformation in Poland, the Czech Republic, and Hungary', *International Journal of Political Economy* 28, 2: 12–43.

Holman, O. and van der Pijl, K. (1996) 'The Capitalist Class in The European Union', in G. A. Kourvetaris and A. Moschonas (eds) *The Impact of European Integration: Political, Sociological, and Economic Changes*, Westport, Conn./London: Praeger: 55–74.

Holman, O., Overbeek, H. and Ryner, M. (eds) (1998) 'Neoliberal Hegemony and the Political Economy of European Restructuring, special issues', *International Journal of Political Economy*, 28(1 and 2).

Hörngren, L. and Lindberg, H. (1994) 'The Struggle to turn the Swedish Krona into a Hard Currency', in J. Åkerholm and A. Giovannini (eds) *Exchange Rate Policies in the Nordic Countries*, London: Centre for Economic Policy Research: 133–64.

Huldt, B. (1994) 'Sweden and European Community-building 1945–92', in S. Harden (ed.) *Neutral States And The European Community*, London: Brassey's: 104–43.

—— (1995) 'New Thinking in Sweden? The Public Debate on Security and Defense (1979–1995)', in R. Lindahl and G. Sjöstedt (eds) *New Thinking in International Relations: Swedish Perspectives. The Yearbook of the Swedish Institute of International Affairs*, Stockholm: 139–62.

Hummer, W. (1996) 'Völkerrechtliche Aspekte des österreichischen Beitritts zur EU: Das vorläufige Ende von 50 Jahren Integrationspolitik', in A. Rothacher *et al.* (eds) *Österreichs europäische Zukunft: Analysen und Perspektiven*, Vienna: Signum: 11–49.

Hummer, W. and Schweitzer, M. (1987) *Österreich und die EWG: Neutralitätsrechtliche Beurteilung der Möglichkeiten der Dynamisierung des Verhältnisses zur EWG*, Vienna: Signum Verlag.

Jankowitsch, P. and Porius, H. (1994) 'The Process of European Integration and Neutral Austria', in S. Harden (ed.) *Neutral States and the European Community*, London: Brassey's: 35–62.

Jerneck, M. (1993) 'Sweden – the Reluctant European?', in T. Tiilikainen and I. D. Petersen (eds) *The Nordic Countries and the EC*, Copenhagen: Copenhagen Political Studies Press: 23–42.

Jonung, L. (1986) 'Financial Deregulation in Sweden', *Skandinaviska Enskilda Banken Quarterly Review* 4: 109–19.

Karazman-Morawetz, I. and Pleschiutschnig, G. (1991) 'Wirtschaftsmacht und politischer Einfluss', in H. Dachs *et al.* (eds) *Handbuch des Politischen Systems Österreichs*, Vienna: Manz: 377–89.

Katzenstein, P. J. (1985) *Small States in World Markets: Industrial Policy in Europe*, Ithaka/London: Cornell University Press.

Kavan, Z. and Palouš, M. (1999) 'Democracy in the Czech Republic', in M. Kaldor and I. Vejvoda (eds) *Democratization in Central and Eastern Europe*, London/New York: Pinter: 78–92.

Keohane, R. O. (1984) *After Hegemony: Cooperation and Discord in the World Political Economy*, Princeton, N.J.: Princeton University Press.

Keohane, R. O. and Milner, H. V. (eds) (1996) *Internationalization and Domestic Politics*, Cambridge: Cambridge University Press.

Koch, K. (1994) 'Austria: The Economic Logic of Accession', in J. Redmond (ed.) *Prospective Europeans: New Members for the European Union*, New York/London: Harvester-Wheatsheaf: 40–58.

Köves, A. (1992) *Central and East European Economies in Transition: The International Dimension*, Boulder, San Francisco/Oxford: Westview Press.

Kramer, H. (1996) 'Foreign Policy', in V. Lauber (ed.) *Contemporary Austrian Politics*, Boulder, Colo./Oxford: Westview Press: 151–200.

Krammer, J. (1991) 'Interessenorganisation der Landwirtschaft: Landwirtschafts-kammern, Präsidentenkonferenz und Raiffeisenverband', in H. Dachs *et al.* (eds) *Handbuch des Politischen Systems Österreichs*, Vienna: Manz: 365–76.

Król, M. (1999) 'Democracy in Poland', in M. Kaldor and I. Vejvoda (eds) *Democratization in Central and Eastern Europe*, London/New York: Pinter: 67–77.

Kunnert, G. (1993) *Österreichs Weg in die Europäische Union: Ein Kleinstaat ringt um eine aktive Rolle im europäischen Integrationsprozess*, Vienna: Verlag der Österreichischen Staatsdruckerei.

Kurzer, P. (1993) *Business and Banking: Political Change And Economic Integration In Western Europe*, Ithaka/London: Cornell University Press.

Laireiter, C. *et al.* (1994) 'Die österreichische EG-Diskussion in den Ländern: Vergleichende Analyse von regionalen Konfliktpotentialen in sechs Bundesländern', *Österreichische Zeitschrift für Politikwissenschaft* 23, 1: 67–88.

Lantis, J. S. and Queen, M. F. (1998) 'Negotiating Neutrality: the Double-Edged Diplomacy of Austrian Accession to the European Union', *Cooperation and Conflict* 33, 2: 152–82.

Lauber, V. (1992) 'Changing Priorities in Austrian Economic Policy', *West European Politics* 15, 1: 147–72.

—— (1996) 'Economic Policy', in V. Lauber (ed.) *Contemporary Austrian Politics* Boulder, Colo./Oxford: Westview Press: 125–50.

Laursen, F. (1993) 'The Maastricht Treaty: Implications for the Nordic Countries', *Cooperation and Conflict* 28, 2: 115–41.

Lehmbruch, G. (1979) 'Liberal Corporatism and Party Government', in P. C. Schmitter and G. Lehmbruch (eds) *Trends Towards Corporatist Intermediation*, Beverly Hills/London: SAGE: 147–83.

—— (1982) 'Introduction: Neo-Corporatism in Comparative Perspectives', in G. Lehmbruch and P. C. Schmitter (eds) *Patterns Of Corporatist Policy-Making*, London/Beverly Hills: SAGE: 1–28.

Lehmbruch, G. and Schmitter, P. C. (eds) (1982) *Patterns Of Corporatist Policy-Making*, London/Beverly Hills: SAGE.

Leitner, G. (1993) 'Der Weg nach Brüssel: Zur Geschichte des österreichischen EG-Beitrittsantrages vom 17. Juli 1989', in M. Gehler and R. Steininger (eds) *Österreich Und Die Europäische Integration, 1945–1993: Aspekte einer wechselvollen Entwicklung*, Vienna/Cologne/Weimar: Böhlau Verlag: 87–108.

Lewin, L. (1994) 'The Rise and Decline of Corporatism: the Case of Sweden', *European Journal of Political Research* 26, 1: 59–79.

Lindahl, R. (1995) 'Towards an Ever Closer Relation – Swedish Foreign and

Security Policy and the European Integration Process', in R. Lindahl and G. Sjöstedt (eds) *New Thinking in International Relations: Swedish Perspectives. The Yearbook of the Swedish Institute of International Affairs*, Stockholm: 163–82.

Lindberg, L. N. (1963) *The Political Dynamics of European Economic Integration*, Stanford, Calif.: Stanford University Press.

Lindmarker, I. (1991) 'How Sweden's Political Parties View Europe and Possible EC Membership', *Current Sweden* 382 (June).

Logue, J. (1989) 'The Legacy of Swedish Neutrality', in B. Sundelius (ed.) *The Committed Neutral: Sweden's Foreign Policy*, Boulder, San Francisco/London: Westview Press: 35–65.

Luif, P. (1988) *Neutrale in die EG? Die westeuropäische Integration und die neutralen Staaten*, Vienna: Braumüller.

—— (1994) 'Die Beitrittswerber: Grundlegendes zu den Verhandlungen der EFTA-Staaten um Mitgliedschaft bei der EG/EU', *Österreichische Zeitschrift für Politikwissenschaft* 23, 1: 21–36.

—— (1996) *On The Road To Brussels: The Political Dimension of Austria's, Finland's and Sweden's Accession to the European Union*, Vienna: Braumüller.

Luther, K. R. (1991a) 'Die Freiheitliche Partei Österreichs', in H. Dachs *et al.* (eds) *Handbuch des Politischen Systems Österreichs*, Vienna: Manz: 247–62.

—— (1991b) 'Bund-Länder Beziehungen: Formal- und Realverfassung', in H. Dachs *et al.* (eds) *Handbuch des Politischen Systems Österreichs*, Vienna: Manz: 816–26.

—— (1992) 'Consociationalism, Parties and the Party System', *West European Politics* 15, 1: 45–98.

Madeley, J. (1995) 'The Return of Swedish Social Democracy: Phoenix or Ostrich?', *West European Politics* 18, 2: 422–8.

Maresceau, M. (ed.) (1997) *Enlarging the European Union: Relations between the EU and Central and Eastern Europe*, London/New York: Longman.

Marginson, P. and Sisson, K. (1994) 'The Structure of Transnational Capital in Europe: the Emerging Euro-company and its Implications for Industrial Relations', in R. Hyman and A. Ferner (eds) *New Frontiers in European Industrial Relations*, Oxford/Cambridge, Mass.: Blackwell: 15–51.

Marin, B. (1985) 'Austria – The Paradigm Case of Liberal Corporatism?', in W. Grant (ed.) *The Political Economy of Corporatism*, Houndmills: Macmillan: 89–125.

Marks, G., Hooghe, L. and Blank, K. (1996), 'European Integration from the 1980s: State-Centric versus Multi-level Governance', *Journal of Common Market Studies* 34, 3: 341–78.

Mayhew, A. (1998) *Recreating Europe: The European Union's Policy towards Central and Eastern Europe*, Cambridge: Cambridge University Press.

Mearsheimer, J. J. (1990) 'Back to the Future: Instability in Europe After the Cold War', *International Security* 15, 1: 5–56.

Meth-Cohn, D. and Müller, W. C. (1994) 'Looking Reality in the Eye: the Politics of Privatization in Austria', in V. Wright (ed.) *Privatization In Western Europe: Pressures, Problems And Paradoxes*, London: Pinter: 160–79.

Miles, L. (1994a) 'Sweden and Finland: From EFTA Neutrals to EU Members', in J. Redmond (ed.) *Prospective Europeans: New Members for the European Union*, New York/London et al: Harvester-Wheatsheaf: 59–85.

—— (1994b) 'The 1993–1994 Enlargement Negotiations: A Critical Appraisal', *Centre for European Union Studies/The University of Hull: Research Paper* 1/94.

—— (1995) 'Sweden, Security and Accession to the European Union', *School of Economics and International Studies/University of Humberside: Occasional Papers in*

Nordic Studies 1.

—— (1996) 'The Nordic Countries and the Fourth EU Enlargement', in L. Miles (ed.) *The European Union and the Nordic Countries*, London/New York: Routledge: 63–78.

—— Redmond, J. and Schwok, R. (1995) 'Integration Theory and the Enlargement of the European Union', in C. Rhodes and S. Mazey (eds) *The State of the European Union, Vol. 3: Building a European Polity?*, Boulder, Co./Burnt Mill, Harlow: Lynne Rienner/Longman: 177–94.

Millard, F. (1999) 'Polish domestic politics and accession to the European Union', in K. Henderson (ed.) *Back to Europe: Central and Eastern Europe and the European Union*, London: UCL Press: 203–19.

Milner, H. (1989) *Sweden: Social Democracy in Practice*, Oxford/New York: Oxford University Press.

Milner, H. (1992) 'International Theories of Cooperation Among Nations: Strengths and Weaknesses', *World Politics* 44, 3: 466–96.

Moran, J. (1998) 'The Dynamics of Class Politics and National Economies in Globalisation: The Marginalisation of the Unacceptable', *Capital and Class* 66: 53–83.

Moravcsik, A. (1993) 'Preferences and Power in the European Community: A Liberal Intergovernmentalist Approach', *Journal of Common Market Studies* 31, 4: 473–524.

—— (1995) 'Liberal Intergovernmentalism and Integration: A Rejoinder', *Journal of Common Market Studies* 33, 4: 611–28.

—— (1998) *The Choice for Europe: Social Purpose and State Power from Messina to Maastricht*, London: UCL Press.

Morawetz, I. (1988) 'Die Legende vom "Europa der Bürger". Zum Kräfteverhältnis von Unternehmerverbänden und Gewerkschaften in der EG', in M. Scherb and I. Morawetz (eds) *Der Un-heimliche Anschluss: Österreich und die EG*, Vienna: Verlag für Gesellschaftskritik: 19–46.

Morton, A. D. (1998) 'Labels on Lapels: Why There is no neo-Gramscian 'School' in IPE and Why it Matters'; *paper presented at the 23rd annual conference of the British International Studies Association*; University of Sussex, UK, 14–16 December.

Morton, A. D. (1999) 'On Gramsci', *Politics* 19, 1: 1–8.

Moses, J. W. (1995) 'Devalued Priorities: The Politics of Nordic Exchange Rate Regimes Compared', upublished PhD. thesis, University of California/Los Angeles.

Müller, W. C. (1992) 'Austrian Government Institutions: Do They Matter?', *West European Politics* 15, 1: 99–131.

—— (1996a) 'Political Institutions', in V. Lauber (ed.) *Contemporary Austrian Politics*, Boulder, Colo./Oxford: Westview Press: 23–58.

—— (1996b) 'Political Parties', in V. Lauber (ed.) *Contemporary Austrian Politics*, Boulder, Co./Oxford: Westview Press: 59–102.

Murphy, C. (1994) *International Organization and Industrial Change: Global Governance since 1850*, Cambridge: Polity Press.

Mutimer, D. (1989) '1992 and the Political Integration of Europe: Neofunctionalism Reconsidered', *Journal of European Integration* 13, 1: 75–101.

Neuhold, H. (1987) 'The Permanent Neutrality of Austria: A Status Similar to and Different from Sweden's "Non-Alignment"', in B. Huldt (ed.) *Neutrals in Europe: Austria*, Stockholm: The Swedish Institute of International Affairs: 5–25.

—— (1992) 'Die dauernde Neutralität Österreichs in einem sich wandelnden internationalen System', in H. Neuhold and P. Luif (eds) *Das Aussenpolitische Bewusstsein Der Österreicher: Aktuelle internationale Probleme im Spiegel der Meinungsforschung*, Vienna: Braumüller: 87–108.

—— (1994) 'EFTA-Erweiterung der Europäischen Union: Eine österreichische

Sichtweise', *Integration: Beilage zur Europäischen Zeitung* 17, 2: 109–12.

Notermans, T. (1993) 'The Abdication from National Policy Autonomy: Why the Macroeconomic Policy Regime has become so unfavorable to Labour', *Politics and Society* 21, 2: 133–67.

Nugent, N. (1999) *The Government and Politics of the European Community* (fourth edition), Houndmills: Macmillan.

Oberhauser, A. M. (1990) 'Social and Spatial Patterns under Fordism and Flexible Accumulation', *Antipode* 22, 3: 211–32.

OECD (1985) *OECD Economic Outlook No. 38*, Paris: Organisation for Economic Co-operation and Development.

—— (1990) *OECD Economic Outlook No. 47*, Paris: Organisation for Economic Co-operation and Development.

—— (1998) *OECD Economic Outlook No. 64*, Paris: Organisation for Economic Co-operation and Development.

Öhlinger, H. (1988) *Verfassungsrechtliche Aspekte Eines Beitritt Österreichs Zu Den EG*, Vienna: Signum Verlag.

Ohmae, K. (1990) *The Borderless World: Power and Strategy in the Interlinked Economy*, London: Collins.

—— (1995) *The End of the Nation State: The Rise of Regional Economies*, London: Harper Collins.

Olsen, G. (1991) 'Labour Mobilization and the Strength of Capital: The Rise and Stall of Economic Democracy in Sweden', *Studies in Political Economy* 34: 109–45.

Oman, C. P. (1995) *The Policy Challenges of Globalisation and Regionalisation*, OECD Development Centre: Policy Brief (12 July 1995).

Overbeek, H. (ed.) (1993) *Restructuring Hegemony in the Global Political Economy: the Rise of Transnational Neo-liberalism in the 1980s*, London/New York: Routledge.

Overbeek, H. and van der Pijl, K. (1993) 'Restructuring Capital and Restructuring Hegemony: Neo-liberalism and the Unmaking of the Post-war Order', in H. Overbeek (ed.) *Restructuring Hegemony in the Global Political Economy: the Rise of Transnational Neo-liberalism in the 1980s*, London/New York: Routledge: 1–27.

Panitch, L. (1994) 'Globalisation and the State', in R. Miliband and L. Panitch (eds) *Between Globalism And Nationalism. The Socialist Register 1994*, London: Merlin: 60–93.

Parris, H., Pestieau, P. and Saynor, P. (1987) *Public Enterprise in Western Europe*. London/Sydney/ Wolfeboro, N. H.: Croom Helm.

Pedersen, T. (1994) *European Union and the EFTA Countries: Enlargement and Integration*, London/New York: Pinter.

Pehe, J. (1999) 'The Czech Republic', in J. Smith and E. Teague (eds) *Democracy in the New Europe: The Politics of Post-Communism*, London: Greycoat Press: 25–46.

Peterson, J. (1995) 'Decision-making in the EU: Towards a Framework for Analysis', *Journal of European Public Policy* 2, 1: 69–93.

Petersson, O. (1994) *Swedish Government and Politics*, Stockholm: Publica-Fritzes.

Pichl, C. (1989) 'Internationale Investitionen: Verflechtung der österreichischen Wirtschaft', *WIFO Monatsberichte* 62, 3: 161–75.

Pollert, A. (1997) 'The Transformation of Trade Unionism in the Capitalist and Democratic Restructuring of the Czech Republic', *European Journal of Industrial Relations* 3, 2: 203–28.

Pontusson, J. (1994) 'Sweden: After the Golden Age', in P. Anderson and P. Camiller (eds) *Mapping the West European Left*, London/New York: Verso: 23–54.

Preston, C. (1997) *Enlargement and Integration in the European Union*, London/New York: Routledge.

Puchala, D. (1972) 'Of Blind Men, Elephants and International Integration', *Journal of Common Market Studies* 10, 3: 267–84.

Putnam, R. D. (1988) 'Diplomacy and Domestic Politics: the Logic of Two-level Games', *International Organization* 42, 3: 427–60.

Radice, H. (1997) 'Globalization and National Differences', *paper presented at the ESF–EMOT Workshop: Globalization and Industrial Transformation in Europe*, Malaga, Spain, 9–12 January.

Riedlsperger, M. (1992) 'Heil Haider! The Revitalization of the Austrian Freedom Party since 1986', *Politics And Society In Germany, Austria And Switzerland* 4, 3: 18–58.

Ruggie, J. G. (1982) 'International Regimes, Transactions, and Change: Embedded Liberalism in the Postwar Economic Order', *International Organization* 36, 2: 379–415.

Rupert, M. (1995) *Producing Hegemony: the Politics of Mass Production and American Global Power*, Cambridge: Cambridge University Press.

Ryner, M. (1994) 'Assessing SAP's Economic Policy in the 1980s: The "Third Way", the Swedish Model and the Transition from Fordism to Post-Fordism', *Economic and Industrial Democracy* 15: 385–428.

—— (1999) 'Neoliberal Globalization and the Crisis of Swedish Social Democracy', *Economic and Industrial Democracy* 20, 1: 39–79.

Sainsbury, D. (1991) 'Swedish Social Democracy in Transition: the Party's Record in the 1980s and the Challenge of the 1990s', *West European Politics* 14, 3: 31–57.

—— (1993) 'The Swedish Social Democrats and the Legacy of Continuous Reform: Asset or Dilemma?', *West European Politics* 16, 1: 39–61.

Schaller, C. (1994a) 'Die innenpolitische EG-Diskussion seit den 80er Jahren', in A. Pelinka, C. Schaller and P. Luif (eds) *Ausweg EG? Innenpolitische Motive einer aussenpolitischen Umorientierung*, Vienna/Cologne/Graz: Böhlau Verlag: 27–269.

—— (1994b) '"Ja" oder "Nein" zu "Europa": Die österreichische EU-Debatte im Vorfeld der Volksabstimmung unter besonderer Berücksichtigung von Konfliktlinien im Parteiensystem – ein Rekonstruktionsversuch', in A. Pelinka (ed.) *EU-Referendum: Zur Praxis direkter Demokratie in Österreich*, Vienna. Signum: 49–85.

Scherb, M. (1988) 'Die Europäische Gemeinschaft – Objekt österreichischer Begierden. Zum Charakter der Europäischen Gemeinschaft und den österreichischen Beitrittswünschen', in M. Scherb and I. Morawetz (eds) *Der Un-heimliche Anschluss: Österreich und die EG*, Vienna: Verlag für Gesellschaftskritik: 47–72.

Schneider, H. (1990) *Alleingang nach Brüssel: Österreichs EG-Politik*, Bonn: Europa Union Verlag.

—— (1994) 'Gerader Weg zum klaren Ziel? Die Republik Österreich auf dem Weg in die Europäische Union', *Österreichische Zeitschrift für Politikwissenschaft* 23, 1: 5–20.

Schultz, D. M. (1992) 'Austria in the International Arena: Neutrality, European Integration and Consociationalism', *West European Politics* 15, 1: 173–200.

Siegel, D. (1992) 'Die Bedeutung österreichischer multinationaler Konzerne für die Internationalisierung', in W. Clement (ed.) *Neue Entwicklungen – neue Formen – neue Herausforderungen. Internationalisierung Band VI*, Vienna: Signum Verlag: 165–89.

Sinclair, T. J. (1994a) 'Passing Judgement: Credit Rating Processes as Regulatory Mechanisms of Governance in the Emerging World Order', *Review of International Political Economy* 1, 1: 133–59.

—— (1994b) 'Between State and Market: Hegemony and Institutions of Collective Action under Conditions of International Capital Mobility', *Policy Sciences* 27, 4: 447–66.

Smith, H. (1996) 'The Silence of the Academics: International Social Theory, Historical Materialism and Political Values', *Review of International Studies* 22, 2: 191–212.

Smith, M. A. (1999) 'The NATO Factor: A Spanner in the Works of EU and WEU Enlargement?', in K. Henderson (ed.) *Back to Europe: Central and Eastern Europe and the European Union*, London: UCL Press: 53–67.

Standing, G. (1997) 'Labour Market Governance in Eastern Europe', *European Journal of Industrial Relations* 3, 2: 133–59.

Ste. Croix, G. E. M. de (1981) *The Class Struggle in the Ancient Greek World from the Archaic Age to the Arab Conquests*, London: Duckworth.

Stopford, J. and Strange, S. (1991) *Rival States, Rival Firms: Competition for World Market Shares*, Cambridge: Cambridge University Press.

Strange, S. (1994a) *States And Markets (second edition)*, New York/London: Pinter.

—— (1994b) 'Wake up Krasner! The World has Changed', *Review of International Political Economy* 1, 2: 209–19.

—— (1996) *The Retreat of the State: The Diffusion of Power in the World Economy*, Cambridge: Cambridge University Press.

Sundelius, B. (1989) 'Committing Neutrality in an Antagonistic World', in B. Sundelius (ed.) *The Committed Neutral: Sweden's Foreign Policy*, Boulder, San Francisco/London: Westview Press: 1–13.

—— (1994) 'Changing Course: When Neutral Sweden Chose to Join the European Community', in W. Carlsnaes and S. Smith (eds) *European Foreign Policy: The EC and Changing Perspectives in Europe*, London/Thousand Oaks/New Delhi: SAGE: 177–201.

Svensson, S. (1994) 'Der Beitritt Schwedens zur Europäischen Union', *Current Sweden* 408 (December).

Swedenborg, B. (1979) *The Multinational Operations of Swedish Firms: An Analysis of Determinants and Effects*, Stockholm: IUI.

Swenson, P. (1991a) 'Bringing Capital Back In, or Social Democracy Reconsidered', *World Politics* 43: 513–44.

—— (1991b) 'Labor and the Limits of the Welfare State: The Politics of Intraclass Conflict and Cross-Class Alliances in Sweden and West Germany', *Comparative Politics* 23, 4: 379–99.

Tálos, E. (1996) 'Corporatism – The Austrian Model', in V. Lauber (ed.) *Contemporary Austrian Politics*, Boulder, Colo./Oxford: Westview Press: 103–23.

Taylor, R. (1991) 'The Economic Policies of Sweden's Political Parties', *Current Sweden* 383 (June).

Tranholm-Mikkelsen, J. (1991) 'Neo-functionalism: Obstinate or Obsolete? A Reappraisal in the Light of the New Dynamism of the EC', *Millennium: Journal of International Studies* 20, 1: 1–22.

Traxler, F. (1992) 'Interests, Politics, and European Integration: Austria's Political System in the Wake of 1992', *European Journal of Political Research* 22: 193–217.

Ucakar, K. (1991) 'Verfassung – Geschichte und Prinzipien', in H. Dachs *et al.* (eds) *Handbuch des Politischen Systems Österreichs*, Vienna: Manz: 81–95.

UN (1991) *World Investment Report 1991: The Triad in Foreign Direct Investment*, New York: United Nations.

—— (1992) *World Investment Report 1992: Transnational Corporations as Engines of Growth*, New York: United Nations.

—— (1998) *World Investment Report 1998: Trends and Determinants*, New York/Geneva: United Nations.

van Apeldoorn, B. (1996) 'The Political Economy of Conflicting Capitalisms in the European Integration Process: A Transnational Perspective', *RIES: Research Paper* 31 (November).

—— (1997) 'Structure and Agency in the Construction of European Order:

Gramscian Transnationalism as an Approach to the Study of European Integration', *paper presented at the 22nd annual conference of the British International Studies Association*; Leeds, UK, 15–17 December.

—— (1998) 'European Unemployment and Transnational Capitalist Class Strategy: The Rise of the Neoliberal Competitiveness Discourse', *paper presented at the Workshop 'The Political Economy of European Unemployment'*, *ECPR Joint Sessions of Workshops*; University of Warwick, UK, 23–27 March.

van Apeldoorn, B. and Holman, O. (1994) 'Transnational Class Strategy and the Relaunching of European Integration: the Role of the European Round Table of Industrialists', *paper presented at the 35th Annual Convention of the International Studies Association*; Washington, D.C., 28 March–1 April.

van der Pijl, K. (1984) *The Making of an Atlantic Ruling Class*, London: Verso.

—— (1989) 'Restructuring The Atlantic Ruling Class In The 1970s And 1980s', in S. Gill (ed.), *Atlantic Relations: Beyond the Reagan Era*, Hemel Hempstead: Harvester-Wheatsheaf.

—— (1995) 'The Second Glorious Revolution: Globalizing Elites and Historical Change', in B. Hettne (ed.) *International Political Economy: Understanding Global Disorder*, London/New Jersey: Zed Books: 100–28.

—— (1998) *Transnational Classes and International Relations*, London/New York: Routledge.

Viklund, D. (1989) *Sweden and the European Community: Trade, Cooperation and Policy Issues*, Stockholm: The Swedish Institute.

Vinton, L. (1999) 'Poland', in J. Smith and E. Teague (eds) *Democracy in the New Europe: The Politics of Post-Communism*, London: The Greycoat Press: 47–75.

Waltz, K. N. (1979) *Theory of International Politics*, Reading, Mass.: Addison-Wesley.

Whyman, P. and Burkitt, B. (1993) 'The Role of the Swedish Employers in Restructuring Pay Bargaining and the Labour Process', *Work, Employment and Society* 7, 4: 603–14.

Widfeldt, A. (1996) 'Sweden and the European Union: Implications for the Swedish party system', in L. Miles (ed.) *The European Union and the Nordic Countries*, London/New York: Routledge: 101–16.

Wieser, T. and Kitzmantel, E. (1990) 'Austria and the European Community', *Journal of Common Market Studies* 28, 4: 431–49.

Wilks, S. (1996) 'Class Compromise and the International Economy: The Rise and Fall of Swedish Social Democracy', *Capital and Class* 58: 89–111.

Wincott, D. (1995) 'Institutional Interaction and European Integration: Towards an Everyday Critique of Liberal Intergovernmentalism', *Journal of Common Market Studies* 33, 4: 597–609.

Winkler, G. (1988) 'Der Austrokeynesianismus und sein Ende', *Österreichische Zeitschrift für Politikwissenschaft* 17, 3: 221–30.

Woschnagg, G. (1994) 'Possible Implications of Accession to the EC and the Complexity of Enlargement Negotiations Seen from an Austrian Perspective', *EIPASCOPE* 1: 6–8.

Wæver, O. (1992) 'Nordic nostalgia: Northern Europe after the Cold War', *International Affairs* 68, 1: 77–102.

Index

advertising/campaigning 45, 96–7, 100, 101–2, 115–16, 119
agriculture 35, 57, 58, 60–2, 64–6, 68–9, 74–5, 79, 86, 90, 92, 95, 96, 100, 107, 113, 150–2
alcohol monopoly 93, 94, 114,
Amsterdam, Treaty of 2, 139, 162
Andersson, S. 132, 167n6
Arvidsson, L. 119
Austria: accession to EU 1, 4–5, 53–69, 85–7, 88, 89–92, 94–102, 126; economic (performance 5, 6–7, 27–8, 39–40, 89 (statistics 40, 48, 54, 55, 57, 89; *see also* employment); policy 27–8; structure 53, 64–5); forces encouraging EC membership 6–7, 12, 57, 59–60, 63, 87, 96–7, 156; forces opposing EC membership 4, 12, 53, 58, 60–4, 66–9, 87, 97–100, 128; historical bloc of capital and labour 27, 66, 85, 87, 156, 159, 160, 161; impact of globalisation 34–41; neutral status 1–2, 5, 55, 57, 60, 64, 67–8, 85, 90, 92, 94, 99, 123–30, 135, 153, 156, 159; political system 28–30, 49–50, 85, 100, 128 (*see also* parties by name); resistance to neo-liberalism 164; social policies 27, 63, 65, 66; transnationalisation of production 37–41, 47, 54–7, 63, 67–8
Austrian: Business League (ÖWB) 49, 56; Chamber of Agriculture (LK) 30, 48, 62, 156; Chamber of Commerce (BWK) 48–9, 57–9, 89, 96, 156; Chamber of Labour (AK) 30, 48, 59, 60, 63, 91, 92, 96, 128, 156; Chancellor's Office 50; Economic and Social Partnership 27–9, 49, 56; Farmers' League (ÖBB) 49. 57, 62, 69, 92; Federation of Austrian Industrialists (VÖI) 48–9, 54–8, 85, 89, 96, 125, 126, 156, 161;

Federation of Trade Unions (ÖGB) 30, 48, 59, 60, 63, 91, 92, 96, 97, 128, 156; Freedom Party (FPÖ) 28–30, 49–50, 57, 97, 98, 99–101, 121, 129, 136, 159, 160; Green Alternative Party (GA) 29, 50, 66–7, 98, 100, 121, 129, 136, 159, 160; League of Blue and White Collar Workers (ÖAAB) 49; Liberal Forum 28–9, 100, 129; Ministries (Agriculture 50, 68–9; Economic 50, 56, 87, 156; Finance 39, 50, 64, 87, 91, 156; Foreign 56, 64, 90, 126, 128; Labour and Social Affairs 50, 68–9; Nationalised Industry 50, 68, 69); National Bank 36–7, 50, 87, 96, 97, 156; Parity Commission 30; People's Party (ÖVP) 5, 28–30, 39, 56–7, 60, 62, 63, 68, 95, 128, 129, 136, 156; Social Democratic Party (SPÖ) 1, 5, 28–30, 39, 57, 60, 63–4, 68, 90, 92, 95, 97, 124, 128, 156

Balcerowicz, L. 146, 150; Plan 143
Baltic States 134, 139, 140
banks 41, 42, 141; central 24; nationalisation of 36; *see also* European Central Bank, financial markets, World Bank
Belgium 5
Bildt, C. 78–9, 91, 92, 102, 119, 133, 134, 135
Blau-Meissner, F. 66
Bretton Woods 18, 37
budget: EU contributions 93, 95, 139; national 2, 28, 43–5
Bulgaria 139, 140
Burnham, P. 15–16

cabotage 105
capital/capitalism 10, 11, 15–1, 24; alliances 45–6, 58–9, 72–4, 155;